## Praise for *Manopause*

"**Manopause** is an entertaining and enlightening read about an important and neglected topic. As a midlife man, I was impressed with the sensitivity of the authors' writing, and as a health psychologist, I was delighted with the solidness of their scholarship. I highly recommend this book to men and women. I know it will help both genders navigate a heretofore challenging passage."

— **Fred Luskin, Ph.D.,** Director of the Stanford University Forgiveness Projects, Professor of Clinical Psychology at the Institute of Transpersonal Psychology, and Best-Selling Author of *Forgive for Good, Forgive for Love,* and *Stress Free for Good*

"**Manopause** is an extremely helpful book that sheds light on an important and seldom-talked-about topic. It's a must-read for both genders!"

— **Marcelle Pick, MSN, OB/GYN NP,** Co-Founder of Women to Women and Author of *Are You Tired and Wired?*

"This is a terrific book! Not only is it well-written and friendly, it's well-researched and enormously informative. I can't wait to share it with the women (and men) I work with who are struggling with the often mystifying physical and psychological changes that take place in men during midlife."

— **Laraine T. Zappert, Ph.D.,** Clinical Professor in the Department of Psychiatry and Behavioral Sciences at Stanford University School of Medicine

"As a urologic surgeon and clinician for over 35 years, I am convinced that both men and women deserve the enjoyment that comes with complete sexual satisfaction. Yet too often I have seen men deprive themselves of that satisfaction at midlife, due to ignorance of normal physical and mental changes. **Manopause** does a stellar job of busting through that ignorance, by giving readers facts about men's hormonal and psychological shifts that will help them to eliminate negativity and self-doubt, while enriching their sexual lives and relationships."

— **Dudley Seth Danoff, M.D., F.A.C.S.,** Founder and President, Tower Urology Group, Cedars-Sinai Medical Center and Author of *Penis Power*

"As a family therapist, I am delighted that **Manopause** gives us a comprehensive way to look at men at midlife and to understand how their psychological and physical changes impact them and all those around them. Just as Passages changed the way we view menopause, **Manopause** will change the way we view the male 'midlife crisis.' After reading this groundbreaking book, you won't be able to look at yourself or your man the same way again."

— **Eva Ritvo, M.D.,** Former Vice Chair of the Department of Psychiatry, Miller School of Medicine, and Co-Author of *Concise Guide to Marriage and Family Therapy*

# MANOPAUSE

## ALSO BY LISA FRIEDMAN BLOCH
## AND KATHY KIRTLAND SILVERMAN

*Dr. Richard Marrs' Fertility Book: America's Leading Infertility Expert Tells You Everything You Need to Know About Getting Pregnant*

# MANOPAUSE

## Your Guide to Surviving
## *His* Changing Life

Lisa Friedman Bloch
Kathy Kirtland Silverman

**HAY HOUSE, INC.**
Carlsbad, California • New York City
London • Sydney • Johannesburg
Vancouver • Hong Kong • New Delhi

*Published and distributed in the United States by:* Hay House, Inc.: www.hayhouse.com® • *Published and distributed in Australia by:* Hay House Australia Pty. Ltd.: www.hayhouse.com.au • *Published and distributed in the United Kingdom by:* Hay House UK, Ltd.: www.hayhouse.co.uk • *Published and distributed in the Republic of South Africa by:* Hay House SA (Pty), Ltd.: www.hayhouse.co.za • *Distributed in Canada by:* Raincoast: www.raincoast.com • *Published in India by:* Hay House Publishers India: www.hayhouse.co.in

*Cover design:* Christy Salinas • *Interior design:* Tricia Breidenthal

**Library of Congress Cataloging-in-Publication Data**

Bloch, Lisa Friedman.
 Manopause : your guide to surviving his changing life / Lisa Friedman Bloch, Kathy Kirtland Silverman.
    p. cm.
 Includes bibliographical references.
 ISBN 978-1-4019-2712-7 (pbk. : alk. paper) -- ISBN 978-1-4019-3106-3 (digital) 1. Middle-aged men--Psychology. 2. Midlife crisis. 3. Middle-aged men--Sexual behavior. I. Silverman, Kathy Kirtland. II. Title.
 HQ1059.4.B59 2012
 305.244'1--dc23
                                2012013046


**Tradepaper ISBN:** 978-1-4019-2712-7
**Digital ISBN:** 978-1-4019-3106-3

15 14 13 12    4 3 2 1
1st edition, September 2012

Printed in the United States of America

First in THE **MANOPAUSE MAN**™ Series

*To my precious daughters and treasured son,*
*Alexis, Caroline, and Jordan, and*
*to my extraordinary man, Jonathan,*
*thank you for your patience, enthusiasm,*
*and immeasurable support.*
*— Lisa*


*To Matt, for the great man he would have been.*
*To Alan, for the remarkable man he is.*
*— Kathy*

# CONTENTS

# FOREWORD

by Louann Brizendine, M.D.
author of *The Female Brain*
and *The Male Brain*

When I met Lisa Bloch and Kathy Silverman at an event in the San Francisco area in the spring of 2010, I realized immediately that we were kindred souls. Like me, they were fascinated by the differences between women and men, and by the robust effect of hormones on men's behavior. I have dedicated my own professional life and decades of work as a neuropsychiatrist, first at Harvard University and today at the University of California, San Francisco, to clinical work in understanding how hormones affect our brains, and how the differences between the male and female brains influence the way the sexes function, feel, and communicate in their everyday lives and relationships. The moment I learned about Lisa and Kathy's research, I knew that *Manopause* would be a wonderful addition to our existing body of knowledge about men at midlife, and, as it speaks to women, that it would enlighten them about the complicating forces that converge on their men during this pivotal, yet somewhat secretive, time.

*Manopause* surpassed my highest expectations. It brings men's midlife change out into the open. It not only makes the reader feel less burdened and alone, but also uplifts her by teaching her how to move through this delicate time period while focusing on its positive aspects—and there are so many to experience. *Manopause* guides women to lovingly assist their men, while making their own lives better in the process.

As the founder of the Women's Mood and Hormone Clinic at UCSF, and the co-director of the Program in Sexual Medicine, I have counseled many midlife couples during the last 25 years, and I am acutely aware of the confusion that midlife hormone changes can produce for both genders—particularly for men, whose brains make them world champions at blocking their emotional reactions. In my practice I have seen that as men's hormones shift at midlife, so does their reality. They feel tendencies that are new to them. They may become more responsive to cuddling and bonding, and, as the authors explain, have an improved capacity to empathize and read subtle facial expressions. And they may be less territorial, and less compelled to fight for a place in the pecking order. While these characteristics may be a welcomed relief to their women, they can terrorize men. Lisa and Kathy expertly, and with anecdotal stories, explain why this is.

*Manopause* will help you to understand that the changes in your man's behavior, including his sexual and emotional changes, are not your fault. They are not occurring because of something you did or did not do. As you read, you will see that manopause men are only trying to fulfill what they believe women and society want and expect from them—to be strong, brave, and independent; to suppress their fear and pain; to hide their softer emotions; and to stand confidently in the face of challenge. What I have discovered through my research is that men's desire to fulfill these expectations is so strong that their brain circuits actually architecturally change to reflect the emotional suppression that is required of them.

If you are dealing with the outward signs of a midlife male shift— with the irritability, anger, and withdrawal that it can produce—this book will help you see that the manopause challenge is only a problem if you ignore your man's veiled doubt, uncertainty, and negative behavior. *Manopause* will help you to unravel his secrets, explore the shameful unknown, alter his goals, and assist him in reshaping his manhood pressures as he starts down the road to inner peace. This could be your man's last chance to find the authentic person inside, to reach his ultimate potential, and to become his "real self." *Manopause* can help you be the midwife who delivers him to himself.

But be careful not to use this book to overthink or overanalyze him, at least out loud. Because, at first, if your man thinks you understand him as intimately as *Manopause* will help you to do, it might frighten him and make him push you away. The book may also give *you* some personal challenges. As you begin to see your man's deepest drives through male-colored glasses, you may realize that you have to take a deeper look at yourself as well. It's only right that you share this time of reevaluation and rejuvenation.

*Manopause* is a goal changer, both for your man and for you. Use it as a secret encyclopedia about your man at midlife. Keep it on your bedside table so you can refer back to it. Let *Manopause* help you gain a greater understanding of who both of you are during his manopause years, and guide you with a wonderful road map for negotiating the potentially rich and plentiful years ahead.

# INTRODUCTION

As Kathy looked around the room, every second booth seemed to hold a couple, lunching together. Men were looking appreciatively at their companions. Hands were being held and meaningful glances exchanged. It was her birthday, but Kathy couldn't have felt more isolated, hurt, and angry. It had been less than a month since she had spotted a woman with her husband's car. A woman half his age. A woman who turned out to be his mistress. He had supposedly driven 100 miles south on a business trip, but there was his car. And there *she* was, loading grocery bags into the trunk. Since then life had been chaos; hours and days had been filled with confusion. Who was this man she had spent decades with, and what had caused this startling shift in his behavior? Were there signs she missed, even subtle ones? How could she have been so stupid? Had their communication faltered? Was she looking old . . . fat . . . undesirable? Maybe she was. Maybe it was all her fault. Kathy stared at a couple in the corner, the man considerably older than his companion. She wondered if some other unsuspecting woman was about to get an emotional gut punch. She wanted to flee. It was torture to sit there, feeling the shame of losing her husband, feeling so very visibly alone. She forced herself to stay. How could she disappoint Lisa and their friends? Checking her watch, she felt worry kick in on top of her anxiety. Lisa knew what pain she was in and how fragile she was. It had taken a week of arm-twisting to get Kathy to agree to come at all. Where could Lisa be?

While Kathy was trying to remain appropriately calm at a beautiful restaurant, Lisa was at Cedars-Sinai Medical Center.

It had been a sleepless night for Lisa. Her husband, Jonathan, had spent it writhing in pain. For the past two weeks, he had taken prescribed painkillers and tried to pretend that his hernia wasn't getting worse. But that had become impossible. Pacing the bedroom, he finally let Lisa call his doctor, reminding her that if surgery was needed, he would have to wait a week, until after he gave a keynote speech at a business conference in New York.

The next morning the doctor confirmed the hernia required surgery, to be done as soon as possible. But from that point on, he might as well have been talking to Lisa and Jonathan in different languages. Lisa heard that the surgery should be immediate; if the hernia burst, it would be a much more complicated operation, with potentially permanent damage. Jonathan, on the other hand, heard what he was hoping for, that it could wait a week. He said he would carve out time for the surgery the following Friday. Lisa was flabbergasted. As Jonathan rose to leave, she protested. Didn't he hear what the doctor was saying? Didn't he understand that if he wasn't treated immediately, there could be serious consequences? Jonathan told Lisa she was overreacting. It was just one more week of pain; he could handle it. Lisa was incredulous. Why would her husband reject the doctor's advice? What was wrong with him? Jonathan shot back. How could she not recognize how important this speech was to him? Lisa asked the doctor whether, if the surgery was performed early the next morning, Jonathan could fly in a few days. He replied that it would be less of a risk than ending up in a New York emergency room, in the hands of a surgeon he didn't know. Jonathan finally came to his senses. Relieved, Lisa looked at her watch and panicked all over again. She was terribly late for her lunch with Kathy. She didn't want her to wait alone at the table, even for a second.

Lisa rushed in and sat down next to Kathy, apologizing profusely. The rest of their girlfriends started arriving. Laurie, juggling an orchid plant, greeted Kathy with a heartfelt kiss. Sarah walked in. She seemed distracted, but still embraced Kathy with a meaningful hug. It was the first time they had seen each other since Kathy's separation. Everyone paused as Natalie entered the room. Her deep brunette hair was now light platinum. Natalie made light of it, saying, "You only live once, right?"

Everyone was worried about Kathy. And as she shared details, revealing her hurt and vulnerability, it became obvious that her husband's actions didn't set the stage for a warm and carefree birthday lunch. Lisa, trying to shift topics, started asking about what was happening in the other ladies' lives. And the answers that came back started revealing a pattern: after the initial niceties, the façades crumbled—each of them eventually admitted to having problems with their men. Laurie's husband, David, had lost his job and had become aimless. He used to be a go-getter, but now he was working toward nothing, and he had become angry and controlling. Sarah's husband, Adam, had become hard to live with, too. He'd been battling their son for months, finding fault with everything he did. The tension had gotten to be more than she could bear. Natalie was having problems with the new man she was dating. Even though they had a lot in common, and they enjoyed spending every minute together, they hadn't been physically intimate. All of the women were confused and upset. All of them had questions—both about their man's behavior and their part in it.

After the meal, Lisa and Kathy were waiting for their cars, and they couldn't help but notice how drastically the conversation had changed over their years of spending birthday lunches together. Fashion, fornication, and frivolity used to be the hot topics. Then, small job promotions, first mortgages, and exciting vacations. After which came mommy talk about sippy cups, school admissions, and kids' sports leagues. But this birthday was different. Now the discussions were suddenly all about problems—all sorts of problems—with men. Were they just being overly sensitive? Or were they uneducated about what was going on and how to handle it?

As you've probably guessed, we are the Lisa and Kathy in the above narrative. And that day in August was a turning point in our lives. Little did we know that the awkwardness, pain, and confusion we felt would push us to search for answers that would ultimately lead to the writing of *Manopause*.

After lunch that day, we started discussing men at midlife more and more. As writers, we'd spent years researching people's interactions so we could craft compelling stories for the big screen, the small screen, and nonfiction books. We had been given insight into the stories of many marriages when we were researching our book on fertility, and we knew from those interviews the varying dynamics of hundreds of couples. Plus, we had observed our own and our friends' couplings over decades. And never before had we heard such a pervasive tone of confusion, frustration, and discontent. Was this just a cluster epidemic, we wondered, limited to our own little world? Or was this more widespread?

We began to put out feelers to friends around the country, and we got some interesting results. Everywhere, women in our age range, and younger, were experiencing similar changes in their men. Maybe they were just getting a little irritable and touchy. Maybe they were getting downright difficult to live with. Or maybe, like Kathy's husband, they had an agenda all their own. We decided we were on to something and had to go full bore into this project.

But we soon learned that our exploration was going to be more challenging than we had anticipated. The fact that men change at midlife is a topic that our society chooses to ignore. When we sit around a dinner table, join together for a family gathering, chitchat at a cocktail party, or strike up a conversation after a meeting, we universally avoid acknowledging, admitting, or discussing the fact that men go through their own version of menopause. We all know they do, but no one talks about it. Unless, of course, you happen to be in a very intimate group of female friends talking about the men who matter to them. There, midlife men being difficult or changing might be a more open—though not very well understood—subject.

A woman's midlife change doesn't seem to carry as strong a stigma. One reason for this is Gail Sheehy's groundbreaking book, *The Silent Passage,* which helped menopause emerge from the shadows. Before she initiated an open discussion, menopause was considered a totally negative, socially unmentionable change of life. After Sheehy's exploration of its many aspects, women realized that while it *was* a time of change, much of that change could be positive. They could embark on a liberated and energized second stage in life. As authors and social commentators, we felt we could do a similarly positive service for men, and for the women who care about them, by examining their midlife changes, as observed from a female perspective.

This is important, because until men's passage is recognized, explored, and socially accepted, we all will be doomed to varying degrees of confusion, misunderstanding, and discontent. Men will continue to suffer through hormonal and psychological changes without the means or knowledge to interpret them. And women will suffer along with them. Change, in varying degrees, is inevitable for all men. That is why it needs to become a topic we can be comfortable with and openly discuss.

Currently, the words that are commonly used to name and describe this pivotal time in a man's life have been rooted in a medical vocabulary. They include such confusing and unhelpful terms as andropause, viropause, endopause, male climacteric, male menopause, climacteric male menopause, and midlife crisis. There doesn't seem to be much consensus among experts as to which term to use or what, exactly, each of them means. Some will tell you that they refer only to hormonal changes and the physical fallout from those changes. Others will advise that they also include psychological and social changes. Ironically, the most commonly used phrase, male menopause, is a contradiction in terms. Menopause literally translated means "stopping of the menstruation cycle." But men do not have a cycle to stop. Only women do. And having experienced a monthly menstrual cycle most of our lives, it is only fair that we claim "menopause" for ourselves.

What happens to men at midlife—hormonally, psychologically, socially, culturally, and physically—was an area that needed to be more deeply explored, clearly defined, and brought into the open. We knew we were the ones to do it.

So we called our literary agent and told her what we were thinking. She wasn't at all surprised. The same sort of uneasiness seemed to be drifting in the wind around her and the women in her world. That's when she suggested the term *manopause*. Hearing it, we smiled. Men pause; they change. It made such sense. It was a way to give them their own term, one that had not already been used and confused, one that would be all-inclusive, appropriate, and easy to understand. When we talked it up with our professional associates and personal friends, they not only smiled, they let out a "been there, experienced that" laugh. And so, our journey began. Over several years, massive research; interviews with medical, psychological, and cultural experts; dialogues with men about their personal stories; and hours of woman-to-woman sharing brought *Manopause* to life. The result is a book that can help to guide you through the most challenging transition in your man's life.

*Manopause* is divided into two parts. Part One is the launchpad for your understanding of *why* men are the way they are. In this section, you will discover the power our culture has exerted over our men, the many ways its influence has shaped their feelings about how they must behave in order to "be a man," and the ways in which women are equally vulnerable to our culture's preconceptions of what "a man" should be. This section also highlights the ways men can be negatively impacted when change occurs that prevents them from fulfilling their perceived manhood requirements. And it clarifies what lies behind the behavioral challenges that may crop up when unrelenting cultural pressures collide with a man's physical decline. Finally, it explores the biological differences between men's and women's brains, and how these differences can complicate the already-complex relationship dance during manopause.

Part Two becomes more specific, exploring a variety of areas and situations that are impacted by manopause on an everyday basis. Here you will find chapters that delve into men's hormones and emotions, and others that discuss the impact of manopause on sex, family, work, and on a man's interaction with the world around him. In this section you will also read about the many admirable and redeeming masculine traits that you should welcome, enjoy, cherish, and encourage in your man. Throughout these chapters, we have provided first-person stories that will help you to better understand what your man is going through, and tip boxes that offer suggestions and guidelines that will resonate with your desire to make life-affirming changes in every challenging situation.

Before you jump in, we invite you to take the Manopause Quiz. This series of questions will first clue you in on where you stand in your knowledge of men in general, and then, on manopause men in particular. The quiz will then ask you to test yourself on ways your personal attitude plays into, and potentially complicates, your mano-pause man's issues. Truly knowing yourself and understanding where you stand will be a precious tool in your efforts to move through this time of life, toward a more fulfilling tomorrow.

The insight you gain by reading *Manopause* will allow you to feel more empathy and patience toward your manopause man and his behavior. Sharing what you have learned with your man will help him to become better adjusted to his own changes and more emotionally aware of what he is going through, plus what you are going through alongside him. This new insight will help to lessen his struggles and release him from the cultural pressures he is laboring under. He will be more at peace in his home, with his family, at work, with his friends, and, most important, with you. You will enjoy improved communi-cation and a more intimate relationship. You will be freed from the constraints that have kept you both from exploring avenues of life that have always been intriguing but seemingly unobtainable. Now is your chance to absorb the message of *Manopause.* With men living longer today than ever before, it's time to take the steps to ensure that you share your future with a man who is happy, well-adjusted, and fulfilled.

# UNDERSTANDING YOUR
# **MANOPAUSE** MAN

**PART I**

CHAPTER ONE

# THE **MANOPAUSE** QUIZ

Men . . . we can't live without them. They make up almost 50 percent of our planet. We are raised by them. We work with them. We live with them. We share our lives with them. And best of all, we make love to them. They are our fathers, our friends, our husbands, our co-workers, and every so often, our bosses. They are our teachers, our mailmen, our doctors, our taxi drivers, our attorneys, our supermarket clerks, our shoe salesmen, and our neighbors.

But while it's true we can't live without them, let's admit that sometimes it's hard to live with them, especially during the unsettled years between 40 and 65. These are the years when noticeable changes in our men can begin to turn them into people we aren't sure we recognize. Why does this happen? And why has there been so little focus placed on this? Why does society as a whole find men's changes frightening and difficult to talk about? It's because our culture has pronounced that this change eats away at the very core of what it means to "be a man."

There are certain ways men must behave, and certain ways they are expected to perform. And most of them conform to these standards, at least for a while. But when they reach midlife, with hormones possibly ebbing, the struggle gets harder. For some men, midlife can be a transition that is relatively smooth, with just a few bumps in the road. For others, it may be disquieting. But for many, it can be earth-shattering, as their declining hormones collide, head-on, with our culture's manhood demands. It is this crash that triggers uncharacteristic feelings and actions in our men. This is the period we call manopause—one word that says it all. Manopause encompasses every aspect of the inevitable change in a man's life.

But don't despair. Your relationship with a manopause man can thrive, as this period of time can also offer a satisfying, rewarding, and fulfilling new stage in life. *Manopause* will turn on the lights for you, expose how important it is to understand how men tick at this precarious time of life, and guide you both to savor a happier shared future.

### The Quiz

Maybe you sense that your man is in the midst of this change. Perhaps you don't. But then again, do you really know and understand your man and the ways he is different from you? To help make the process of change more comfortable, you need to appreciate and empathize with what he is going through. You must also begin to analyze how you may be contributing to his stress. The following quiz will help you take a more honest and forthright look at your knowledge of the differences between men and women, and it will help you to recognize the inner cultural programming that affects both of your expectations. In addition, it will shed light on how both of your behaviors individually influence and color this confusing, sometimes tumultuous, but potentially fulfilling time of transformation.

### Part One:

How well do you know and understand men? How different are they from us? The following short quiz will help you determine your depth of knowledge about some all-important male and female traits—traits that could impact your relationship and your ability to communicate as you navigate through manopause. Your score on this quiz will show you just how much you know about men, and their changes at midlife. After all, knowledge is power.

QUESTIONS

**1. A man who has sex at least twice a week can boost his infection-fighting cells by:**

    a.  45 percent

    b.  30 percent

    c.  20 percent

    d.  0 percent

**2. Who has more neurons in their brain?**

    a.  Men

    b.  Women

    c.  They are equal

**3. Generally, as a man ages, the semen he ejaculates:**

    a.  Decreases by up to half

    b.  Decreases slightly

    c.  Becomes thicker

    d.  Increases slightly

**4. Studies show women recognize signs of sadness in a face 90 percent of the time, whereas men recognize them:**

    a.  40 percent of the time

    b.  60 percent of the time

    c.  75 percent of the time

**5. On average, a man begins losing testosterone at the age of:**

    a.  60

    b.  45

    c.  30

    d.  18

**6. When faced with something dangerous and life-threatening:**

    a.  A woman's brain activates faster than a man's

    b.  A man's brain activates faster than a woman's

    c.  Both brains activate at approximately the same rate

**7. Whose brain can better analyze a dangerous situation before acting on it?**

    a.  Women's

    b.  Men's

    c.  They do it equally well

**8. Which sex has a better built-in lie detector?**

    a.  Men

    b.  Women

    c.  They both recognize a good lie when they see one

**9. Men's testosterone levels fluctuate:**

    a.  Hourly

    b.  Daily

    c.  Seasonally

    d.  Both a and b

    e.  All of the above

**10. More often over the age of 50, it is:**

    a.  The woman who asks for a divorce

    b.  The man who asks for a divorce

    c.  Equal between men and women to demand a divorce

**11. Can a placebo be as effective as Viagra for a midlife man?**

    a.  Yes

    b.  No

**12. If our ultimate fear is death:**

    a.  Both sexes fear it to the same degree

    b.  Women generally fear it more than men do

    c.  Men generally fear it more than women do

**13. Whose brain has a better "camera" to record details of experiences?**

    a.  Men's

    b.  Women's

    c.  Recollection of detail is not gender-specific

**14. When men and women communicate:**

    a.  Women use twice the words that men use

    b.  Women use 20 percent more words than men use

    c.  Women use half the words that men use

**15. Baby boomers, on average, believe that middle age ends at:**

    a.  55

    b.  67

    c.  79

**16. A common sign of a man's innate testosterone level is:**

    a.  The number of children he fathers

    b.  The job he chooses

    c.  The number of wives he has by the age of 50

**17. Researchers believe that during midlife, at one time or another, depression affects:**

    a.  Up to 60 percent of men

    b.  Up to 50 percent of men

    c.  Up to 40 percent of men

    d.  Up to 20 percent of men

**18. Studies indicate that a man's age:**

    a.  Has no effect on the health and brainpower of the children he fathers

    b.  Can influence the IQs of the children he fathers

**19. As a man ages:**

    a.  His brain reacts to rewards more fully than before

    b.  His brain reacts to rewards less fully than before

    c.  There is no particular change in the way his brain reacts to rewards

**20. It is possible to predict genetically whether a man is likely to be faithful to you.**

    a.  True

    b.  False

**21. The percentage of men who have their first child over the age of 35 is:**

    a.  15 percent

    b.  20 percent

    c.  30 percent

**22. In the last decade, the number of women receiving college degrees has:**

    a.  Drawn to within 10 percent of men

    b.  Drawn equal to men

    c.  Exceeded men

**23. Regular sex can:**

    a.  Raise a man's pain threshold

    b.  Cut down on his sick days

    c.  Help lift a depression

    d.  Both a and c

    e.  All of the above

**24. According to the 2010 Census, the highest American divorce rate is:**

    a.  In couples from 20 to 30

    b.  In couples from 30 to 45

    c.  In couples from 45 to 64

    d.  In couples over 64

**25. At midlife, the performance of a man's penis can be a predictor of future heart attacks.**

    a.  True

    b.  False

**ANSWERS**

Give yourself one point for each correct answer.

    1.  (b)

    2.  (c)

    3.  (a)

    4.  (a)

    5.  (c)

    6.  (b)

    7.  (a)

    8.  (b)

    9.  (e)

10. (a)

11. (a)

12. (c)

13. (b)

14. (a)

15. (c)

16. (b)

17. (c)

18. (b)

19. (b)

20. (a)

21. (c)

22. (c)

23. (e)

24. (c)

25. (a)

## What Does Your Score Mean?

**21–25 Points:** You are very knowledgeable! You are beginning your journey with a solid understanding of the different traits of the sexes. Building on this strong base, you can now learn a new way to comprehend the struggles men experience during manopause, as well as myriad ways to cope with their situation and improve your relationships. Armed with the new knowledge about your manopause man that is presented in *Manopause,* you will be able to achieve positive, productive, and meaningful communication and your relationships will be greatly enhanced. Read on.

**12–20 Points:** Your score shows that you have been paying attention, and you appreciate the importance of understanding what it takes to be a man, both physically and emotionally, what the differences between the sexes are, and how deeply those differences affect your relationships. Through reading *Manopause,* you will gain the facts and ideas you need to make your relationship thrive. You will understand what makes your manopause man tick, and you will be able to help guide him through any rough patches that might lie ahead.

**1–11 Points:** Be glad you picked up this book! As a novice in the field of men, you need to learn as much as you can, not just about this tumultuous time of life, but also the physical and societal forces that affect men. With this knowledge, you can live happily with your manopause man. Start by paying special attention to Part One of the book, as it will explain what makes a man "a man" and how manopause affects this. After you've learned the basics of manhood and manopause, the second half of the book will give you more detailed information, as well as concrete advice you can put into practice. As your manopause man is changing, you will be on secure footing with your improved knowledge of his biological and psychological characteristics, and you will understand how they can impact his everyday life—and your relationship.

## Part Two:

This portion of the quiz is designed to help you discover how well you truly understand the pressures our culture places on your manopause man. Cultural conditioning strongly influences all of us. Where do your beliefs and those of your manopause man fall on the traditional manhood scale? If they are not in alignment, it can be a source of great contention, as these beliefs dictate what you expect from him and the sort of support he hopes to get from you. This quiz will illuminate how *your* attitudes and actions impact your man. There is the possibility that he is sensing beliefs in you that are making his own inner struggle worse. Beliefs you may not be aware of, but that you are projecting.

This quiz can also be used as a tool to assist in telling you whether you and your man view the world from the same point of view. If your man is open to it, each of you might, individually, want to take the following portion of this quiz. While doing that, you will answer as to how you would act, and your manopause man will answer as to how he would *expect you* to act.

If you connect with several answers, choose the one which most honestly represents how you would feel and act. Being completely truthful will offer you the best chance of learning how you are influencing your manopause man, and how you are helping or hindering him in moving toward being more open-minded and comfortable with his changes. How sensitive are you? How fine-tuned is your empathy? This section of the quiz will help you take a look at yourself, and better understand your contributions to his manhood pressures.

QUESTIONS

**1. You and your manopause man watch your four-year-old son at preschool. When your son moves from the trucks to the dolls, your manopause man calls to him, in front of other parents and students, saying that dolls are for girls; he should go back with the other boys and the trucks. Your reaction is to:**

a. Tell your husband he's wrong; your son can play with whatever he wants.

b. Tell your son that daddy is right. Trucks are more fun.

c. Stay out of it in the classroom, and discuss gender roles with both of them later.

**2. The teacher, having heard this shout-out to your son, informs your husband that comments like his are not acceptable in her classroom. Seeing that your husband is upset, your reaction is to:**

a.  Quietly tell the teacher he is just a caring father.

b.  Quietly tell your husband she is right and suggest you talk about it later.

c.  Quietly tell your husband that even though the teacher was overly harsh, he needs to pull her aside, discuss it with her, and apologize.

**3. Your manopause man is experiencing erectile dysfunction. You:**

a.  Attempt to get advice from your friends; they may have experienced a similar problem.

b.  Encourage him not to worry; he should initiate sex when he feels comfortable doing it.

c.  Do your homework on sexual problems, and then share it with him.

**4. Your manopause man begins to cry in public when your preteen son receives a sports award. You:**

a.  Quietly suggest he step outside; he may not want people to see him like this.

b.  Let him cry.

c.  Excuse yourself and go to the ladies' room to give him some space.

**5. Your manopause man catches your 13-year-old daughter necking in the family room. He blows his top and kicks the boy out of the house. As your daughter bursts into tears, you:**

    a.  Tell her she deserved the reprimand; Daddy is just trying to protect her.

    b.  Tell your manopause man that his temper is going to drive a wedge through your home.

    c.  Tell him you understand that he was trying to protect your daughter. You suggest that he was also protecting himself.

**6. Your manopause man is angrily and frequently attacking you verbally, seemingly for no apparent reason. When he denies that something other than your actions are behind this, you:**

    a.  Defend yourself, pointing out his flaws.

    b.  Avoid confrontation, hoping this is a passing phase.

    c.  Tell him you love him, but if he can't change, he has to leave.

**7. Your manopause man is being overly flirtatious with a woman at a party. You:**

    a.  Tell yourself boys will be boys and, while ignoring his behavior, stand at his side and smile.

    b.  Remind your manopause man that he is married.

    c.  Interrupt the conversation and ask your manopause man to step aside to have a private word with you.

**8. Your manopause man is demoted at work. You:**

a. Encourage him to talk out his feelings, then suggest ways in which he could share his expertise with others.

b. Offer to pick up more hours at work, or offer ideas to cut down on the household expenses, so he doesn't feel the financial burden.

c. Share with him how worried and insecure this is making you feel. Assure him you can only imagine how bad he is feeling.

**9. You discover that your husband has been frequently visiting X-rated sites online. You:**

a. Confront him and insist on talking it out, telling him it must be addressed.

b. Begin to call friends for advice.

c. Worry about whether you have disappointed him and change your sexual behavior.

**10. While playing in the doubles tournament at the tennis club, your manopause man blows several shots and constantly blames you for being out of position. You:**

a. Ignore the comments and play harder, hoping to change the rhythm of the game and give him time to renew his concentration.

b. Ask the other team to weigh in on it; who is out of position, you or him?

c. Suggest that the goal of the day is to have fun. Winning is secondary; he doesn't need to be so competitive.

**11. Your manopause man admits to being attracted to the 28-year-old woman he works with. You:**

    a.  Strongly suggest that he find a new place of employment.

    b.  Tell him that while you appreciate his honesty, this news hurts. You insist that he spend more time discussing, with you, the reasons he is feeling this way.

    c.  Are relieved that he shared instead of acting on it; you make a concerted effort to spice up your relationship.

**12. Your manopause man's best friend dies after a prolonged battle against cancer. At the funeral, trying to be strong for his friend's family members, he doesn't shed a tear. You:**

    a.  Commend him for his strength.

    b.  Ask him why he is acting as if he doesn't have feelings and encourage him to let his emotions out.

    c.  Decide to ignore it, understanding that this is a very male reaction to tragedy.

**13. It's your anniversary and your manopause man takes you to an expensive restaurant. Upon arrival he discovers that the special table he reserved is not available. He begins to loudly berate the hostess, threatening to leave. You:**

    a.  Suggest there is another restaurant down the street. It's his choice.

    b.  Comment that people are staring, and suggest he lower his voice.

    c.  Tell him that you know the two of you deserve better, but things can't always go as planned. You insist on accepting the table.

**14. After his father's illness, your manopause man decides he has to quit his job and take his family to live out his dream of opening a bed-and-breakfast in the country. You:**

    a.  Lovingly remind him of how badly he will feel if he falls short in supporting his family.

    b.  Tell him that if this is truly his dream, since you believe in him, you will try it.

    c.  Give him conditional support, dependent upon him examining his reasons for his decision.

**15. Your manopause man's best friend drives over to show off his new sports car. When they return from taking a spin, your manopause man is glum and irritable. You:**

    a.  Tell him you understand him feeling down. It's unfortunate he doesn't earn enough so he could have one, too.

    b.  Assure your manopause man that someone like him doesn't need a car to be noticed.

    c.  Tell him you are open to cutting down other extra expenses if a sports car means so much to him.

**16. When your children are off to college and you announce that you need money from your joint account to start a business of your own, your manopause man says no. You:**

    a.  Tell him this is something you need to do for yourself. Ask him to examine his reasons for objecting; you will consider them.

    b.  Find ways to make it happen without extra money; it's selfish to use family savings on a whim or desire.

c. Tell him that half of that money is yours. You are doing what you need to do at this time in your life.

**17. After you buy a new home, your husband invites his father over to see it. His father tours the house finding faults. Your manopause man is ticked off. You:**

a. Tell your husband to ignore his father's comments. His father could be jealous of his hard-earned success.

b. Tell your husband that instead of feeling hurt, he needs to understand that his father is trying to maintain his position as head of the family.

c. Tell your husband to stop being so sensitive; many of his father's comments were valid.

**18. Your manopause boss begins to cut you out of the information flow. You:**

a. Confront him, preferably in a private meeting.

b. Think carefully, then decide whether it is necessary to go over his head and report what he is doing to his superior.

c. Discreetly survey your fellow workers to get their opinion of why he might be doing this.

**19. Your manopause man discovers Viagra, and the amount of time he wants to spend in the bedroom with you quintuples. You:**

a. Participate, despite your exhaustion. You don't want him to feel deprived and go elsewhere.

b. Find new ways to be intimate in addition to inter-course. If that becomes frustrating for him, encourage him to communicate his thoughts.

c. Tell him that he's overdoing it; ask him to be more sensitive to you.

**20. When his co-worker has a heart attack, your mano-pause man begins to spend excessive hours in the gym. He is looking better, but your relationship is losing out. He drops into bed exhausted and rushes out early every morn-ing. He makes commitments, but is always running late trying to squeeze in everything. You:**

a. Encourage him; he's never looked better, and you be-lieve he is healthier.

b. Don't worry about it, since you know he won't be able to keep going at this pace forever.

c. Commend him on his dedication and strength, while exploring the deeper reasons for this new behavior.

**21. You book a surprise weekend away to celebrate your husband's milestone birthday. When he says he needs to stay home to do some work, you:**

a. Insist that he go. He deserves a celebration—you both do.

b. Postpone the reservations, and hope that he will be-come available then.

c. Push him to delve deeper as to his reason for avoiding the trip.

ANSWERS

1. a=0, b=2, c=4
2. a=2, b=4, c=0
3. a=0, b=2, c=4
4. a=0, b=4, c=2
5. a=2, b=0, c=4
6. a=0, b=2, c=4
7. a=2, b=0, c=4
8. a=4, b=2, c=0
9. a=4, b=0, c=2
10. a=2, b=0, c=4
11. a=0, b=4, c=2
12. a=0, b=4, c=2
13. a=2, b=0, c=4
14. a=0, b=2, C=4
15. a=0, b=4, c=2
16. a=4, b=2, c=0
17. a=2, b=4, c=0
18. a=4, b=0, c=2
19. a=2, b=4, c=0
20. a=2, b=0, c=4
21. a=0, b=2, c=4

**What Does Your Score Mean?**

Your score reflects the level of your sensitivity to your manopause man's pressures, while also exploring your contribution toward easing or complicating his feelings. Ideally, once you understand how your attitudes and actions affect him, you can use what you learn in this book to help him move beyond his traditional thinking, and into a new, satisfying, and more fulfilling way of life. So if you score:

**66–84 Points:** Feel blessed that you have an innate grasp of the importance of shedding the cultural pressures that are weighing on your manopause man, and that you have the gift of empathy. You have made a healthy start toward helping him restructure his thinking in order to move smoothly through this time of change. Using *Manopause* as a guide and a tool, your contributions will become even more constructive. You will learn new techniques that will help you approach a variety of male challenges, and will deepen your understanding of the value of constant and honest communication, no matter how difficult or awkward.

**32–64 Points:** You are to be congratulated on your sensitivity, but your strong empathetic skills need to be tempered with an appreciation of how cultural manhood pressures conflict with the physical and psychological changes your manopause man is going through. Otherwise, you may be unknowingly and unintentionally handicapping him, instead of helping him to easily move forward through this inevitable passage. *Manopause* will help to open the door to your self-exploration by exposing the cultural biases that so many of us unknowingly fall into. It will also help you pinpoint which reactions you need to keep in check. Remember, your man isn't the only player in this game—your actions affect how well your man deals with life during manopause. After reading this book, and better understanding how the manhood pressures society imposes on him shape his behaviors, not only will you employ your magnificent skills of empathy to comfort your manopause man, you will also be able to contribute to his personal growth and happiness.

**0–30 Points:** You are comfortable seeing the world through your own eyes. Feeling empathy toward your manopause man and his challenges does not come easily to you. Maybe you don't understand the weight of his culturally based manhood pressures, you don't believe they negatively impact his everyday existence, or you don't feel you need to cater to him because of them. Nevertheless, the fact that you are reading this book means that you very much want to help your relationship during this period of his life. Pay particular attention to the chapters on what it means to "be a man" and on "The Manopause Problem" for guidance in reshaping your view of the world. And then the chapters in Part Two will give you hints on how to navigate empathetically through specific situations. You have made an important move by picking up *Manopause.* Hopefully, after you have completed this book, you will become more attuned to your manopause man's way of seeing the world, and more sensitized to his feelings. With this as your goal, you can look forward to a healthy relationship filled with respect and meaningful communication.

## So Let's Get Going!

*Manopause* will help you decipher the manopause men in your life, see the world through their eyes, and comprehend what they are feeling and experiencing. Understanding how different they are from us will be a pathway to improving your relationships. There may be stumbling blocks on this road to Nirvana, but you are not tackling them alone. We will teach you to navigate through this period of life with eyes open, as you explore it in relation to our culture's complexities.

Along the way, you will be learning the benefits of a new way of thinking about manhood. One you will want both yourself and your manopause man to absorb and live by—one that will free him from burdensome and archaic cultural pressures, while enriching the second half of his life. Each man should use this new style of thinking in a way that is uniquely personal, based on his own psychological predispositions and cultural conditioning.

Your journey will involve compromise. In certain situations, you will have to push beyond your personal comfort level. In others, since the culture has had a powerful impact on you as well, you will dig in your heels, feeling it is not possible for you to change to such a great degree. But don't despair; this is not an all-or-nothing proposition. Feel secure that with your newfound knowledge, you will make good choices and compromises—ones that will enhance your relationship with your manopause man.

So dive in to *Manopause* and open your mind. The more you know, the more you will understand. The more you understand, the more secure you will feel. The more secure you feel, the more likely you will be to communicate effectively and take the one small step toward relieving manhood pressures that can lead, if we all work together, to a big leap for our culture. Our manopause men live many more years than they ever did before. Help make those years, shared in a relationship with you, the best years of your lives.

CHAPTER TWO

# WHAT IT MEANS
# TO **"BE A MAN"**

Imagine you are ordering dinner at your neighborhood Chinese restaurant. You will be choosing one dish from Column A, another from Column B, and a third from Column C. Put them all together and you have a typical Chinese dinner. What it means to "be a man" similarly has its own set of components. They include powerful influences from our culture, added to well-established biological factors within a man's brain and his fluctuating hormonal system, combined with psychological reactions and behavioral tendencies. That is why, in order to truly understand what it means to "be a man," we need to examine the many elements that help to make up the men we know and love today.

Keep in mind that "being a man" is very different from "being a woman." Medical technology is highlighting biological dissimilarities every day. And these disparities are reinforced by our culture. Even the most subtle differences play an enormous role in how the sexes perceive reality, how they individually react to that vision, and, most important, how they communicate. These differences complicate your attempts to interpret your man's actions and reactions.

That is why it is so important for you to understand what these many differences are.

## The All-Important Quest for Manhood

*"The search after the great men is the dream of youth, and the most serious occupation of manhood."*

**— Ralph Waldo Emerson**

To understand what is happening to our men, we need to delve into the biological and psychological roots of manhood. To see the world through their eyes, we need to learn how their brains function. To appreciate their special brand of energy, we have to look at the male hormones that drive them. To grasp their psychology, we must explore their purpose for living, their drive to achieve their goals, their feelings about their roles in society, their need to emotionally connect, their position in the family, their expectations of unchanging physical abilities at any age, and their struggle to find their own comfort and happiness in relationships.

Every man *should* have the freedom to define and live out his own individual version of manhood. But unfortunately, because of society's cultural dictates, maintaining "manhood" has become a one-size-fits-all quest, a set of standards men are being challenged to conform to every day. Gabriel Byrne, playing Dr. Paul Weston, the psychiatrist dealing with his own inner turmoil on *In Treatment,* said it clearly when he told his personal therapist that, "as a man, you're like an animal in the wild. You're living day-to-day. You're trying to protect your territory and provide for your family. That's what a male is—a hunter, a dominator."

## Womanhood Is Biological, Manhood Is Doubtful!

World-renowned anthropologist David Gilmore, Ph.D., in his book, *Manhood in the Making,* says that in most cultures "femininity is more often construed as a biological given,"[1] that achieving woman-hood takes place with the onset of menstruation. This absolute marker of attainment is not so obvious for men. "There is a constantly recurring notion that real manhood is different from simple anatomical maleness."[2] A man has to meet "rigid codes of decisive action in many spheres of life: as husband, father, lover, provider, warrior."[3] In other words, manhood is only achieved by unremitting and never-ending tests of bravery, endurance, strength, and skill. Dan Kindlon, Ph.D., and Michael Thompson, Ph.D., in their book *Raising Cain,* concur, telling us that a man's "masculine identity is virtually impossible to achieve in any lasting way."[4] When young, "a boy lives in a narrowly defined world of developing masculinity in which everything he does or thinks is judged on the basis of the strength or weakness it represents: you are either strong and worthwhile, or weak and worthless."[5]

We, as women, don't have to think, on a daily basis, from the moment we rise until the time we go to sleep, of trying to prove ourselves as women. Our womanhood is preestablished. It is different for men. They feel an undefined, but constant, pressure to prove their manhood. With every action, the question becomes "Is this what a *man* would do?" or "Is this the way a *man* should act?" Men are always looking for ways to prove their masculinity. This unfair burden was established eons ago, yet it is still imposed on them today. Our culture has raised men to believe they need to be heroes to be real men. And culturally, both sexes have bought into these old beliefs.

### Men Must Be Heroes

Michael Gurian, author of *What Could He Be Thinking?,* suggests that Sigmund Freud, Carl Jung, and many other psychoanalysts and psychologists who studied the human psyche believed that "the hero is biologically wired into men's minds."[6] Gurian goes on to say, "Testosterone, vasopressin, greater spinal fluid in the brain, less serotonin, less oxytocin, and the way the male-brain system projects life into an abstract and spatial universe, lead men to see the world in terms of action, heroes, warriors, even lovers who must negotiate landscapes of challenge."[7] Another way of saying this is that most men are on an extraordinarily burdensome quest.

And societal pressure kicks in early, too. Young boys are told to "be a man" when they stumble on the Little League field. Hold back those tears, brush off the hurts, and get right back in the game. Never show weakness, especially in front of opponents. Never reveal emotion because that's a sign of vulnerability. The culture has taught our young boys to focus on the goal of winning at all costs, showing unbelievable physical strength, and never betraying emotional weakness.

Take a look at the plethora of action figures our children grow up with. They come from books, comic strips, and movies. Superman, Iron Man, and the Incredible Hulk—even Mighty Mouse—are characters that display muscular physiques and physical prowess. As action heroes, they make sure goodness overcomes evil, and by doing so, they gain respect in their imaginary worlds. Growing boys identify with and emulate them. This is the kind of cultural conditioning that teaches them they must become heroes.

If you're thinking that we don't put pressure on men to succeed at a heroic quest, take a look at a successful website called Dateahero.com. Founded by a firefighter and his wife, its homepage tagline is, "Tired of dating zeros? It's time to date a hero." Firefighters, law enforcement, and military officers are promoted on the website. Heroic pictures of these men in action are plastered across its pages, and the website's success confirms, beyond a doubt, that women find pleasure in looking at, fantasizing about, and dating heroes. So it's no wonder that in your man's heart—and all men's hearts—he wants to be Hercules, the son of a god and the greatest hero in Greek mythology. Yet, as men grow older, it becomes more difficult to live up to this ideal, and somewhere, deep down, they know it.

And it's not simply physical heroics we demand of our men. We also expect them to carry an invisible shield that protects them from feelings and emotions coming in or going out. When describing "manhood," "masculinity," or what it is to "be a man," emotions and feelings are never included. Our culture has socialized men away from feelings—away from recognizing them, getting in touch with them, expressing them, or recognizing them in others. And this inability to healthily deal with emotions can lead to some serious problems.

The men in the military, our real-life warriors, are extreme examples of the price men pay for quashing their emotions. Dr. Heidi Squier Kraft, author of *Rule Number Two*, who has devoted her life to treating U.S. combat patients with post-traumatic stress syndrome, says that feeling and showing emotion is the ultimate stigma that men have to fight. The military has "a long-standing culture that has had no tolerance for anything that looks like less than emotional perfection."[8] But of course no human being can be emotionally perfect. This requirement to hold back emotion and remain strong is one of the reasons that so many soldiers—and men in general—have to deal with stress-related conditions.

As you can see, in so many ways, our culture has been a catalyst, an antagonist, and a negative influence on our modern men. This is why it is time to change our culture's thinking.

## Ubermen, the Ultimate Heroes

Some men take their pursuit of manhood to an extreme. These are the "Ubermen." Webster's Dictionary tells us that anything that is "uber" is a superlative example of its type or class, a thing taken to an excessive degree. The 19th-century German philosopher Friedrich Nietzsche had this in mind when he coined the term *Uberman* to describe those special men who had it within them to rise above their fellows and create a new type of world.

Today's Uberman is a high achiever who is goal-oriented to the point of ignoring other precious aspects of life. He is driven to succeed beyond expectations, as power and success are the very linchpins of his identity. So much so that for an Uberman, there is never quite enough, even if he has reached a pinnacle above the rest. The more success he finds, the greater an Uberman's goals become, and the more difficult it is for him to reach them.

Ubermen head the world's industries, run corporations and investment funds, control real-estate empires, wield scalpels in surgical

31

suites, govern countries, and excel in the world of sports. On the surface, they appear strong and impervious; but underneath that veneer, they are most likely suffering more than most as they struggle to maintain their own high standards.

## Today's Lifestyle Is Setting Men Up for Failure

*"The tragedy of machismo is that a man
is never quite man enough."*

**— Germaine Greer**

Since the earliest days of human existence, if a man was not respected by his peers it was evolutionary death. "The need for respect is at the core of manhood,"[9] says Jed Diamond, Ph.D., author of numerous books and an expert on the psychology of male behavior. According to Diamond, without respect, a man would not have been invited to participate in masculine activities such as hunting for food. If he wasn't good at hunting for food, then he didn't have the ability to provide for a family. And if he could not provide for a family with his strength and warriorlike abilities, then women were not interested in him. If women were not interested, then he was not able to reproduce. Obviously, his survival and the survival of his genes were directly dependent on his power and strength. The more ability he had to provide and to lead, the more women he would attract, the more success he would find, and the more control he had over his destiny. Today's men no longer hunt for food, but this prehistoric insistence on earning respect through power and strength has not changed to reflect our modern society. Men have remained trapped by antiquated definitions of manhood.

*"Masculinity is not something given to you, something
you're born with, but something you gain . . . And you
gain it by winning small battles with honor."*

**— Norman Mailer**

Unfortunately, modern men, unlike their ancestors, have few obvious chances to show off their heroics. The hundreds of thousands of men who used to prove themselves on the battlefield have largely been replaced, as wars are increasingly fought through technology. Men no longer risk their lives by hunting and killing wild animals to bring home food and clothing for their family, or by cutting down trees and building homes for shelter. Our modern society has evolved beyond that.

When becoming a financial success is more controlled by the world economy than by a man's individual achievement, it can be debilitating. This can lead to frustration, feelings of worthlessness, disillusionment, and confusion—feelings Hercules would never have had. So which came first? Did our culture form our ideas of "manhood," or did our men's biology dictate our cultural ideal of what a man should be?

### *It All Begins with Testosterone*

Let's talk hormones. If estrogen is a bicycle built for two, testosterone is a Harley-Davidson Electra Glide, fully loaded with a Screamin' Eagle twin cam 110. It powers your man. Women do produce some testosterone in their ovaries and adrenal glands, but only a tenth to a twentieth of what men generate. Testosterone is considered the most male of all the hormones—the one that puts the "Joe" into your man's mojo.

Becoming a man begins in the womb. Around six weeks after conception, the testicles in male fetuses begin to pump out large amounts of testosterone, causing the genitalia to grow and transforming the brain into a distinctly male structure. Another flood, at puberty, triggers the development of male secondary sexual characteristics, deepening squeaky voices, causing facial and body hair to grow, changing the physique, and increasing muscle mass and strength. Truly, from womb until death, testosterone is the hormone that is responsible, more than any other, for initiating and maintaining your man's normal adult male characteristics.

Testosterone increases your man's ratio of lean muscle to body fat, and helps to keep what fat there is, properly distributed. It boosts his strength, particularly his upper body strength. It helps to sustain his male hair pattern. It keeps his skin thick and supple. It facilitates his bone development and helps to preserve his bone density. It is his leading metabolic hormone, assisting the conversion of food into energy, and burning protein. It aids in supporting his red blood cell production. It accelerates his rate of recovery from injury. It improves his cognition, boosting his mental alertness and focus. It works as an antidepressant. It helps to maintain his male reproductive tract. And, it assists in both his production of sperm and their maturation.

Most important of all, at least to your man, testosterone helps to provide his sex drive and to boost it into "overdrive." It kick-starts his desire and increases his sexual thoughts and fantasies, and, by doing that, it makes him feel like a "real man."

## What Is a Normal Testosterone Level?

The perimeters are as wide as the oceans are deep. Let's rephrase the question. Instead of asking what a normal testosterone level is, we should be asking what is normal for *your* man. Because, in case you are one of the few women who *hasn't* noticed, men come in different models. Some are just naturally high in testosterone. Some are lower. Think Tony Soprano versus Mahatma Gandhi; at its most extreme, the testosterone variation can be as great as theirs. Chances are, your man is somewhere in the middle. Just understand that each and every man has his own natural level of testosterone, and where that level falls can affect him, and you, in many ways.

A study done on college fraternity members by James McBride Dabbs with Mary Godwin Dabbs bore this out. Fraternities with lower mean testosterone levels had a calm and polite atmosphere and responded quickly to a female visitor, making her feel at home. High-testosterone fraternities, on the other hand, had wrecked furniture in their living rooms and were crude and rude to the same female visitor.

They were less interested in making her feel at home than in solving the problem of how to get her into bed.[10]

A common sign of a man's innate testosterone profile is the kind of work he chooses. Another Dabbs study showed that ministers, as a group, had the lowest levels of testosterone of any profession studied, while actors had the highest.[11] Blue collar workers had higher levels of testosterone than white collar men.[12] And other studies have shown that testosterone levels for trial lawyers surpass those of tax lawyers.[13]

## High Testosterone Can Be Big Trouble

Just as there are testosterone benefits, there are some very distinct drawbacks. Testosterone may be the hormone of vigor and drive, but it is also the hormone of aggression and risk-taking. Having overly high testosterone levels tends to get a man into trouble. It is a very real contributor to the fact that men lead shorter lives than women. Without it, they would not be signing up to be Navy SEALs, jumping into boxing rings, or getting into physical confrontations. Testosterone is the reason that while men may be just 50 percent of the population, they account for 89 percent of murders committed in the United States.[14]

And it is not just physical risk that high testosterone encourages. High testosterone can lead to bad decision-making. Look no further than your teenage son for proof of that. It makes men tenser, more stressed, more stubborn, and more easily frustrated if things don't go their way immediately. No wonder a man who flies off the handle at the drop of a hat is called "testy." Even his body can get "testy." Since high testosterone levels can be correlated with heart disease and susceptibility to infectious diseases, some experts theorize that it can act as an immune suppressant.

High testosterone is also an ingredient that can muck up the recipe for a long and happy marriage. There is a reason why single men are, generally, higher in testosterone than married men. A young man needs it to give him the confidence to compete for an attractive mate. But ironically, at the same time that it makes him attractive to women, it also makes him want to maintain his separateness and avoid emotional entanglements, and thus will keep him emotionally remote from his woman.

There's a reason why testosterone levels tend to decline in men who are in long-term marriages. They no longer need to impregnate as many women as possible. Their levels drop even further when they become fathers. Mother Nature helps men to become caretakers for their families by lowering their testosterone levels and raising their care-giving prolactin levels during these bonding years.

High or low, hormones are a very important part of what makes up your man. But without the contribution of his brain, how male would he be?

### The All-Important Male Brain

Why won't he ask for directions when he's lost? Why can't he learn the right way to load a dishwasher? Why does he do a "drop and walk" when he takes off his dirty clothes? Face it ladies, if this is your man, his behavior is wired into him, and you already know that in some things, he is not likely to change. If you are lucky, he may try to for you, but it could prove to be futile. Blame it on differences between the male and female brains.

Thousands of years ago, facing down a saber-toothed tiger, men had to be aggressive, strong, and emotionless. "Biology does represent the foundation of our personalities and behavioral tendencies,"[14] says Louann Brizendine, M.D., neuropsychiatrist, and best-selling author of several books including *The Female Brain* and *The Male Brain.* She continues, "Men have . . . larger brain centers for action and aggression."[15] In other words, men are built to take action and react to threats, not to talk things over. This could be the seed from which our culture has perpetuated the concept of heroics. Rutgers University professor Helen Fisher, Ph.D., adds, "The two brain hemispheres are less well connected in men than in women. This gives men the ability to focus on one thing at a time and be very goal oriented."[16] Women, on the other hand, have 11 percent more neurons in the language area than men, and a larger hippocampus, the principle hub for emotion and memory. They also can easily read facial expressions and body language, and sense that "something is wrong."

Clearly our culture's idea of what constitutes "manhood" and "womanhood" is rooted in the fact that our male and female brains are constructed and wired very differently, partially because of what each sex needed to accomplish in order to survive thousands of years in the past.

## Dissecting the Male Brain

For centuries scientists studied the brain using information gathered from cadavers, or from the symptoms of brain-damaged individuals. Today we are much more enlightened, thanks to noninvasive technologies that have been developed for measuring and studying the living brain. Doctors and scientists are now able to view and analyze the brain in real time as you are reading, writing, and speaking, and while you are experiencing pleasure, fear, depression, and anxiety. This complex organ can be observed solving problems, retrieving memories, recognizing facial expressions, listening to babies crying, and even falling in love. Modern technology helps doctors and scientists to compare and contrast the sizes of various portions of the male and female brain, and to decipher how our dissimilar brains guide us to function in distinctly male and female ways. The differences they have found can be traced all the way back to the most essential and primitive parts of the brain.

Inside the brain, there are two "ancient, ever-watchful eyes of the emotional system,"[17] says Rush Dozier, Jr., Pulitzer-nominated science author, scholar, and author of *Fear Itself.* Deriving their name from the Greek word for almond, the amygdalae sit underneath each temple about an inch and a half deep in the brain. All the information that enters your senses flows through them. They play a pivotal role in the emotional system. "The amygdala appears to be vital in generating all primitive emotions, from ecstasy to terror,"[18] Dozier continues. These two clusters, each about the size of a nickel, are where fear, anger, and aggression originate. They remember that you are fearful of a growling Doberman pinscher, like the one you met up with years ago

37

while walking down an unfamiliar street. Or the bee-infested hive you accidently stumbled onto in your friend's wooded backyard.

The hippocampus is your brain's memory center for details. You have two hippocampi, each about the size of your little finger. They rest right next to their respective amygdala. The hippocampus is responsible for details—for remembering exactly where you were standing when you first saw that Doberman pinscher, and what you were wearing as you fled from those bees.

Even when you are sleeping, the amygdalae and hippocampi are awake. Think of them as all-night security guards, watching your back, ready to call on your other faculties if an emergency presents itself. Because of them, if there is a loud crash while you are deeply asleep, you awaken ready to respond and protect yourself and those around you. Now, thanks to cutting-edge technology, scientists have discovered that the size and function of these structures are different within male and female brains. This helps them to explain the difference between some of the actions, and reactions, of the sexes.

Generally, the amygdala is larger, and the hippocampus smaller, in the male brain. This is one of the reasons men can be more aggressive, their temperatures can rise faster, and more energy rushes to their muscles in an emergency. During prehistoric times, it was this series of traits that helped men to attack and defend at the first sign of danger, and to efficiently kill when hunting for food without feeling empathy for their prey. In women, the prefrontal cortex, which is the control center for fear, anger, aggression, and other emotions, is larger. If danger intruded on a woman or, God forbid, her children, her prefrontal cortex gave her the ability to take a moment to assess the dangerous situation and decide how best to protect her young. These sex-based traits have been wired into our brains over millennia, but they still affect how the two genders behave today.

## The Male Brain Behaves Differently than Yours

How many times have you vividly remembered physical details of emotional events when your man wasn't able to? The larger hippocampus in women's brains acts like a camera, photographing moments and storing them on your own personal, internal hard drive. The stronger the amygdala's response is to happy, sad, or stressful situations, the more likely it is that the hippocampus will be signaled to memorialize them. This is not so for men. Because less of their brain energy is given to the processing of feelings, they store fewer emotional memories. Dave and Jenny are a case in point.

Years after Dave and Jenny were married, she realized he didn't remember what she wore on their first date. She was disappointed that he had forgotten the jump-off to their lifelong love affair. Jenny was wrong to assume that Dave would remember the details. Had he spilled hot coffee on her dress, he might have recalled it. The threat to her would have activated his amygdala, and that memory would have been printed into his hippocampus. But since nothing dramatic or threatening happened that night, Dave had no reason to remember exactly what Jenny was wearing. Dave was not losing his memory, the imprint never made it to his male brain.

### He's a Systemizer with a Spatial Brain; You're an Empathizer with a Verbal Brain

Herein lies the difference between the brains. Simon Baron-Cohen, Ph.D., and author of *The Essential Difference* says, "The female brain is predominantly hard-wired for empathy. The male brain is predominantly hardwired for understanding and building systems."[19] Assuming your man is a systemizer, he is driven to ferret out the nature of events or objects. He approaches a situation by intuitively deciphering how things work and by understanding the underlying rules that govern the behavior of that system. This is done in order to understand and predict the system or to invent a new one. Boys choose to build with blocks, select toy vehicles, and play with toys that have clear functions. Girls, more often, choose to play with dolls and to lean toward imaginary play. As men mature, most of them become ever-more fascinated with what makes things tick, fixing items around the house, and examining the strategies of their favorite sports teams in an effort to see which one is going to win.

It is not a coincidence that there are certain professions, as Dr. Baron-Cohen points out, that are primarily male, such as construction, crafting musical instruments, metal working, and weapon making. Success in these fields comes from being able to focus attention and perfect processes, which are some of the things a systemizer excels at. The key to being a systemizer is control. Your man is probably driven to take control throughout every step of a process; once he can figure out what drives it, he can move to the next step.

Don't misunderstand though; both sexes have a combination of systematizing and empathizing skills. It's just that most likely, you lean toward empathizing, and your man leans toward systematizing. In order to systematize, your man must detach himself and step back to evaluate situations, monitor information, and track factors that cause variation in the information he's receiving. To do that, he has to approach a given situation without feeling empathy toward it. But is that natural? "Empathizing occurs when we feel an appropriate emotional reaction, an emotion triggered by the other person's emotion, and it is done in order to understand another person, to predict their behavior and to connect or resonate with them emotionally."[20] "To empathize you need some degree of attachment in order to recognize that you are interacting with a person, not an object, but a person with feelings and whose feelings affect your own,"[21] says Dr. Baron-Cohen. It is not about knowing what another person thinks, but rather, about having an emotional reaction to what that other person is feeling.

It is imperative to recognize the difference between your brain wiring and your man's. Traditional men thrive with a lack of empathy; it allows leaders to establish themselves. They disconnect from other people's feelings in an effort to get ahead. On the other hand, if you naturally attach to other people, it becomes hard to charge to the front, because you may want to reach out to others and help them. Being an empathizer, you understand the people in your world by connecting to their feelings. Michael Gurian explains this in a slightly different way. Male brains are spatial, and female brains are verbal. The male brain devotes more outer-layer areas to "spatial and mechanical strategies in the brain,"[22] while the female brain tends to devote more outer-layer areas to word use and word production. In fact, on average, men use just half the words that women use. That is why your man may choose to spend his time playing ball or mastering a video game, because he is more comfortable engaging his brain in the areas of mechanical strategies and "systemizing." You, on the other hand, would rather meet friends to talk, choosing to engage your brain in the area where you are most comfortable: your verbal skills and communication.

A great example that shows the difference in how male and female brains work can be seen in the interaction of Zack and Lianna, two-and-a-half-year-old male/female twins. Zack wanted a toy Lianna was playing with, so he aggressively yanked it out of her hands. Zack was content—he had systematically and single-mindedly set out on a mission and accomplished it. Lianna felt violated. As Zack loaded her toy into his dump truck, she asked him to return it, but Zack remained focused on building a system of toys in the bed of his truck. He wasn't feeling her loss or connecting with her feelings of violation. Hurt, Lianna decided to make him understand how she was feeling. Spotting Zack's coveted blue pedal car on the other side of the room, Lianna sat in it. She wanted Zack to feel violated, too. Instinctively trying to protect his property, Zack dashed over, pushed her out of his car, and got in it. Empathy was the farthest thing from his mind. Lianna picked herself up, ran back to the dump truck, and grabbed the original toy. After a moment, Zack realized he had never intended to be in his blue car. How did he get there? Wondering what had just happened, he looked toward Lianna. She smiled back at him, holding the original toy. At that moment, Zack understood what his sister felt when he took her toy. She had communicated a lesson about feelings. In a perfect world, every little boy would have a savvy sister. But in this world, you may need to teach your man about empathy.

### The Male Brain Is Less Sensitive to Emotional Nuance

Men's brains are not thick; they are just less sensitive to emotional nuance. "Part of the reason that a woman's memory is better for emotional details is that a woman's amygdala is more easily activated by emotional nuance,"[23] says Dr. Louann Brizendine. She adds, "The female brain is gifted at quickly assessing the thoughts, beliefs, and intentions of others, based on the smallest hints . . . Men don't seem to have the same innate ability to read faces and tone of voice for emotional nuance."[24] This is because they have less brain circuitry for language and for observing emotion in others. We easily recognize feelings and subtleties in situations that our men don't see. According to Dr. Brizendine, women can pick up the subtle signs of sadness in a face 90 percent of the time. Men, by comparison, can only recognize subtle signs 40 percent of the time.[25] It isn't that women have a sixth sense; it's just that we can collectively read signals, faces, and situations through body language, tone of voice, and facial expressions much more keenly than men.

If you want an example, just look to the 2009 case of Jaycee Lee Dugard. Despite 18 years of probation officer checks and routine surprise home visits by local male police officers, no one detected the horror taking place inside Phillip Garrido's home . . . until the paroled sex offender was spotted by two *female* police officers. They noticed that Garrido was "clearly unstable." He was frenetic and he rambled. The young girls who were with him were unusually subdued, had unnaturally pasty skin for the end of the summer, and appeared rehearsed when they spoke. Female officer Campbell, "got a really bad feeling about it" after looking at the two children the rapist had fathered.[26] How unfortunate it is that male parole officers and policemen didn't detect strange behavior in the past. But how understandable, given the deficiencies of the male brain with respect to emotional nuance.

### Men Lie More, but Women Lie Better

Pat yourselves on the back, ladies. Because of our insight into emotional nuance, we are superior lie detectors. So be confident. If you are convinced that your man is cheating on you or doing something that you don't approve of, just ask him. If you confront him, it is likely he won't be able to fool you. Clinical neuroscientist, psychiatrist, and brain-imaging expert Daniel G. Amen, M.D., author of *The Brain in Love,* says, "Men tend to be more impulsive than women. They tend to have more affairs and tend to say things without fully thinking it through and often find themselves in hot water. Women also lie, but they get caught less. One reason is that women have better access to the right hemisphere and thus read social cues better than men. They notice the small things, like looking away or down or clearing the throat, that are typical in people who are not telling the truth. Since men tend to be in denial a lot of the time, they do not see when their partner is lying."[27] Generally, women don't get caught as often as men because men's lie detectors are not at full strength.

Outside their personal and romantic relations, men lie to maintain respect in the eyes of their peers. They do this because the pursuit of respect and honor is one of the cornerstones of their manhood and masculinity. In fact, men do anything they can to appear to adhere to our culture's strict rules dictating what it means to "be a man."

### The Mandates

With biology, psychology, and cultural pressures guiding them, our men strive to win, take action, be productive, and set and reach goals. At their core, men are striving to perform tests of bravery, to gain power and respect from their peers, their community, and, most important, their women. Proving and sustaining manhood is a lifelong goal for our men, and the game is ruled by a complex set of traditionally male guidelines—which we have dubbed "the *man*dates."

Many experts propose very similar lists of guidelines for the way men should think and act. Ronald Levant, Ed.D., ABPP, author of *Masculinity Reconstructed,* and Michael Kimmel, Ph.D., a researcher, writer, and author on men and masculinity, are two who have independently presented their checklists after doing in-depth studies.[28] Their findings have helped us create the following "*man*dates":

1.  Be a big shot. Your worth is only as great as your power, money, and status.

2.  Push down your emotions; never reveal them.

3.  Always be aggressive, daring, and strong. Don't let fear be part of your vocabulary.

4.  Never do anything that can be considered "feminine" or weak.

5.  Avoid any association with homosexuality.

6.  Disconnect sex from emotional intimacy.

7.  Be self-reliant. Never let others know you need them.

8.  Make duty and self-sacrifice the center of your life.

Keep in mind these are male rules taken to an extreme. Scaled-back versions of some or all of them may be recognizable to you. All are intended to prevent a man from showing any sign of "weakness" or "feelings." You have seen hints of the *man*dates at work in the personalities of men you interface with every day—your children's schoolteachers, government workers, your boss, or the men at your family gatherings. Some qualities are more pronounced in certain men. Like any spiritual belief, the stringency of a man's adherence depends on the commitment of the *man*date observer. Some men consider breaking these *man*dates to be a venial sin; some consider it to be a mortal sin. It all depends on how steeped they are in tradition.

### Traditional Traits to Cherish

Happily, not all of your man's ingrained beliefs are counterproductive. There are many traditional male traits that are positively treasured, and never to be forfeited. Dr. Levant's extensive research has guided us to this list of admirable manhood characteristics:

1.  The willingness to sacrifice their personal needs to provide for the ones they love.

2.  The willingness to experience pain and hardship to protect loved ones.

3. The desire to express their love by taking action and doing things for those they care about.

4. The desire to dive in to help solve a problem, even if the act involves danger.

5. The desire to remain loyal to commitments and stay connected until a problem is solved.

Most likely it is your man who will be the one to drive on a treacherously stormy night, not you. Or, he will take his hard-earned bonus, and, instead of rewarding himself, he will invest it in his children's education. Or he will be quick to help a female stranger struggling to lift a heavy box of groceries at a superstore. These irresistible traits, the ones that show our men's generosity of spirit, sit at the top of a long list of cherished manhood qualities that will forever display our men's everyday heroics, even as some of the other manhood qualities he has learned to lean on begin to dissipate.

### The Pursuit of Manhood at Midlife Comes at an Even Higher Price

Men feel pressure to live up to the *man*dates every day of their lives. If they can't be a modern-day Hercules, their manhood may be in question. This has been inculcated into our men over so many centuries, it's now innate. Your man may not be conscious of the pressures of manhood, since every man is carrying the same weight. And if he is aware of his heavy load, he may not tell you about it. Why would he reveal that he feels vulnerable? If, in his heart, he wants to be Hercules, to you and in front of the other men and women in his life, why would he risk showing weakness? He could be judged, shamed, and perceived as less of a man.

As Steven Z. Leder, senior rabbi of Wilshire Boulevard Temple in Los Angeles, wrote in an article for *Reform Judaism* magazine, "Most of the men in my life were either competitors, clients, or strangers. Like most men, I had never really left the junior high school locker room where the main thing was to measure up. For me and for so many others, to be a man among men meant to talk around things and keep my guard up; to carry the unique weight of manhood in mighty silence. Men are God's loneliest creatures."[29]

And the weight of manhood only gets more intense when the game changes. At midlife, the body, emotions, and actions a man has worked to sculpt and perfect all those years begin to morph into something he doesn't feel comfortable with or recognize. Being a man may be hard. But, as we will discuss in the next chapter, being a manopause man is even harder.

CHAPTER THREE

# THE **MANOPAUSE** PROBLEM

Manhood is fragile, more than ever at midlife. How is *your* man feeling about his manhood at this point? How do you think he sees his life's choices, his romantic connection, his family relationships, and his career path? Is he wondering whether he will have the time to accomplish the goals he set for himself? Does he see and feel biological changes? You bet he does, both consciously and subconsciously. And now that life is changing in ways that are beyond his control, his quest for herohood is that much more of a challenge. He probably won't admit having manopause fears to you, or even to himself. He may say he is not aware of his physical and psychological changes, but most likely, at least when it comes to his physical changes, he is. He just doesn't want to admit it, even to himself, because that breeds feelings of uncertainty, insecurity, unfamiliarity, and fear. That's right . . . fear. Our strong, invulnerable, even Herculean men are, underneath it all, afraid. They are frightened of changes in their bodies, and in their sense of themselves. And they are afraid of being vulnerable, aging, weakening, and being mortal.

Until fairly recently, men did not live long enough to have recognizable hormonal changes. A hundred years ago, they were not expected to live past 50. The U.S. census for the year 1900 reported that the average life expectancy of a man was 40. Today it's 78.[1] In 1900, people didn't worry about mood swings, depression, and erectile dysfunction, because 50 was not midlife, it was end of life. Today, life past 50 is a growing area of study, because men are living so much longer. And longevity is a glass half-empty, glass half-full proposition. You can see the problems it may present, like outliving the career that is paying the bills, or, you can refocus and see these extra decades of life as an opportunity to grow into a new self, with the depth to appreciate things that were passed over in earlier years. But one thing is for sure, you can't ignore the signs of manopause.

### The Cracks in His Herculean Armor Begin to Show

Men go about their business, shoving manopause away, smothering their fears and hoping that tomorrow will give them a brighter outlook. And all the while, as they refuse to acknowledge it, the pain of this resistance infiltrates their psyche, putting a cloud over their heads.

He says he's really "fine," and you want to believe him. But suddenly he has those moments. He's overly sensitive, cranky, irritable. You push them aside, telling yourself they are just aberrations. He's stressed about work. He didn't sleep well the night before. You find all kinds of excuses. But as time goes by, you become suspicious. You wonder what's happening to your husband . . . to your father . . . to your friend. Is he having a collection of bad days? Are you beginning to have to adjust your behavior around his?

Then you spend an evening with some friends and you start to recognize changes in their husbands—familiar changes. Why is he being rude to her, when, in the past, he has been so attentive? At home your husband's mood swings grow. Maybe he becomes angry in an instant. Maybe he's self-destructing by overindulging. It begins to occur to you that he's not just hurting himself, he's hurting you.

Why is he acting this way? Why is he saying these things? Why isn't he happy? You ask yourself where you have gone wrong. What have you done to cause this? Most likely, nothing. Very simply, he is rebelling against midlife changes that leave him with less and less control over his ability to maintain his manhood. We keep telling ourselves that he's just having a midlife crisis. That it will pass.

But is it a crisis? While *midlife crisis* is a common term, it has never been proven to be a valid scientific condition. The term was coined by Elliot Jaques, M.D., Ph.D., in 1965, in a paper he authored on the working patterns of creative genius. It was popularized by Gail Sheehy in her revolutionary book *Passages: Predictable Crises of Adult Life,* which she wrote ten years later. But over all of these years, no scientific study has shown that a *midlife crisis* exists for most men. It is much more probable that your manopause man is having a *midlife adjustment.*

This adjustment is every bit as powerful as the one he experienced during adolescence. And yet it is gradual, making it difficult to recognize, and even harder for him to accept. Hard to accept because, bottom line, men don't view change the way women do. Women are accustomed to having their bodies alter. Every month we menstruate. We go through the transformation of pregnancy, watching ourselves swell with new life and then, hopefully, grow thin again. To women, change is a positive. Not so for men. They view change as a negative; their shifts are to "less strength" and "lower testosterone." In their minds, change is bad.

And the media tells them that this perception is right. Every day sexy, shirtless men parade on beaches and perform in bedrooms on film, on television, and in magazines . . . *young,* sexy, perfect men. When was the last time we saw a 60ish man being touted in the media as a sex symbol? When Clint Eastwood bared his soul and his chest in the outdoor shower in *The Bridges of Madison County* at the age of 64, the world was shocked to see an "older" man displaying himself. Is there any compliment more backhanded than "he looks good for his age"? It's no wonder men don't want to cop to change.

## Physical Factors in Manopause

Of the physical changes that affect men at midlife, perhaps the most influential is a lowering of their testosterone levels. Daniel D. Federman, M.D., and Geoffrey A. Walford, M.D., both of Harvard Medical School, explained in *Newsweek* in 2007: "Levels of a man's main sex hormone, testosterone, begin to drop as early as the age of thirty . . . the testosterone levels drop very slightly (about one percent) each year—for the rest of his life. Some of the experts in the field maintain that this downhill slide can begin as early as in a man's 20s, while others feel it rarely starts before his 40s. Either way, this change is so gradual that many men may not notice any affects until several decades have gone by. Yet, by 50, 10 percent of all U.S. men have low levels of testosterone."[2] And as testosterone levels lower, hair begins to thin, muscles begin to shrink, energy begins to wane, moods begin to swing, bellies begin to enlarge, bone mass begins to lessen, sadness begins to creep in, and sexual performance begins to suffer. Losing one's "hunkdom" is deeply upsetting. Our men see and feel these shifts, and it's all terribly frightening.

But the gradual nature of this decline actually has some positives. Unlike women, whose hormones fall off a cliff at menopause, men rarely experience most of the more obvious and uncomfortable symptoms of their hormonal readjustment—things like hot flashes. On the other hand, since their lower testosterone levels have "snuck up on them" over decades, they often find themselves confused, even totally stymied, by inexplicable changes in the way they feel, both physically and mentally. At some point, they may find themselves wondering, *What happened? Where did this de-energized and unwelcome feeling come from?* Given the stealthy disappearance of this very pivotal male hormone, it's no wonder your manopause man is confused.

So he may be struggling. Is he alone? How common *are* low testosterone levels? According to John Morley, M.D., professor of geriatrics at St. Louis University School of Medicine, about one-third of men over 50 have testosterone deficiency.[3] And since a man turns 50 in the United States every 16 seconds, that adds up.

But life is, indeed, unfair. And testosterone is no exception. While it's a given that every woman will undergo menopause, there is a great variability among men. Not all of them will experience a low testosterone level or its symptoms. Some men maintain "normal" levels of testosterone well into old age. But as we discussed before, there actually is no "normal" testosterone level, which is one of the big complications in the testosterone debate. If you're living with a manopause man, you need to get a handle on where he falls on the testosterone curve. Why? Because a man who starts with a high testosterone level, which then drops, can suffer considerably more symptoms than another man whose testosterone level ends up even lower than the first man's, assuming the second man's level started lower in the first place. Imagine that Steve lives in New York City, where the average temperature in July is 77 degrees. He then moves to Cleveland, where it's 71, a six-degree drop. Then compare Steve to Jack, who lives in Arizona, with an average July temperature of 95 degrees. Jack then moves to New York, with its 77-degree average. Even though Jack is in a warmer climate than Steve, since he has experienced a 28-degree drop in temperature, he feels colder. So, although it's important, it's not only your man's current testosterone level that matters. It's where it is ending up in relation to his starting point.

How do you know which type of man you are with? It would be perfect if your man had asked for a baseline reading of his testosterone at age 30. Then you could clearly see where his current level falls in relation to the apex of his hormonal strength. But how many 30-year-old men are planning ahead for hormonal decline? None. So, you have to look for other clues. The hints you should watch out for range from physical and psychological, to sexual. Some signs you may be able to see; some you can't.

## The Effects of Testosterone Loss

Remember how that rush of testosterone during a man's teenage years changes his physique, increasing muscle mass and strength? Well, declining testosterone reverses the process. Starting in their early 30s, even men who maintain the same weight begin to lose muscle mass and replace it with fat. Between the ages of 40 and 70, the average man will drop between 12 and 20 pounds of muscle.[4] And, along with that, he can drop a good part of his self-image.

When pecs begin to turn to pooch, a man just naturally feels differently about himself. Muscles and strength have been drilled into him as part of the *man*dates since boyhood. What kind of a hero is he without muscles? And make no mistake, as muscles shrink, only to be replaced by love handles, his stamina is declining as well.

Your manopause man, who was once a lean, mean sports machine, may now be heading for the sidelines sooner than he is willing to accept. As his muscle mass decreases, so does his strength and endurance. Not only in sports, but in life in general, including at work, where it may be becoming harder to keep pushing like a madman to get ahead.

At the same time, aches, pains, and stiffness ratchet up. And recovery from injuries, or even illness, is not as fast as it used to be. As if this isn't enough, his body hair may be thinning, or moving to new and less attractive places, as his skin is drying and becoming less supple. Worse yet, he may be getting shorter. Since testosterone helps to build and maintain bone, as it goes down, bone density decreases. Some studies have shown that between the ages of 40 and 70, men lose an average of 15 percent of their bone mass and two inches in height.[5]

But the lowest blow of all for manopause men—both physically and psychologically—deals with the all-important topic of sex. Some research indicates that almost 40 percent of men will begin to feel a decrease in their sex drive, fewer spontaneous erections during sleep, an increased difficulty in attaining and sustaining their erections, or even a total loss of sexual pleasure as they move through their 40s.[6] Any of which may lead them to believe that they are "losing it." Since sexual prowess has dominated their lives, it is not surprising that men become terrified when they feel their sexual grip slipping. This hits at the very core of their masculinity. Whether they have some loss of libido and become less interested in sex, or whether their penises begin to betray them, panic can set in. Yet fear of losing their sexuality is something men wouldn't dare admit to anyone, possibly even you.

If your manopause man is moving toward a lower testosterone level, don't assume this is totally bad news. Low testosterone is helpful in keeping your man emotionally connected in a marriage. It can leave you with a kinder, mellower, and more loving partner. One study of middle-aged professional men showed that lower testosterone levels were related to higher marital satisfaction and better relationships with adolescent children. High testosterone men are less likely to marry, and less likely to stay married if they do make it to the altar, a fact that is borne out by a rise in married men's testosterone levels once they divorce. So lower testosterone can be good. We'll discuss testosterone in greater detail in Chapter 7, but for now, just know that this drop isn't necessarily bad.

### Psychological Factors in Manopause

Loss of testosterone, and the physical changes it causes, is only one wrench in the system. Most men undergoing hormonal changes at midlife are also experiencing psychological stress. Your manopause man's mind is churning, as he tries to decipher what's happening to the hero he has worked so hard to perfect. He feels as if he's losing his life, literally. Sleep problems, an energy deficit, poor performance at work, a loss of short-term memory and concentration, depression, and even panic attacks—all due to a loss of testosterone—have made him start to think, for the first time, about his mortality. He can sense it laying in wait for him, just over the next hill. He believes that his years of success are behind him, and years of struggling to maintain the status quo are the only things that lie ahead. But being a man means he's a problem solver. So why can't he figure this one out? Because he doesn't want to. It's better just to ignore what he's feeling and the signs that are slowly surfacing, which just leads to more worry and more psychological pain.

Often, this downward spiral is triggered by some sort of alarming event or change in your man's daily routine. Maybe it's a call from the doctor, telling him that something might be seriously wrong. Or it happens following the death of a friend or family member. It could be triggered by the failure of a business, a job layoff, or a younger co-worker moving fast up the ranks. The goals that have been so important to your man suddenly may not seem as attainable as he once thought, and perhaps not as meaningful after all. Men begin to realize at some point that they may not remain on the top of the heap. Their children will be leaving for college before they know it. Their wives may rejoin the workforce. They fear they may not be valued anymore. And if they are not esteemed in the ways to which they are accustomed, what meaning do their lives have?

With their worlds changing around them, and with mortality staring them in the face, manopause men come to a place of reevaluation. They may find themselves walking through a "mind-field," with no training on how to maneuver around old concepts that can explode with serious repercussions. On their present course, they have fewer real-life goals to strive for, with less ahead of them than behind them. They may worry about their endgame, death's unknown abyss. And for some men, their financial picture is not as bright as expected, which makes things even more of a struggle. As they worry about continuing to fulfill the *man*dates at midlife, men's sense of insecurity and their feelings of mortality are amped up. Secrecy magnifies their actions and reactions, as they are culturally forced to hide their changes. It's no wonder they are suffering as they wonder who they are. So how does this all play out? Let's look at an example: Olivia, 35, spent months planning a 45th birthday party for her husband, Derrick. Finally the evening arrived. The surprise went off without a hitch; everyone was happy to be there, except Derrick. He sat on one of the couches, nursing martinis and watching everyone else have a great time. Olivia tried to encourage Derrick to participate in the festivities, but he declined. She didn't understand. Why was he being selfish and inconsiderate, unappreciative and incorrigible during a celebration in his honor? Why didn't he appreciate all of her hard work? He told her she just wouldn't understand. In fact, he was struggling to understand himself.

Ryan, Derrick's best friend, pulled Olivia aside and explained that Derrick's behavior had nothing to do with her. Derrick was hurting. He didn't think he deserved the celebration. His business had taken a hit; he wasn't the big cheese he thought he would be by 45. Feeling like a failure in front of all his friends was no way to celebrate a milestone. Ryan understood, having gone through something similar himself. And recently he had noticed Derrick with that same lost and disillusioned look in his eyes.

Ryan's words rang true. Olivia felt awful—she was aware of Derrick's down behavior, which was why she decided to surprise him in the first place. But what she hadn't realized was that the party was celebrating the very thing that Derrick was trying to dodge—the realization that as he had hit midlife, and with his journey almost half over, he wasn't feeling good about his choices and his accomplishments, and he was extremely worried about being successful in the future.

Olivia realized that Derrick's party had a hidden purpose for her, too. Her cultural conditioning had taught her she should be with a "hero." The way to have other people recognize she had achieved that was to publicly celebrate him. Understanding her own selfish motivations to throw the party helped to lessen her hurt. Her anger turned into empathy toward her husband. She approached Derrick and apologized. She shouldn't have planned the party without his consent. He appreciated her sensitivity and accepted her apology. But it was his fault, too. He hadn't explained to her what he had been feeling; he was running away from it himself. She told him that she would help him figure it out. He appreciated her support and together they rejoined the party as a unit, connected by their empathetic understanding of each other's point of view.

Like Derrick, your manopause man has fears—fears that he tries to push down. But he can't, and the anxiety and stress of continuously trying evidence themselves in his behavior. Don't be fooled by his cover-up. Know that he has his own very special set of worries. It is important to understand what they are, how they originate in his brain, how they multiply during his manopause years, and how they dramatically affect your daily lives together. Keep in mind that like any feedback loop, your fears play into his, and his anxieties increase yours. The factor most instrumental in increasing your man's age-related apprehensions is the manhood pressures our culture has placed on him. Understanding his cultural programming, and how it has impacted his fears, is key to moving toward a less fearful and happier existence.

## Fear Is His Driving Force

*"A man who says he has never been scared is either lying or else he's never been any place or done anything."*

**— Louis L'Amour**

Your manopause man's actions will reveal the areas in which he is feeling weakest. Will he make a play for a last grasp at youth? Buy a fabulous new sports car? Climb Mount Kilimanjaro? Change careers or sell his hard-built business? Move to an exotic island to become the next Iron Man or, God forbid, find a sexy young thing? All of these are defenses employed to relieve his anxiety. In some cases they can cause your manopause man to behave unrecognizably. Whether he is in denial; acting irritable; avoiding your help; blaming you for his difficulties; or camouflaging his pain by overindulging with alcohol, drugs, or food; it can get nasty. He could suggest that it's your fault for being less sexually appealing, and more difficult. That is why he is having an affair. As Meg Ryan so correctly stated in the October 2008 issue of *In Style* magazine, "When a woman has an affair, it's her fault. When a man has an affair, it's her fault."

And if it's not you, it's someone or something outside of himself. At home, it is the kids who are unreasonable. That is why he can't deal with them anymore. At work, it is management that doesn't know what it's doing. That is why he wants out. And, of course, it is the economy and the illogical stock market that is preventing him from reaching the financial pinnacle he always hoped he would get to.

Still, he can't allow himself to get down, since heroes never do. So he tries to suppress his feelings. It is a better option than admitting or exposing weakness. But his anxiety begins eating at him from the inside out. You may begin to notice he is getting irritable, impatient, restless, and having bouts of anger. Your lovemaking begins to diminish. You try to communicate with him, but can't seem to get through. He may even be experiencing depression. And success, power, and status are no protection. In fact, since bigger achievement means greater loss, they may make his reactions to changing circumstances even more intense.

### What Is Fear?

Ask your manopause man what scares him. If he registers high on the *man*date scale, he will probably have difficulty putting a list together. The idea that a man should never be afraid is embedded in his brain. So he convinces himself, and everyone around him, that he is really not fearful. What he is not focused on is that every action he takes, every thought he has, engages either desire or fear. Since he has been socialized to steer clear of vulnerability, he has to work hard not to show or acknowledge these fears, even to himself.

*"Just as courage imperils life, fear protects it."*

**— Leonardo da Vinci**

But fear is not necessarily a bad thing—especially when you realize that fear is the emotion that protects us from danger, even death. From the beginning, fear has been the engine that drives your man's brain. Fear is the "quintessential human emotion,"[7] says Rush Dozier, Jr. We all go through life experiencing the gamut of emotions, but fear is the most primal. Fear—whether an emotion felt and expressed in an instant or expressed occasionally, over time, as a repetitive, protective wake-up call—is good in moderation in that it serves to balance our lives. Having evolved as an early warning system for pain and death, fear protects us.

Fear is processed by the most primitive centers of the brain, the ones we have in common with other animals. Because saving our lives is a biological imperative, it is processed with lightning speed. The fear system in your brain is watching you front and back, 24/7, sleeping or awake. When a threat is perceived through the senses, the first fear response is for the brain to react instantly, recognizing circumstances that can cause injury or death. Within a tenth of a second our primary fear system is engaged. We react with a fight-or-flight response, girding our bodies to shield us from harm. When this emotional reaction occurs, every other biological need, even for food, sex, and love, shuts down. This is nature's way of throwing all of our energy into the matter at hand, hopefully getting us out of danger. The second fear-response system is what Dozier calls our "rational fear system." "It allows us to assess rationally the nature of a specific fear and weigh many different possibilities and options"[8] to protect ourselves. The rational fear system plans our escape. A third system, the conscious fear system, is the final decision maker. It determines what to do after weighing in on the conflicts between the primary fear system and the rational fear system. In other words, the third fear system is the final judge of who wins, between emotion and reason.

We must always keep our fear systems alive, but under control. If our conscious fear system stops keeping our primitive fear system in check, our apprehensions will restrict, stagnate, even paralyze us. Once fear takes over, it can have pervasive effects on our partners, our families, and our friends. But when there is proper balance between these systems, our fears help us to face and overcome our biggest obstacles and enable us to reach and obtain the greatest fulfillment of our human potential.

### Push or Pull, Fear or Desire, It's Why We Do What We Do

*"There are two levers for moving men: interest and fear."*

**— Napoleon Bonaparte**

Two opposing forces, fear and desire, guide us and help to determine our emotional state. They are part of every decision we make. Every action is dictated by our desire to do something, weighed against our fear of the consequences of doing it. That is exactly the quandary Mike was caught in.

Mike, 47, was playing catch with his son, tossing his son's beloved baseball. His son threw a wild pitch. The ball flew over Mike's head and rolled into the street. His immediate reaction was to dash after it. But he saw a car, followed by three others, approaching. As his son watched "his hero" faltering, Mike's eyes darted between the ball and the cars. His brain was weighing his desire to run after it, against his fear of getting hit by a car. Anxiety built. His fear of getting hit won out. He froze as the cars passed. Once the street was clear, he raced to retrieve the ball. Luckily, it was unscathed; his son could still look up to him. Every decision in life works this way; it is a push-pull battle until either fear or desire wins out.

### Some Fears Are More Painful than Others

All kinds of fears fill our minds, competing for attention. Depending on the day, their pecking order can change. The one that produces the strongest response in our brain's fear systems at a particular moment is the one that controls our behavior at that time.

For example, let's say that you and your manopause man are taking a long hike on a very hot day. After a while the two of you get thirsty. Your partner has already finished his water, so you reach into your backpack. As you take yours out, it slips through your fingers and drops onto a small outcropping of rock, jutting from the wall of a deep crevasse. You look at each other, knowing that without that water, the two of you risk dehydration as you hike back to your car. Motioning you back, responding with self-sacrifice, a cherished traditional trait of manhood, your manopause man starts to put one foot on the wall of the crevasse, hoping to get low enough to grab the water bottle. Rock and dirt begin to cascade from under his foot. He quickly steps back. Yes, he fears dehydration, but he fears falling to his death even more.

As more rock loosens, the bottle topples, crashing down into the gully. You are relieved, knowing your man's fear system saved him. Two fears competed—dehydration versus death. His fear of death won out.

### Death Is Your Manopause Man's Ultimate Fear

When you are afraid, the brain, using previously accumulated data, prepares your body to protect itself. If there is no prior data, there is an unknown. This, in itself, is frightening. "The greatest unknown is death . . . fear of death becomes in most people the primary fear,"[9] says Dozier. It's no wonder that your manopause man's realization that his life is halfway over is a difficult pill to swallow. Not only is he incapable of stopping the trajectory toward this unknown abyss, he has already lived half his life, and he can't erase or go back. This may be fine for some men. But most still have many dreams to live out and goals to accomplish.

If he's like most manopause men, your man is feeling out of control, vulnerable, and helpless to some degree. But one thing is for sure: He can't show you he's worried. He can't even admit it to himself, much less talk about it. Remember, according to the mandates, he must show no weakness.

Your man may buy into that idea and deny that manopause is happening, hoping it will go away, knowing in his heart that he is powerless. But as he begins to feel a loss of control, his sense of helplessness increases, and with that helplessness comes fear. Manopause men realize they cannot stop the ride they are on as it moves in the direction of death. The concept of mortality hits most men hard, as signs of aging pop up—proof that they are, in fact, on a course they cannot stop.

Your man may be leapfrogging from one hot rock of a feeling to another, trying different things to ease his mind, fighting like a champion against a subconscious that's tugging at his sleeve, telling him, "You've hit the top of the mountain. It's all downhill now." And heaven knows he doesn't want to think about what's waiting at the bottom of that hill.

People are programmed to avoid death at all costs. If they didn't, they might not survive their reproductive years. And then what would happen to the human race? Unlike other species, humans are endowed with a heavy dose of self-awareness. Most of the animal world only has a fear of death when it's nipping right at their heels, when the trap is about to snap shut. But your man, like *all* men, is different. Whether or not he is able to acknowledge it consciously, he is aware of the fact that he is mortal, and the sense of foreboding that understanding stirs is lurking in the back of his subconscious when he hits manopause.

### He's Conditioned to Fear Death

What part does cultural conditioning play in your manopause man's fear of death? Some would argue that the fear of death plays an integral role in maintaining the *man*dates. In his Pulitzer Prize–winning book, *The Denial of Death,* Ernest Becker argued that all of the norms and conventions of civilization are nothing more than a complex defense mechanism against this awareness of our own mortality. Men try to convince themselves that they will never die by embarking on "heroic quests," by trying to involve themselves in something that—unlike their physical bodies—will never die. Some men do this by comforting themselves with religion and thoughts of eternal life. Some do it by building a legacy, whether financial or philosophical. For others, it is their involvement in the continuing lives of their children. Whichever it may be, a man's heroic quest is a stab at giving life some feeling of purpose, despite the knowledge that it is inevitably fated to end. And this desire to participate in something bigger than themselves will only grow during manopause.

Men whose heroism quests are not succeeding are continually reminded of their insignificance. They can become tormented over past failures, or they may spend their time worrying about missed opportunities and regrets. This tendency is even more pronounced during manopause because of the realization of mortality. Manopause men may try to re-create a feeling of importance by seducing new or younger women, and even go as far as creating new families in order to feel potent. Or they can resort to any number of denial or blame strategies, none of which make mortality go away. In Greek mythology, King Sisyphus managed to trick death and evade his clutches not once, but twice. And maybe your man will be able to pull off a similar mental escape act, at least temporarily. But in the end, Sisyphus was dragged back to Hades. Just like our men, he could run, but he could not hide from death.

The sad thing is that fears can actually contribute to death. When your man doesn't acknowledge them, his fears can internalize and grow, and eventually that can have a negative effect on his immune system. If you suspect that his mind is in a constant state of fear, your man may be suppressing his anxieties so his "weakness" won't be revealed. If he doesn't acknowledge what he is feeling, his body will secrete hormones and chemicals that are harmful to him. This is because, according to Eva Selhub, M.D., instructor in medicine at Harvard Medical School, clinical associate in medicine at Massachusetts General Hospital, and author of *The Love Response*, "If the Fear Response continues too long or unregulated, the body stays in a constant state of stress and pathological problems inevitably arise, including increases in blood pressure and thickening of and tears in blood vessel walls. Excess production of fatty acids and blood sugar may lead to deposits in these tears and formation of atherosclerotic plaques, eventually resulting in heart disease and stroke."

The most obvious symptom of this stress that your man might display is anxiety. It's been said that anxiety is the alarm that alerts people to possible danger, and that fear of mortality can become, for some, the alarm that never stops ringing. When this happens, and coping skills are overwhelmed, a man stays in a state of constant stress. Rush Dozier, Jr., offers, "Intense prolonged fear and anxiety depress the activity of the immune system, a happy relaxed attitude rejuvenates it."[10] Studies have shown that it is people with strong self-esteem who are least likely to be laid low by fears of mortality.

But even with a high self-esteem, according to Gail Sheehy, "There are real reasons men fear death more than women."[11] And they should. Just like their innate ability to run faster, men are moving faster toward death. As she points out, the greater risk begins in the womb at three months. Female fetuses are two times more likely to survive than male fetuses. And today the Social Security life expectancy table reports there is a higher probability of death for men at every age. While men are alive, they grey earlier, lose their sexual drive faster, and are less adaptable to healthy living as they age.

If all movement leads toward death, it is best to stay put. Let's not age, right? No wonder your manopause man fears change; it's movement toward death.

### Your Manopause Man's Fear of the Unfamiliar

Your manopause man is already burdened with having to constantly prove his manhood. He is already familiar with his obstacles. Change only multiplies his vulnerable feelings. And as we have said, vulnerability is the enemy of the man who has a strong belief in the *man*dates.

*"The soft-minded man always fears change. He feels security in the status quo, and he has an almost morbid fear of the new. For him, the greatest pain is the pain of a new idea."*

**— Martin Luther King, Jr.**

When he experiences something "new," something unfamiliar, how is your man able to remain in control? He's not, and it scares him. Have you ever offered a new idea to your manopause man that might change a decision in the household or in his career, only to be met with stubbornness, denial, or disinterest? Maybe you found a good refinancing deal for your house, or on a new car, or you suggested a new job opportunity he can pursue, only to have your partner react negatively? Is this behavior becoming more frequent, making you increasingly aware of it? He may fear that you are questioning his ability to act as a provider, or as an expert in cars, or are no longer seeing him as being on top of his career. If he refuses to entertain those possibilities, then in his mind, he remains in control. But is he really? We live in an ever-changing world. Trying to stop change is impossible. Nonetheless, if you suggest a new idea that challenges your man in the area of manhood, men who espouse the *man*dates will work hard to push it off or avoid it.

## Is It Fear of Change? Or Fear of Changing Into Less of "a Man"?

It is important to distinguish between a basic fear of change and a fear of changing into less of a man. Which one do you think your manopause man fears most? To answer this, let's try another approach. Take the need for your manopause man to "be a man" out of the equation. Would he still be fearful of changes if they didn't impact his manhood? Most likely not. When Baskin-Robbins changes their 31st flavor, is he threatened? Not at all. It does nothing to change his view of himself.

In theory most men understand that they are going to age. Our world is in constant flux; the law of impermanence rules our universe. Having been raised in this environment, it's possible your manopause man recognizes that the physical changes to his body at midlife are similar in intensity to his changes at puberty, in that they are life altering. The adolescent changes were easy to accept. But these changes aren't, because they are weakening him, and to "be a man," one must be strong. Since his physical prowess is fundamental to his manhood, his reaction is to want to stop his hormonal decline, or at least control it.

Keep in mind that helplessness is the enemy of happiness. A vital element of feeling happy is having a sense of control. As things are changing for your manopause man in ways that are unsatisfactory to him, and he feels his control slipping, his first response is to fight the changes or to deny they are happening, out of fear of being judged less of a man. Take Joe for an example:

Joe got into a pickup game of basketball and tore a ligament in his knee. It wasn't surprising. Despite his regular exercise routine, he hadn't played basketball in years. While Joe was laid up, his wife, Cynthia, got a promotion at work, and a raise that put her salary slightly above his. She was thrilled to help with their additional expenses. Was Joe happy they now had more money to spend and enjoy? No. Joe, who was already feeling vulnerable due to his injury, was afraid of this change. He felt he had lost his position as "the man" of the household, the one who is in charge. He started picking on Cynthia's opinions, and putting down her new ideas. He became more demanding of her and more short-tempered with the kids. He did everything he could to put himself back on top.

When things like this are happening, it is a sign that your manopause man is afraid—afraid of losing control, afraid of losing his manhood. Joe felt helpless, so he took out his frustrations on his family, but subconsciously he knew that Cynthia getting a promotion wasn't the problem; it was the possibility that he was neither respected, nor needed any more. Hewing closely to the *man*dates was making life more difficult for Joe.

### *The Omnipresent Manopause Fear – Losing His Manhood*

Because manopause men can't assure themselves of permanent masculinity, they feel helpless. This helplessness is not only an enemy of happiness; it is a friend of fear. Let's examine the most common manhood fears: being a failure, losing respect, being dominated, and being vulnerable. See if you recognize your manopause man in any or all of them. This will help you gain an understanding of, and an appreciation for, the struggles he confronts every day.

### He Could Lose His Manhood – Fear of Failure

Our culture has taught us to believe that a man's worth is tied to his success. That success is judged in every aspect of his life. Boys learn at an early age that they have to do well, whether it is on the ball field, in school, or with their peers. The winners always rise to the top, and our culture always rewards those at the apex. As men mature, the pressures on them intensify, while the unrelenting nature of judgment remains the same. To remain a man, one cannot fail. A man must always strive to be a hero, a warrior, a leader, a protector, and a provider. He has been socialized to believe in setting goals and reaching them. He must succeed in his relationships—as a father, as a lover, and as a friend—because being a failure could affect his perception of his worth. As a man, consciously or subconsciously, he fears failure, especially as his abilities in some areas are declining, due to physical changes in his body and thoughts of mortality.

## Fear of Not Being Respected – He Could Lose His Manhood

Hercules was judged by his fellow men to be the most esteemed warrior of them all. In our society, all men want to command this kind of respect in the eyes of their peers. To your manopause man, the only way to know that he has passed muster is to be recognized by his world and acknowledged for his actions. At work he needs to be told that he is doing a good job, and at home he needs to be recognized and honored as the head of the household. He needs confirmation that he is a good father and a good lover. In the community, he needs to be looked up to by his peers. As your manopause man becomes more aware of the changes occurring to him, his need to be recognized grows that much stronger. One of the ways men command regard is by showing off their accomplishments. Material goods such as sports cars, boats, and big houses telegraph to other people just how successful and accomplished men really are.

At the core, your manopause man fears that if he is not respected, he could be replaced—replaced in the community, replaced in his love relationship, and replaced at work—by a more energetic man. One who has the one thing a manopause man does not have: youth.

## Fear of Being Controlled or Dominated –
## He Could Lose His Manhood

"A man's greatest fear is of being dominated or humiliated by a stronger man or in front of other men,"[12] offers Gail Sheehy. As the *man*dates dictate, your man strives to remain in control in some form or another. Worst of all is being dominated by a non-leader, such as a younger member of the household or a lower-level or female co-worker. The fear of being dominated creates an even greater sense of helplessness as your manopause man begins to feel some of his strengths slipping. Threats can even come in the sanctuary of his own home. There are times when threats to his manhood come from you, and others when they come from his progeny. At some level, men are competing with their children—especially male children. Around middle age, when sons become powerful physically, this can be menacing. Hercules was unable to be controlled. In his heart, your manopause man wants nothing less. How, then, can he continue to demonstrate his manliness in a healthy way? By carving out areas where he can still be in control. These may be different ones than he's accustomed to. They may involve him using his expertise, leadership, and generosity of spirit in lieu of brute strength. David, after all, dominated Goliath by using a slingshot and his wits. Your manopause man can learn to do the same.

## Fear of Revealing His Vulnerabilities –
## He Could Lose His Manhood

Our culture socializes men to believe there is no place for weakness, no room for cracks in their armor. That is why they desperately try to hide their vulnerabilities. But, as we all know, men are human. Men make mistakes, men get hurt, and men act out of weakness. They do this, even though these actions are against the *man*dates. But being void of emotions and vulnerabilities is as much a myth as

Hercules. Men sense they are vulnerable, so they are forced to strain unbelievably hard in an attempt to hide weakness and to avoid being viewed as less of a man. This is a heavy burden to carry, especially when, at midlife, they are biologically less aggressive and more emotional. That's why this fear can become, at times, terrifying.

### Ubermen – The Manhood Problem Magnified at Manopause

If all men carry a heavy burden because of their self-imposed high standards, Ubermen carry an even heavier load. Part of the problem stems from the fact that often, consciously or subconsciously, they feel they are not subject to the same set of rules that apply to other men. This is further complicated by their struggle to reach the exponentially expanding, unobtainable goals they set for themselves. As a result, Ubermen can become extremely difficult to work with, live with, or even associate with during their midlife passage, the time when, ironically, most of them have hit their greatest success. This is because they are accustomed to controlling everything around them, something they can't do with manopause. In truth, they are afraid— afraid of failing, of being vulnerable, and of forfeiting respect, and, most important, of losing control. This is when the typical Uberman clings harder to some of the *man*dates, and turns to his power and influence for help. If these strategies fail, the Uberman may be headed toward destructive behavior. At times like this, communicating with an Uberman and penetrating his shield is extremely difficult. But he doesn't see that. Nor does he waste time feeling empathy for the people he is affecting, since the world revolves around him. One of America's most respected authors recognized that because of our culture's bias in favor of success, reducing the Uberman's fears is nearly impossible. As John Steinbeck once said:

"It has always seemed strange to me. The things we admire in men, kindness and generosity, openness, honesty, understanding and feeling are the concomitants of failure in our system. And those traits we detest, sharpness, greed, acquisitiveness, meanness, egotism and self-interest, are the traits of success. And while men admire the quality of the first, they love the produce of the second."

## *Women in a Manopause World*

As women dealing with manopause men, we really need to tap into our amazing ability for empathy. Being able to feel what they feel makes us especially suited to help our men through this trying time.

On the other hand, we have to be aware that our empathy can lead us to look for issues that don't exist, which can be damaging to *us*. Since we are sensitive to everything our men do, we assume that if he is not smiling, he is upset with us, when perhaps his mind is simply on something else. At work, when a boss becomes particularly critical or difficult, we wonder how we could have done a better job, instead of asking ourselves what his problem is. In our families, when our fathers seem to overreact to something we have done, we worry whether we should have tried it differently. In our marriages, when we are attacked, we may work even harder to please. Living with these fear-filled reactions causes us anxiety, frustration, and confusion.

Nevertheless, we buy into our cultural conditioning and feel we should maintain our manopause man's heroic image. It is hard to confide our problems or doubts to friends. So, instead of getting support, we become "secret keepers." We hesitate to discuss our man's difficulties in public, because we fear we will undercut him. By keeping them to ourselves, we are left alone with our fears. Let's admit it, watching our men change is frightening to us, too. And so, when we see it happening, we put on blinders. We conjure up excuses in our own minds, because we are afraid. But it's time to face our own fears so we can help lessen our manopause men's fears. We cannot let our own preconceived notions of what it means to be a man interfere.

### Redefining the Mandates

The first step toward getting a man out of society's man trap is to help him understand that he has stumbled into it. Start by helping your man distance himself from hard-lined, traditional manhood ideals and strict beliefs in the *man*dates—and do the same for yourself. In order to be happy in a changing life, he has to become more comfortable connecting with his emotions, and then he has to reconstruct his definition of what it is to "be a man." Doing that will take loads of weight off of his back, and yours.

In our modern society, conflict arises as men age and cultural pressures collide with reality. Widening your horizons and understanding your man's burden can help you to better accept his actions, his choices, and your actions, as well. Accepting your biological differences and showing him how to become more emotionally sensitive can assist in communication between you. Feeling more empathy toward your man, and helping him to experience it himself, will reduce your confusions and frustrations. And, most important, having an awareness of what it means to "be a man" can help you to get inside his head. Once you do, you will be better equipped to help your man rediscover, reevaluate, and redefine his manhood, and to alleviate his pressures. Remember, a less burdened man is one who will be better able to participate in a happy and successful relationship.

### Learn to Combat His Manopause Fears

Luckily, you've already begun helping your man—you're getting educated. Our culture has shied away from thinking about men's midlife and beyond. One of the greatest causes of fear is anxiety about the unknown. That can be calmed by making it more known.

*"Courage is resistance to fear, mastery
of fear—not absence of fear."*

**— Mark Twain**

With the help of research, and open discussion, we can begin to push our cultural boundaries in a healthier direction. Making *mano-pause* a familiar word is a first step. There is nothing wrong with men changing—what is wrong is our culture's inability to accept it.

Rush Dozier, Jr., suggests a way for your man to cope: "Science has uncovered one important technique for managing fear and stress . . . Try to avoid whenever possible, circumstances in which you feel help-less and vulnerable."[13] But the "manhood pressures" our men are dealing with as they physically change are so numerous that it be-comes hard to totally avoid situations that press their "loss of control" button. That is why, instead of thinking we can keep our men out of the line of fire, it may be more effective to redirect their thinking and approach to life. So work toward establishing a mood of optimism in your lives by moving your man's focus *away* from things that are uncontrollable, *to* things that give him more happiness.

When Kevin Mittan began to feel a sense of angst about treading water at midlife in the job he had worked at for decades, he decided to devote part of his time to the crazy dream he had for years: starting a small winery. In 2003, together with his wife, Jill, he bought land in Paso Robles, California, and started The Midlife Crisis Winery. He had to keep his day job, but he was able to begin devoting a portion of his time to something he really loved—something real, and totally different from the work he had been doing up to that point in his life. Today, the land he has purchased for growing his grapes says it all: it's "The Crisis Solved Vineyard."

## Mastering the Manopause Problem

Merriam-Webster tells us that a *problem* is a question or matter involving doubt, uncertainty, or difficulty. The manopause *problem* is only a problem if you don't make an effort to move away from doubt and uncertainty, to learn what this period of life is about, and to understand what forces are affecting your manopause man. He needs to be open to finding ways to adjust to his changing life, to al-leviating struggles he may be experiencing, and to searching for ways

71

to make life more satisfying. Like Kevin Mittan, your man can look at this manopause period, not as a downward swing in life, but as a stepping-stone to an even richer and more fulfilling time. Remember that the ability to maintain a healthy, long life in the face of stress is in your manopause man's control. He just has to be a willing participant.

The oft-quoted Chinese proverb, "May you live in interesting times," can be interpreted in two ways. The first way is as a curse and a problem, since "interesting" times are often those that are filled with turmoil and upheaval. The other interpretation is as a blessing, since the same "interesting" times are filled with change, and the opportunity that is its companion. You and your manopause man are about to embark on, or are already living through, your own interesting times, ones which can lead you to new experiences and opportunities.

Experts say that strong proponents of the *man*dates allow their fears to control them, and will suffer the most during the manopause years. How a man reacts to his changes is a direct result of how he perceives his masculinity and manhood, thanks to his cultural conditioning. And, as we are about to see, these perceptions can affect his behavior, and your shared happiness.

# CHAPTER FOUR

# GOOD MEN,
## BAD BEHAVIOR

How is *your* manopause man acting? Is he growing impatient? Does he seem hypersensitive toward you and others around him? Do you sense that he is feeling unappreciated and unrecognized? Is he irritable and frustrated at times? Is he drinking more, driving faster, pushing past his limits as he exercises? Is he turning into a man who is quick to shift blame to everything and everyone around him? Is he becoming increasingly anxious, tense, dissatisfied, and argumentative? All of these are common behaviors displayed by manopause men.

So let's take a step toward helping our men by learning more about the defense mechanisms good men use and abuse when they reach midlife. Your understanding will help you interact with your man in a better way and help you to show him the pitfalls of his reactions to his anxiety.

### Recognizing Bad Behavior

*"Behavior is what a man does, not what he thinks, feels, or believes."*

**— Anonymous**

If your manopause man is displaying bad behaviors, understand that they are a reaction to his inner turmoil, his dread of being less of a man, and the shame that this engenders in him. Psychologist Steven Krugman, Ph.D., of Harvard University tells us that "Shame is the emotional response to feeling exposed as inadequate, insufficient, dirty, vulnerable, and helpless."[1] When men experience shame, they feel as if they have failed. And being men, they will do just about anything to not expose the fact that they feel ashamed. This includes resisting help that might expose their "shortcomings." This can be particularly true at midlife.

Bad behaviors are your manopause man's outward relief valves for his inner anxiety—evidence of his fight to remain in control. And the more he believes in the *man*dates, the more his internal anxiety will grow at the thought of losing that battle. You should not ignore small signs. Little things can grow into larger issues. By slowly uncovering what is distressing your manopause man or causing him anxiety, you can better understand his behavior, and help him find ways to deal with his feelings of shame and fear.

### Fight or Flight?

As we discussed in Chapter 3, fear is the driving force behind all of your man's uncharacteristic behavior. On the most basic level, the response to fear is to fight or to flee. Rush Dozier, Jr., explains, "Fear is designed to be self-correcting, to turn itself off by motivating us to take the appropriate action to eliminate the source of the stress. In that manner, it is like hunger. We turn off hunger by eating. We turn off fear by fighting or fleeing."[2]

Animals have to choose between these two extremes. We humans are more evolved. When our brains react to fear, we are motivated to take more nuanced action to eliminate the source of the stress. Our desire to self-correct leads to a variety of behaviors that help us to feel in control, at least temporarily. But, in the long run, we learn that these behaviors don't do the trick. No man can command time, the environment, the economy, his physical changes, or the feelings of others. Despite this, our men have been culturally conditioned to believe that they can, and that they should. At midlife, men employ a multitude of behaviors, consciously or unconsciously, to combat their fear of losing control; of losing their manhood.

## Your Manopause Man's Most Primitive Response – Fighting Back Physically

Isn't that what Hercules would do? What about your man? Instinctively, he fights helplessness and vulnerability by trying to prove his physical strength to himself and to others. It's no wonder men who approach midlife, and fear mortality, participate in marathons, triathlons, and intense biking trips. They throw themselves down black diamond ski runs, and compete for hours in tennis tournaments in the blazing sun. Experiencing fear is painful. Exhausting your body is a good way to turn off your brain to the pain. When your manopause man's fears are reduced, he feels better, even invigorated. Physicality is the perfect antidote for his trepidations about aging; it helps him ignore and deny the changes that are taking place.

In extreme cases, men, who are working hard to hold on to their herohood—and through it their sense of worth—dare death by involving themselves in dangerous physical acts. Attacking a threatening feat and coming out a winner empowers them. By conquering things like bungee jumping and rock climbing, open-ocean sailboat races, or 100-mile-an-hour motorcycle rides, these daredevils attempt to prove to themselves that they can withstand the test of time. If your manopause man has this tendency, be on the alert. He might be cruising for a bruising—or worse. Recognize there are gradations of this attitude, but all of them put your man at risk to one extent or another.

So your man is putting up a good fight. He's battling change, punching to prove his manhood, grasping for control, rising up against weakness, and, most importantly, struggling against mortality. The problem is, his opponent is himself. How does he fight himself? He can only do so much physically to secure his manhood. Still, the anxiety remains within him. So he copes by moving on to the next line of defense. He begins fighting back mentally with some distinctive, and quite varied, defense mechanisms.

### Denial . . . Let's Talk about It

As your man walks through the "mind-field" of manopause, denial is often the first defense deployed to move anxiety out of his brain. According to the *Encyclopedia of Mental Disorders*, denial is "the refusal to acknowledge the existence or severity of unpleasant external realities or internal thoughts and feelings."[3] If your man fears change, but convinces himself it doesn't exist, his anxiety is averted. By denying reality, he can go on his merry way, fooling everyone, including himself . . . at least for the time being.

Denial helps us turn our back on the truth and, possibly, avoid feeling pain. How can you tell if your manopause man is a "master of denial"? When you notice that he is gaining weight, does he claim his pants are shrinking? When you tell him CD rates have gone down, and you think it is time to find another investment, does he ignore you? When you suggest that he is drinking or using drugs to deaden himself to his fears and to deny his feelings, does he quickly dismiss your "ridiculous idea"? When you ask him to visit a doctor for the sore shoulder he continues to rub, does he shrug you off, saying it will go away? Most likely he knows that what you are suggesting is correct. But at the moment you make your point, he feels his manhood slipping, and he can't stomach it. As "a man," he wants to be treated with respect. He has been taught to lead, not to follow. Denial is deep-seated. Even if your manopause man doesn't have a problem going to a doctor, once he is there he may fight advice about losing weight, drinking, smoking, or altering his lifestyle. The doctor doesn't really know his body, only he does. Or sometimes, particularly in bad economic times, your manopause man will deny financial problems that are beginning to grow, hoping they will go away on their own. In every case, denial gives him a sense of control. But it is a false sense. Ironically, by failing to take action, he has even less control.

While this "denialamania" may help your manopause man to maintain the illusion of invulnerability, it can have negative impacts. Your relationship may get tense if he is recoiling from the idea of taking advice from you, afraid to show weakness. He may be frightened of learning bad news about his body or his world. Or, he may be avoiding hearing from a doctor what actions he needs to take to fix a physical problem.

If this sounds familiar, you may be baffled. As a woman, you seek outside counsel to talk out problems and changes, and you welcome other opinions. So when you, or a doctor, or another kind of professional, or an offspring suggests what your manopause man should do, and he ignores it, it is hard to fathom. Consider the possibility that he is feeling his control slipping, and understand that denial is his defense against the situation, not against the suggestions he is hearing.

Greg was a poster child for the denial of physical weakness. He loved to cycle. He would venture out on long rides every weekend with a group of guys. And every Sunday night, he would limp around the house, complaining about his sore knee. When his wife, Donna, suggested it was the cycling, he denied the possibility. He had difficulty admitting weakness; he didn't want to give up his fresh-air time with his buddies, and he didn't want to face the possibility that his cycling days were over. But when he was forced to pass up several weekends of cycling due to business trips, Greg's knee stopped throbbing. Then he returned to his cycling. After another painful Sunday night, Donna begged him to consider that his sport was causing his problems. But this time she did it differently, with empathy. She acknowledged his deep desire to cycle, but also explained her fear that the physical damage Greg was doing to himself could be permanently life altering. When she presented it that way, she was able to convince him to take a long break. Greg felt sympathy for her when she clearly explained how her worries about his health were causing her stress. Months later, Greg picked up a weekly golf game. The bonding time with the guys filled the same need as his cycling had offered. And while he still missed biking, he realized it wasn't worth the price of permanent pain. His wife had been right.

When deception overrides truth, serious damage can result. As we have said, denial is used when your man is afraid. And fear is the emotion that serves to protect us. If we do not acknowledge the reality of our fears, then we are at risk. And denial doesn't just come in physical forms. Your manopause man can utilize emotional denial, as Ted did while his marriage with Jill was going through a difficult time.

Jill did not question Ted's love and devotion, nor did she question his faithfulness. But his behavior at midlife was beginning to reflect a man struggling with, and fearing, the changes that were overtaking his body and his world. He was becoming more irritable, hypersensitive, and more controlling. He even lashed out in angry fits from time to time. When Jill pointed out his actions and reactions, he would deny their existence, or make excuses. Jill began to press him to join her in marriage counseling. He insisted they were not experiencing any significant problems that would require professional help. The truth was, Ted was in emotional denial. He was unwilling to admit, accept, or take responsibility for his actions. Jill grew frustrated and felt caged. She tried to be patient. Months passed. Ted's denial remained intact, as their marriage fell apart. Jill realized she had only one choice. She moved out. Ted couldn't believe it.

Feeling miserable and helpless, Ted sought therapy on his own. Through hard work, he learned that his stubborn inflexibility was an outgrowth of his fear of vulnerability and lack of control. The *mandates* had done a number on his psyche. His therapist explained there is nothing wrong with having these self-preserving feelings, but they often produce precisely the outcome that is being avoided. In Ted's case, the harm he was currently experiencing—the loss of his wife— was far more painful than facing his midlife feelings of weakness. With this in mind, Ted was now willing to admit his fears, accept the changes in his life, and recognize that his behaviors were an outgrowth of his suppressed emotions. He was ready to begin the process of adjusting, starting with an apology to Jill. After he did this, they began the long journey of renewing what they had lost. Whether your manopause man's denial is emotional or physical, they share one common denominator. At some point he will find that he can't continue to run from the truth.

## Baby Boomers Are Masters of Denial

Baby boomers—everyone born post–World War II through 1964—have done everything they can to deny the very fact that they age. In a *New York Times* article from January 2009, consumer research firm Yankelovich reported that on average, boomers believed that old age begins at 79.5 for men.[4] This is astounding, considering the average life expectancy of a man in the United States today is 78. If middle age ends at 79.5, when does it begin? Boomers practice denial by trying to conduct their lives as if they will be forever young. They try to redefine midlife by taking any and all steps to remain vital, active members of society, while camouflaging the truth about age. The boomer generation spends hundreds of billions of dollars each year on antiaging "solutions." Unfortunately, the "ageless generation" is lying to itself; it is still aging. In 2006, 193,000 Americans ages 45 to 64 had knee replacements; 39 percent of all knee and hip replacement surgeries in the United States were done on boomers, reported *The New York Times* in February of 2009.[5]

Most likely your manopause man is one of the 79 million American boomers.[6] So there's a good chance that he wouldn't dare notice, acknowledge, or accept the beginning of his decline in his early 40s.

## *Other Defense Mechanisms*

Denial is not your manopause man's only way out. Since his brain is complex, he can find many ways to defend against his stresses, and to self-correct in an attempt to soothe himself. The higher his level of anxiety, the more forcefully his defense mechanisms will be employed.

His "go-to" list includes: displacement, intellectualization, projection, rationalization, reaction formation, regression, and sublimation.

## He Hands You a "Gift" Intended for Another — Displacement

Has your manopause man unexpectedly, and without reason, unleashed aggression or hostility on you? You are minding your own business when suddenly he lets loose with an angry tone, a nasty comment, or a harsh action. It's not really because of the last thing you did or said. It's because he is feeling anxious and is trying to transfer those feelings away from their real cause and onto you. By displacing them, he is finding relief. At least he hopes to.

Unfortunately, you are likely one of the few people in your manopause man's life he feels safe attacking. He can't unleash his anger on his boss, his friends, or his associates. It might be too dangerous to offend them. Keep in mind that the cause of his anxiety does not have to be a person. It can just as easily be a situation that caused him to feel out of control. Either way, you are the focus of your man's outburst.

Andrea experienced this unwanted "gift" from her manopause man when she decided to make a special dinner for him. As she was lighting the candles and putting the final touches on her beautifully set table, Dan walked in from a day of sales calls. He looked at the rib roast and Yorkshire pudding and started to berate her for serving something so fattening when she knows that he has been watching his weight. Andrea was confused. She had seen him step off his diet several times that week, and she wanted to surprise him with one of his favorite meals. He told her she shouldn't assume anything. All she cares about is doing what *she* wants to do. Andrea couldn't believe his reaction. All she did was cook him a beautiful dinner. Why was he gunning for her? The evening continued in silence.

The next morning, over coffee, Dan apologized. He explained that a younger associate had gotten an account he had been hoping for. When he questioned his boss, he was told the decision was final. He was feeling disappointed, weak, vulnerable, and incapable—a manhood failure. Andrea was the perfect target for his anger. Once he exploded at her, he felt more in control of his life.

## He Thinks and Reasons, but Doesn't Feel — Intellectualization

Men are considered to be the less emotional sex, but all humans have feelings. Our cultural conditioning has just guided men to suppress theirs. To make things even worse, men are uncomfortable expressing how they feel because of the way in which their brains are wired, and the way in which they have been socialized. Then, along comes an incident that makes suppression impossible, and the vulnerability alarm is sounded. What to do?

Intellectualization, an often-employed defense mechanism, helps men to distance themselves from their feelings by focusing instead on objective qualities or real events. By doing this, they can sidestep internal conflicts and the emotional stress associated with them. Intellectualization enables your manopause man to continue to feel strong, less vulnerable, and more in control, as Steve did when he dropped his daughter off at college.

Steve and his wife, Lori, prepared for the big day when they would move their firstborn, Kristin, into her first dorm room. After a six-hour drive, they were weary. Upon arrival, they quickly realized the myriad of things that needed to be done to get Kristin settled in. Roommate issues, closet-space problems, and security concerns were just a few of the many complications they faced. Finally, after 12 hours, Steve and Lori said their good-byes and began their trek home.

Within five minutes in the car, Lori burst into tears. She already missed her baby. How was Kristin going to survive there all alone, far from home, in that small, dirty room? Steve rattled off the facts: Kristin had a seemingly nice roommate. Her clothing fit into the extra containers they bought. The meal plan was extensive. Security was efficient. And the washer and dryer could be used around the clock. Steve's distant and impersonal recitation infuriated Lori. Did he actually feel comfortable leaving Kristin there? Didn't he miss her already? Wasn't he concerned about her well-being? In the face of Lori's emotional outburst, Steve withdrew and drove the rest of the way home in silence. If only Lori understood that Steven was processing the same things she was experiencing, it could have reduced her level of frustration. He was using intellectualization to help calm his anxiety. By stringing together facts, he distanced himself from his painful thoughts, blocked himself from feeling, and maintained his façade of manly strength.

## He Plays the Blame Game — Projection

The blame game isn't fun, especially when you are the target. Have you ever wondered how you ended up on the receiving end?

*"The superior man blames himself.*
*The inferior man blames others."*

**— NFL coach, Don Shula**

The *man*dates tell your manopause man that if he is going to be a hero, he can't afford to make mistakes. But then a blunder occurs. Your man knows responsibility is attached to that mistake, and it doesn't feel good. Anxiety builds. His mind tries to protect him from this discomfort. One common defense, projection, may have been learned in childhood, a time when most of us are fearful of accepting blame. Projection is what happens when your manopause man shifts his unacceptable or inappropriate thoughts to someone else instead of acknowledging that they are his own, and in so doing, he alleviates his inner tension.

What if his anxiety isn't caused by a specific mistake? What if it's a more generalized fallout from feelings he is experiencing at midlife? As we mentioned earlier, your man's manopause changes make him uneasy. But if he doesn't understand or chooses not to acknowledge that the source of his discomfort is within, he may look outside himself for outlets to relieve his anxiety. Some of those outlets, sexual affairs for example, may be forbidden to him. Since his loyalty to you won't let him act on those urges, he begins to blame you and project his discomfort onto you.

Could this be the reason he seems to point the finger at you for so many things? Could this be why you, or your children, or his work associates are so often his victims, for no apparent reason? Does he accuse you of provocative thoughts or feelings, when in truth he is the one who is experiencing them? By projecting his feelings onto you, he can fool himself into thinking that he is not having those ideas himself. And by doing that, he alleviates his stress, as George did when he projected onto Cindy.

George and Cindy took a long-overdue vacation with another couple, Dave and Lacey. George had been going through a difficult year at work, with younger hotshots nipping at his heels. Finally, watching a televised golf tournament with Dave in the hotel's bar, George began to relax. Meanwhile, Cindy and Lacey were catching up with each other at the other end of the lounge, when two men engaged them in friendly conversation. It turned out that one of them went to the same college as Cindy. As they compared notes and shared laughs, George and Dave appeared. Cindy introduced everyone, and then happily joined her husband for dinner. The conversation was strained. George was being difficult. Cindy wasn't sure why. After everyone ordered, George excused himself and Cindy to speak privately. Once out of earshot, he accused her of flirting with her college "sweetheart." Cindy was appalled. She wasn't flirting; she was merely being friendly. She is happily married. George didn't let her off the hook. He kept blaming her for actions she never took, and thoughts and intentions she never had.

From Cindy's point of view, George had no reason to be saying these things. But Cindy wasn't attuned to the anxiety George was experiencing. He had been feeling threatened at work, and he needed validation as a man. At midlife, he had been sensing that his life lacked excitement, goals, and challenges. Maybe an extramarital affair would bump things up a notch. Having this idea festering in his head made him anxious. By projecting his fantasy onto his wife, he escaped responsibility for his own negative feelings. Unfortunately, this left Cindy confused and hurt. In order to help him, she needed to understand that his behavior was caused by his own anxiety toward midlife, not her actions.

## He Attempts to Explain Himself — Rationalization

Your hero never wants to fail. But the truth is, he will. Your manopause man can't possibly succeed in everything he does. So how will he react? Every situation is as different as the man who experiences it. But you can be sure, the more traditional your manopause man is, the harder he will be on himself when he fails. To deal with the anxiety this produces, he may employ a defense mechanism that will save him from feeling weak and vulnerable. He will rationalize, finding reasons outside himself to explain why things went wrong, or why he failed to accomplish something he set out to do. Offering a realistic explanation excuses him from having a personal failure, and allows him to continue to hold his head high as a man.

Rationalization is common when your manopause man participates in sports. Skiing, for example, takes strength and skill. But as your manopause man's body matures, he may not be able to attack the slopes the way he did as a younger man. Disappointed, maybe embarrassed, and most likely anxious about his failing abilities, your man may blame the snow conditions, his new boots, or the skis he rented. By doing this, he is explaining away his poor performance in a way that superficially makes sense, and avoids the painful truth. He's just not skiing as well as he did when he was younger. Nonetheless, by rationalizing, your manopause man can temporarily feel better.

## He Takes the Opposite Position — Reaction Formation

An event occurs. Your manopause man reacts. And you're surprised, because what he says is the polar opposite of what you know he believes. What's happening to him? Your manopause man has been trained to be a hero. And when he has trouble fulfilling that role, he may have to fumble for a way to explain it. Espousing opposite beliefs and goals is a way to avoid admitting he failed to live up to the principles in which he truly believes. This is how Harold defended against the anxiety he felt as a result of not being able to pay for his children's college education.

Harold is a highly educated, respected, and much-honored doctor in his field. Despite the fact that he advocates higher education as a stepping-stone in life, especially for his own children, he began telling his friends that his children must pay for their own college. They should be able to identify loans and apply for scholarships by themselves. After all, that was what he did. By espousing this belief, Harold avoids carrying the burden of providing an education for his children. But is this really what he wants? Or is it a defense mechanism? In truth, Harold would love to provide for his children's education. But unfortunately, because of reduced health-insurance payments to doctors, he has been forced to use the savings he put away for his children's education for necessary household expenses. So, in order to maintain his pride in being perceived as a good provider for the family, he presents an opinion to the world that totally opposes his deeply held beliefs.

## He Resorts to Childlike Behavior — Regression

He has tantrums, he makes a racket, he acts angry . . . Does this sound like a little boy? When your manopause man employs these tactics, he is regressing to childhood—a time when he was short on words and big on feelings. Back then, this behavior got results. So when an anxiety-inducing problem arises in adulthood, he may fall back on these immature methods of defense. Beware: regression, as a defensive mechanism, can become dangerous. A child in a tantrum can be controlled; a man is a very different matter, especially one who desperately wants to hold on to power and control.

## He Defends in Positive Ways — Sublimation

At last! A more mature defense mechanism. Sublimation surfaces when your manopause man faces a conflict between the selfish part of his psyche and his moral compass. The selfish part perches on one shoulder, pushing forth all kinds of desires that are, most likely, unacceptable. In extreme cases, it may even tell him to become violent. But his moral compass is whispering in the other ear. It doesn't quit. Fighting hard, it begins to take charge. And when that happens, your manopause man sublimates his aggressive and unacceptable impulses by substituting positive actions to manage—and hopefully alleviate—his stress. This is what happened to John when he started having to deal with unexpected pressures.

John and Sarah's marriage was strained. John had lost his job. They were experiencing severe financial pressures. Sarah was forced to go back to work but still maintained most of the parenting and household responsibilities. Her frustrations grew, as John became more complacent with unemployment. So complacent that he began retreating for part of every afternoon into a local bar. Their marriage slid downhill. Childcare became more difficult. All their communication was filled with conflict. John realized he'd fallen prey to unhealthy impulses, but he didn't know how to find his way out. Sarah suggested replacing the bar with the gym. It was there that John discovered boxing classes, which he thoroughly enjoyed. Using aggressive physical exercise, he was able to knock out his unhealthy impulses. By sublimating them, he found great relief. He gave up drinking and began to feel better about himself. Soon he had regained his self-confidence and found a new job.

### Doing Away with Defenses

As we have seen, many of a manopause man's bad behaviors are actually defense mechanisms in disguise, protecting him from feelings of disappointment, loss of control, and shame. He has quite an arsenal with which to fight back. He may have used variations of these weapons throughout his life, but they are more common—and more exaggerated—as the battles within him multiply during manopause. While defense mechanisms can, in small doses, do away with anxiety and internal stress, if they are used over a long period of time, they can camouflage feelings or alter perceptions. If too many are employed too often, or at the wrong time, they can have a detrimental impact on your manopause man's reality and on his behavior, and their effects can become chronic and more serious in nature. We will be talking about that in Chapter 6.

So while there are many ways in which a man can deflect his fears, it's better if he can recognize, acknowledge, and examine them and then learn to express his feelings about them in a calm and rational manner. We'll explore ways for him to accomplish that in the next chapter.

# LIVING WITH YOUR
# **MANOPAUSE** MAN

# CHAPTER FIVE

# YOUR **MANOPAUSE** MAN'S EMOTIONAL AWAKENING

So now that you have the knowledge of what it means to "be a man," plus an understanding of why your good man is acting out, it's time to jump into actually helping him through this transition. Let's start with perhaps the most important aspect of aiding your man: helping him to learn about and accept emotions.

Emotions and the feelings they produce are essential to survival. So it is extremely unfortunate that many men have trouble recognizing, defining, expressing, and communicating their feelings in ways that are effective, satisfying, and productive. Often, when men experience this inability, anxiety results, and manifests itself either in poor or unpredictable behavior.

Why are emotions so challenging for men? Hearken back to the fact that their brains are not wired to be as sensitive as ours to emotional nuance, nor are they as conducive to emotional expression. It's not that men can't learn to be sensitive to emotions, both theirs and those of the people around them—they can. The problem is that our culture has quashed their innate drive to understand and express what they are feeling. Hewing to the *man*dates, men must "push down their emotions, and never show them."

When your manopause man gets emotionally wounded, can he easily describe his feelings? Most likely he backs away, shelves the pain, and tries to move on. Eventually evasion turns to anxiety and surfaces in the form of negative behaviors. Wouldn't it be better for him to avoid that by examining his hurt and learning to communicate about his pain, in the hopes of better dealing with his feelings? A trip down the road to Nirvana begins when your manopause man learns to open his mind to his emotions, process what he is feeling, and communicate those feelings, when appropriate, to others. In order to make a happy, and mentally and physically healthy transition into their manopause years, men need to free themselves from the tight hold of emotional repression.

This is a tall order for a man who likes to be in control—especially during the manopause years, when men are flooded with unfamiliar feelings and are buffeted by emotional gyrations. If he releases his inner thoughts and feelings, he risks showing vulnerability and weakness. His lack of herohood could be revealed. The way he can claw himself out of this cave is by better understanding what he is going through, in order to learn how to help himself. And part of this involves acknowledging, not ignoring, his fears and his weaknesses.

Manopause is the time, more than ever, for men to be liberated. The path toward accomplishing this is by exploring and discovering their genuine selves, and what they are truly feeling, instead of continuing to act and feel the way they believe society expects them to. To help in the process, men need to learn a broader vocabulary in which to convey their feelings, especially the negative ones. And as a part of this honest examination, they especially need to learn to feel comfortable showing vulnerability and communicating the negative or weak feelings they are experiencing. In addition, they need to learn how to better recognize what *others* are feeling. Summing it up, your manopause man needs to become "emotionally intelligent."

According to Dr. Ronald Levant, emotional intelligence is "the ability to have emotional self-awareness, emotional expressiveness, and emotional empathy." Your manopause man needs to learn how to "feel and express emotions and how to be sensitive and responsive to other people's feelings."[1] The good news is that because of his hormonal decline, your manopause man may be less driven and more inclined to expand his emotional awareness—as long as the *man*dates don't get in his way. By doing so he will gain greater support from you, and from his other human connections such as friends and family members, all of whom can aid him during times of disappointment and change. Reaching that state of emotional awareness will have its challenges, thanks to his natural brain makeup, coupled with the cultural conditioning he has experienced throughout his life.

### Authenticity: The First Step Toward Emotional Intelligence

*"Feelings or emotions are the universal language and are to be honored. They are the authentic expression of who you are at your deepest place."*

**— Judith Wright**

To begin his journey, your man needs to become his most honest self. Our culture encourages our men to gild themselves with all sorts of trappings—trappings of wealth, achievement, and stature. The authentic man is the one who would be left standing if all of those artificial additions were stripped away. In order to clearly examine himself and his emotions, your manopause man must strive to be the most true-to-himself person he can be. Know that he can reach this better place by moving beyond societal constraints and looking at his life through a more focused lens. What is truly important to him? Who is really vital to him, and who can he do without? Who does he feel closest to in his heart? What is imperative for his happiness, and what can he live without? What new directions does he want to explore? What has he always wanted to do, if only he had the opportunity and the confidence to try? Manopause is the time to let go of his inhibitions. He needs to get in touch with who he really is and what he desires.

Part of that involves becoming a more passionate, feeling person in relationship to his interests and hobbies. These may already be obvious to him, or they may have been held within and never explored. Maybe he will develop an enthusiasm for the arts, or he will become a gardener, a gourmet, or an inveterate collector. Sometimes a manopause man's challenge lies in learning to modify the way his existing passions are expressed. The runner who has always entered every marathon may stay both physically and mentally healthier if he skips a few and gets his satisfaction from coaching other runners to victory. Compromise is key. Happily, many manopause men, with a nudge from declining hormones, are already on a path toward their essential selves. Dr. Louann Brizendine reinforces this need for self-exploration when she says, "The happiest people are the ones who are able to express and be their most authentic selves." Those who are living in the center of their authenticity will pass through the manopause years with the least struggle and frustration.

Keep in mind that authenticity can clash with cultural expectations. It is the culture that misleads us into believing that internal strength and security are based on external things. The tighter your manopause man is holding on to the *man*dates and other societal dictates, the harder he will have to work to get to a life filled with happiness, tranquility, and peace. The process of self-discovery may seem frightening to your manopause man. The good news is that today's societal trends are beginning to move in his direction, as the culture slowly grows more open to men's change.

Trust is vital to helping your man search for, discover, and reveal who he really is. Encourage deep and honest communication with you, his trusted partner, to help him find his internal confidence and strength. Be patient as he takes the time to pursue and explore. Help him let go of the need to control. Be free to discover and savor honest intimacy. Your relationship is only as good as the authenticity that you and your manopause man bring to it.

------------------------------------------------------------

**TIP:** To help this process, your manopause man needs to shed his routines. Encourage your man to venture out—alone or with you at his side—and experience life differently, away from the trappings and surroundings that he leans on to define himself. These adventures will give your man a fresh perspective. They will free him to get in touch with his honest thoughts and his true beliefs, and that will define the way he wants to experience this new passage in his life. And if you do this together, it will bring you even closer to one another.

-----

*The Harvard Business Review* published an article in 2008 called "The Existential Necessity of Midlife Change." Its authors, Carlo Strenger, Ph.D., a psychoanalyst, philosopher, and associate professor of psychology at Tel Aviv University; and his businessman partner, Arie Ruttenberg, cried out, "Roll up your sleeves—midlife is your best and last chance to become the real you." Because of life experiences leading up to midlife, it is at this time that "we try listening to ourselves in order to discover who we are and what we want." Realizing that midlife affords the greatest opportunity for inner growth, the authors conclude that men at midlife "can become enriched beyond recognition as they take steps toward what Carl Jung called individualization: the process of becoming your true self."

## Accepting Change: The Second Step Toward Emotional Intelligence

The *man*dates dictate that men should remain strong, powerful, and in control, even in the face of inevitable change. Since we all know this *man*date is impossible to strictly adhere to, the very thought of change can stir up confusion and fear—fear of weakness, fear of aging, even death. These thoughts move our men in such a negative direction that they close their minds to them, hoping they will never gain momentum. Yet we live in a world of impermanence. Time moves on. Nothing stays the same. Positive and negative changes occur every minute, and we are faced with their effects. It is the *man*dates that create deep conflicts, which are an enormous burden to carry, and an even harder one to conceal. It's no wonder your manopause man is struggling.

So what can be done? He needs to face reality. Change is a part of the circle of life; it's not necessarily negative. Change can open the door to new definitions of strength, to deeper recognition of inner manly virtues such as wisdom and caring for others, and to an appreciation for the expertise he has developed over decades. To start down this positive path, you need to help your man develop a new emotional vocabulary.

------------------------------------------------------------

**TIP:** Challenge yourself to match every positive change in your manopause man with a positive comment of recognition. Your verbal acknowledgment and appreciation are a powerful motivating force.

------------------------------------------------------------

### Developing a New Vocabulary:
### The Third Step Toward Emotional Intelligence

> GEORGE: We don't need your help, because we are Lopezes! We don't ask and we don't get help, and even when we get help we don't take it . . . 'cause we don't deserve it!
>
> ANGIE: What are you saying?!
>
> GEORGE: I don't know, but I don't need your help!

**— George Lopez as George Lopez and Constance Marie as Angela "Angie" Palmero, the George Lopez show**

As comic as this exchange on the *George Lopez* show may be, it makes a serious point about a common manhood problem. George is unable to define and express what he is feeling, and that is complicating his struggle to maintain his herohood. By identifying emotional words, George, and other men, can understand more about themselves and can express themselves in ways that will let them get real help. "Naming an emotion helps to clarify it. The more emotion words you know the better you'll be able to identify and verbalize your feelings,"[2] says Dr. Levant.

Your manopause man should observe the words that he uses, as they will give him clues as to how he is reacting emotionally and viewing the world. Being more precise with words can help him fine-tune his recognition of his emotions. A larger working vocabulary will also help your manopause man better understand the feelings *you* express to *him*. The good news is that while the female brain is innately more verbally equipped, the male brain can still learn the skills to be sensitive to emotions, and to verbally communicate feelings.

The ability to learn these new skills is a fortunate by-product of the brain's plasticity. As Dr. Brizendine explains, both male and female brains have plasticity; they can reshape, rewire, and remap. The more a man does something, the more his brain will remold itself to be adapted to that activity. If Henry spends hours a day playing the piano, it follows that a greater amount of space within his brain will be devoted to piano prowess. If he decides that he would prefer to play basketball, at first basketball skills will take up only a small section of his brain. As he continues to practice, the amount of space devoted to the game will grow. The same concept can be applied to Henry's language skills. If Henry is encouraged to talk and communicate, and continues to do so, the neurons devoted to that activity will begin to strengthen, and soon talking and communicating will become much easier for him. It is too bad Henry wasn't encouraged to do this when he was a boy. By midlife, his neural pathways for talking would have been built and reinforced over decades. It is much more difficult to reroute established behaviors than to start down the right road from scratch. Still, Dr. Levant believes it is very possible.

## Getting the Wake-Up Call

Okay, so it's possible to rewire his brain. But how many men are going to volunteer? You can lead a horse to water, but when, if ever, will it decide to drink? Even men who are feeling lost during this confusing time of life may not want to admit it, even to themselves, because of manhood pressures. What will make them put down their heads and take that first swallow? Sometimes it is the rising anxiety they are experiencing as they battle their feelings and worry about their mental and physical health. Other times, it's that their relationships begin to seriously suffer because of their inability to handle all of the emotions and anxiety they are experiencing. And some men only realize they need to change emotionally after experiencing a life-changing event—men like David.

David was in his 50s when he lost his wife to breast cancer. Six months later, he remained overwhelmed by his inability to emotionally support his teenage daughters. The girls were managing to get back into the routine of life as best they could, with the help of their friends and teachers. But David knew he wasn't fulfilling their needs the way their mother once did. He wondered what was wrong with him. Why didn't he know the right questions to ask his daughters? Why didn't he understand the feelings that were behind their moods and painful moments? How could he help them with their "girl stuff" and "boy stuff"? After seeking professional help, he was fascinated to learn that his failure to connect was, in part, because of his cultural conditioning. He had never been taught to be aware of or sensitive to these areas. And knowing that his wife excelled in emotional skills, he never felt he needed to fine-tune his. Like many couples, David and his wife had a division of labor that let each of them take charge of the areas in which they felt the most comfortable. Their family tragedy forced David to see that a void in his insight and emotional skills was short-changing his relationships with his daughters. With the help of his therapist, he immediately began cultivating emotional intelligence, in an effort to better understand and help them, himself, and their relationships.

When all is said and done, the size of the wake-up call your manopause man will require to move him toward developing emotional intelligence will depend on the depth of his adherence to the *man*dates. But once he gets that wake-up call, and he becomes more aware of and in tune with recognizing and experiencing different kinds of emotions, his ability to communicate his feelings and understand yours will improve exponentially.

## How to Expand His Emotional Vocabulary

What if your man doesn't get that wake-up call? What if he just suffers, holding back his emotions? To help him, whether he asks for it or not, you can get to work expanding his emotional vocabulary. So let's look at some of the tools that will help him.

Sometimes it is just a matter of you being proactive. Start by asking him, for example, if he knows the difference between feeling isolated, sad, or discouraged. Yes, those differences are subtle, but without understanding this sort of nuance, how can your manopause man understand and explain to you precisely which emotion he is experiencing? Another way to do this is by discussing the emotions various characters were feeling and acting out, after you and your manopause man watch a television show or movie together. Or, after witnessing an argument between friends, the two of you can describe the feelings and points of view that were expressed, as well as how each of the opponents might have more accurately communicated their ideas. A special emphasis should be placed on vulnerable emotions like neediness, helplessness, disconnection, and doubt—the emotions your manopause man may have the greatest difficulty recognizing and acknowledging, especially after a lifetime of being stymied in this area.

---

**TIP:** Your manopause man can learn a lot from you about expressing his emotions, so having a strong grasp on your own emotional vocabulary is a good way to start. Go to eqi.org//fw.htm for a long list of feeling words you can start incorporating into your vocabulary. You can even share this list with your manopause man if he's open to it.

---

With an enriched emotional vocabulary, your manopause man may return home from a frustrating day at work, and instead of being quiet and guarded, he can explain his feelings to you. Maybe he's feeling diminished because a younger co-worker is maneuvering around him. He fears that his job is in jeopardy, and not knowing what action to take is heightening his unsettled and uncomfortable emotions. Now that he has been able to explain this to you, together you can strategize how he should act within the company, and discuss alternatives outside the company. This will decrease his anxiety by renewing his sense of control. With true communication, the trust between the two of you can become immeasurable. Your manopause man just has to get comfortable expressing how he feels, and recognizing emotion in others. Happily, he may be at the perfect stage to do just that. However, if your manopause man shows no interest in expanding his emotional vocabulary, you can start to discuss *your* emotions—not necessarily while you're feeling them. Eventually, your man will become more aware and open to the subject matter in general.

### Empathy, an Outgrowth of Emotional Intelligence

"Empathy makes us human. Empathy brings us joy. And empathy is an essential part of living a life of meaning,"[3] says Daniel Pink in his bestseller *A Whole New Mind*. But empathy is an emotion that is in short supply for many men who have yet to have their emotional awakening. "Empathy is the ability to imagine yourself in someone else's position and to intuit what that person is feeling,"[4] says Pink. And it's not surprising that a man who is afraid to experience his own emotions is unwilling and unable to immerse himself in the emotions of the people around him. But your manopause man may deserve a bye from time to time, both because his male brain is not wired emotionally like yours and because of his cultural conditioning. Keep in mind that as you expose him to your needs and feelings, your manopause man has the potential to grow in this area.

Remember the concept of a man's selfless generosity, the spirit of giving that is evidenced by the traditional manhood qualities we should forever cherish? As he travels toward emotional awareness, your man will need to learn another type of generosity—emotional generosity. The emotionally generous man has the ability to feel what others are feeling, and act in a way that shows his sensitivity to those feelings.

To better understand these different types of generosity, picture yourself on an airplane. A woman enters the plane carrying an infant. She struggles to lift her heavy bag into the overhead bin. Most likely, your man will rise from his seat to help her. This is a display of his selfless generosity. Later in the flight, the woman's baby begins to cry. Your man, who so kindly displayed selfless generosity, may feel annoyed. This is because he is lacking in emotional generosity. You now have a perfect opportunity to help him cultivate his own feelings of empathy. Point out how helpless the woman must be feeling, unable to control her baby's crying in this small crowded space. Explain how frustrated she must be, perhaps even worried that her baby isn't settling down because something is seriously wrong. It is best to take every opportunity to guide your manopause man into learning the skills of empathy. The more he becomes aware, not only of his own emotions, but also of those being felt by the people around him, the more easily he will recognize and intuit what you and others are feeling. When your man turns to the woman, offers her a sympathetic smile, and asks if there is anything he can do to help, you know that he has begun to learn emotional generosity.

Stress can dampen empathetic feelings. So when your manopause man is anxious, his ability to feel for others may be altered. This is another time when you can help. Remain grounded as you help him untangle the true source of the conflict he is experiencing. He will, hopefully, learn from your example to identify the real problem, understand its ramifications, and take the necessary actions to solve it. In the process he will reduce his poor behavior. Your example will also teach him to be sensitive to *your* emotions, identify with what you are feeling, as well as show him how to help you the next time you are anxious.

Once men add emotional generosity to their repertoire, and practice it regularly, their ability to generate an empathetic reaction to other's feelings becomes second nature. Men live one life. The enlightened man, who feels empathy for others, has the ability, through them, to live many. Hopefully, your manopause man can grow to be one of these enlightened men. This is an essential piece of his emotional awakening.

## Bridging the Communication Gap

One of the most important tools in helping your man establish his emotional intelligence is to make sure you are able to communicate well. Poor communication will lead to your man shutting the door to your help. As we learned, men's and women's brains are wired differently. Dr. Louann Brizendine explains that, "Scientists have documented an astonishing array of structural, chemical, genetic, hormonal, and functional brain differences between women and men."[5] With all of these differences in the brains, it is easy to understand why communication between the sexes can be innately difficult. Since men don't think, act, react, love, hate, or hurt the way women do, both sexes are at a disadvantage in the "understanding game." The many differences in our brains, added to our cultural conditioning, and hormonal shifts, equals a clear communication gap. But with a greater knowledge of these variables, plus some work, you can bridge this gap. Let's explore some of the ways that gap appears, in an effort to close it.

## Facts Versus Intuition

It's no wonder men are not as communicative as we are. Dr. Brizendine explains that, "In the brain centers for language and hearing . . . women have 11 percent more neurons than men." Women also have a larger hippocampus, the principle center for emotion and memory. By midlife, men usually recognize we have a special gift for emotional nuance; they call it "women's intuition." Since we are gifted with additional perceptions, shouldn't we use them to help our relationships with our manopause men?

As we have said, emotions are less likely to be enjoyable brain sensations to him than design problems to be solved. He would much rather problem-solve than talk about feelings. Michael Gurian reports that when a group of college students were given PET scans as they tried to categorize the emotions expressed on faces shown to them in pictures, the women scored better than men. He suggests that, "Men inherently distrust feelings, and women inherently trust them."[6] Think of your own experiences. Does your man rely on his emotional reaction as the final comment on an experience, or must he see some additional logic, proof, or back-up, like Jake?

Melanie felt instinctively that her children's new middle-school principal was not going to fit into the school's established values, and she was worried for the future of the school. Jake, her husband, insisted on getting facts and reports on the man's recent decisions, before he could be convinced. He told Melanie that without them, her judgment was mere speculation. She defended her position by saying that at the morning's PTA meeting, after the new principal spoke to the parents, she didn't sense appropriate enthusiasm going back to him. Jake encouraged her not to make a judgment without solid evidence, but acquiesced, knowing her intuition was right in the past. Understanding Jake's brain, Melanie didn't take his lack of agreement with her personally. Two months later it became obvious to Jake that his wife's intuition was valid, when the school board began a search for a new principal midterm. Melanie's "intuition" was actually an ability to read emotional nuance, such as the subtle hints in body language conveyed by other parents during the PTA meeting.

As we have said, because of their brain circuitry, men's innate ability to read faces and tone of voice, and thus to sense emotional nuance is not as strong as women's. The good news is your manopause man's receptivity to emotional nuance becomes more finely tuned as he gets older, says Gary Small, M.D., director of the UCLA Memory and Aging Center, professor of psychiatry at UCLA's David Geffen School of Medicine, and best-selling author. An older male brain is better in face-to-face communication. At middle age, men are usually more easily able to look people in the eye. "And because they have had more life experience and more emotional maturity," Dr. Small continues, "they have better frontal lobe skills and can put the big picture together better."

If you are lucky enough to have been with your manopause man from your early 20s through to midlife, you may have noticed that he is now more aware of and responsive to your emotional needs. He may also be more keenly attuned to the people and situations he is exposed to. He can probably identify your emotional reactions, as well as those of family members and other people he is close with, by observing body language much more intuitively than he used to. This is one way in which manopause men have an advantage over their younger counterparts in the area of communication.

------------------------------------------------------------

**TIP:** Think back—has your extra sensitivity become obvious at times when you and your man observe other people in a social situation? Have you ever walked away having sensed what is going on in people's minds behind public faces? And if so, when you discuss it with your man, does he seem as if he is completely out of touch with what just happened? Don't blame him. It's his biological makeup. It isn't that your man is blind, there are just things he doesn't see. Be sensitive to his male brain deficiency.

------------------------------------------------------------

## Be Prepared for His Shutdown

Sometimes your manopause man's seemingly cold reactions can be misleading. Instead of indicating a *lack* of feeling, they can be the product of emotions that are *too strong*. When men get overwhelmed, they turn off. John Gottman, Ph.D., renowned psychologist and author, and expert on marriage and relationships, calls this "emotional flooding."[7] Picture your manopause man in an argument. Adrenaline and cortisol flood his nervous system. He goes into survival mode. His body prepares for physical action. Once a man's brain is flooded with fight-or-flight chemicals, it becomes nearly impossible for him to communicate his feelings. If this happens during an argument, it would be better to delay and talk another time, when his brain will once again have the capacity to communicate. Men are usually sorry for their distant behavior, once their emotional flooding is over. You should remember that when your manopause man is emotionally underwater, he is not being stubborn or closed due to midlife hormonal changes. He is simply being overwhelmed, which could happen at any age. Be patient, give him some time, and don't be surprised if you have your own shutdowns. They are more common in men, but the same thing could happen to you.

## Women Naturally Overreact

When people's brains anticipate something frightening or hurtful, scans show that women's amygdalae, their brains' center for primitive emotions, activate more than men's. On average, we find it harder to suppress our reactions to anticipated danger or pain. Have you ever screamed when someone unexpectedly appears and frightens you, or when a large spider scuttles across your pillow? It's a natural female tendency. And of course your manopause man thinks you are overreacting. Since his brain doesn't process things in the same way yours does, it is hard for him to understand your response. And because his behavior may be more irritable at this time of life due to his hormonal shifts, he may be less patient than ever with you, again widening the gap.

## Women Overlap Men's Speech

One of the obvious ways in which our brain differences evidence themselves is through speech. Women have two speech patterns which are particularly irritating to men and which can affect the communication gap. One of them is overlapping speech.

Sally and Mitch are conversing about their day. Mitch is recounting a situation at work. Sally interjects with different trains of thought, tangential to his work story, as they occur to her. While, in her mind, she is staying on topic, to his ear she is overlapping his words with unrelated ideas and questions. He grows frustrated. She doesn't understand why. As far as Sally is concerned, she is just trying to get a more complete picture of Mitch's story. There is a communication disconnect for three distinct reasons. First, Mitch's male brain is comfortable thinking in a linear fashion, while Sally's female brain is comfortable moving in multiple directions. Next, because Mitch's brain is less adept at language skills, he can't keep up with her rapid-fire questions and overlapping comments. Finally, because of Mitch's cultural conditioning, Sally's interruptions make him feel weak and not in control, something he is more sensitive to at this time of his life. They also make him incapable of getting the story out. Would Hercules allow himself to be interrupted? Probably not! Mitch has to learn to comfortably communicate his frustrations. And Sally needs to be more understanding of his brain wiring and manhood pressures. Once she is, she can curb her verbal interruptions, out of respect for her manopause man. When talking with your man, while you can't be expected to change how your brain is wired to make everything okay, you can use your well-developed empathy skills to recognize when it is important to simply stop and listen. This will encourage your man to talk more and will help open lines of communication and trust between you.

## Women Make Abrupt Topic Changes

Another female speech pattern that is problematic when talking to men is abrupt topic changes. This is something we need to remember when talking with our men. Mitch's description of his workday problem reminds Sally of an article she read in that morning's business section, and she veers off in that direction, stopping just long enough to catch sight of her watch. That reminds her that she has to pick up their daughter from volleyball practice. While she is still encouraging Mitch to talk, she interjects that one of the other volleyball moms has to go into the hospital for tests. Mitch's brain is still systematically on the work track. He is uncomfortable switching topics without completing his linear thought. Instead of recognizing this as the clash of two brain types, he thinks Sally is being rude and disrespectful. "A man" deserves better. Sally, meanwhile, is simply giving free rein to her multitasking, emotionally empathetic female brain—a pattern another woman would easily understand and follow.

## Help Him Win in the Communication Game

Sally and Mitch are running up against a language barrier. She speaks female, he hears male. This is one common way that, instead of being communicators, men and women can be "communifailures." From the time they are boys on the playground, men learn not to enter a competition they have little chance of winning. Why risk failure and possible ridicule? They know that in the talking game, women are the probable winners. Because of their cultural conditioning, men often take a backseat in communicating, as women push the game ahead.

Once they are feeling defensive about their verbal shortcomings, it is that much more dangerous if we choose to critique. Manopause men may not receive what we say as constructive. Their frame of mind may steer them into thinking we are pointing out that they are deeply flawed, widening the divide in our relationship.

------------------------------------------------------------

**TIP:** As you communicate with your manopause man, you should check the emotional nuance cues that he gives off, and ask yourself if your brain's complex verbal wiring is overtaxing his manopause brain. If so, you should help to bridge the communication gap by slowing down.

------------------------------------------------------------

### *Emotions That Are Game-Changers*

Now that we have slowed down enough to have our men's full attention, we can begin to communicate some of the emotions that will make their lives fuller, richer, and happier during these years of change—emotions that will help men expand their emotional intelligence.

## Gratitude

*"Think of all the beauty that's still left
in and around you and be happy!"*

**— Anne Frank**

Great mental and physical health begins with a positive outlook on life. An important component of this is gratitude. Being and feeling grateful can be extremely beneficial to your manopause man. Michael McCullough, Ph.D., and Robert Emmons, Ph.D., found that when you remind yourself of being grateful for the life you have, there is a positive result. Maintaining this "attitude of gratitude" can improve psychological, emotional, and physical well-being. It requires self-reflection, the humility to realize one's own limitations, and the ability to admit that one is dependent on the help of others.[8] Under our cultural conditioning edicts, which dictate that a "real man" needs no one, this may be a challenge for your manopause man.

Despite the inherent challenge, gratitude can be learned, and should be, because feeling grateful will provide your manopause man with a more energetic, positive, and happy spirit. That is why he should count his blessings every day.

------------------------------------------------------------

**TIP:** Make sure to express your gratitude for things in *your* life. This will prompt your man to start thinking of what *he* appreciates. And if the situation is right, perhaps you can even ask him what he's grateful for.

------------------------------------------------------------

## Optimism

Optimistic thoughts can relieve stress and anxiety, and in doing so, can eliminate some of your man's bad behaviors. But experts believe that only 50 percent of the population is naturally optimistic; the other half needs to be taught. Pessimistic thoughts, on the other hand, can contribute to a man's stress. Studies show that even using derogatory words can negatively influence a man's mood. So tell your man about the positive effects of optimism—men do respond to facts, after all. And then make sure to express yourself and your emotions optimistically. This will help convince your manopause man that it is best to fill his head with positive thoughts. And remember to express your pride when he looks at a situation positively that could easily be cast in a negative light. This shift to positivity will not only help your man, it will also make your life better. And remember to encourage optimism in your man, even when applied to everyday situations. For example, if he is reluctant to go to a social or family gathering, encourage him to think about the good feelings and lasting bonding that can be a part of the experience. Expressing it in that positive way will give your man optimistic feelings that can influence him to enjoy the gathering.

## Altruism

Altruism is another positive way to counter stress. When you do service for another, or for the public, a positive, rewarding feeling ensues. The best way for a manopause man to stop feeling bad about what is happening *inside* himself, is to look *outside* himself. Improving the lives of others can help him to better his own. Comparing his blessings with their needs can wake him up to gratitude. Using his gifts, either material gifts or his skills, for good can make his life fuller and more meaningful. A dentist or doctor, for example, could donate time to a free clinic. An attorney could do pro bono work. A teacher could tutor a child who might fail without his help. Filling a need for others who can't otherwise afford services will not only make your manopause man feel useful, it will remind him of how lucky he is.

## Spirituality Brings Emotional Receptivity

Just as a field needs to be plowed and fertilized before seeds are sown, your manopause man's psyche needs to offer receptive soil for his emotional growth. Finding or reconnecting to spirituality can help to create that fertile field. It can help him gain a sense of control, as well as compassion, conviction, and connection to help guide him through this time. One way to do this is to look to organized religion or religious teachings, which offer alternative answers and explanations to his questions about the unknown.

Research has demonstrated a multitude of positive effects that result from exposure to religion, or to groupings of people with similarly aligned belief systems. These positive side effects can work wonderfully well for men during their manopause years. Duke University presented a study that showed people within religious groups seemed to be less depressed, and less anxious than people who were not members of a religious group. The members of religious groups also coped better with illness, bereavement, and divorce. In a study by Smith, McCullough, and Poll, it was found that the greater the religiousness, the fewer symptoms of depression.[9] And it does not have to be a specific religion. In Michael McCullough's work, he noticed that as long as there is a framework of belief, such as secular humanism, the benefits are similar. He says, "There are remarkably consistent findings that religiosity correlates with higher self-control."[10] And control is what your manopause man is searching for at a time when he feels he is losing it. In another study performed over a 16-year-period in Israel, secular and religious kibbutzim were examined. This study found that those who were inclined to have higher levels of trust in religion tended to live longer.[11]

Some explanations about why spirituality produces these benefits were pointed out in a conversation with Rabbi Steven Z. Leder who said, "There is no question that religion can give men a deeper sense of meaning and purpose on an individual and spiritual level. Religion can reacquaint us with ennobling ideas. Prayer can give us a greater sense of gratitude and awareness. But there is another benefit to men reconnecting to their religious heritage and church, synagogue, or mosque, which is a greater sense of community and the satisfaction of service to others. Religion can and should be about so much more than what we believe; it should also be about how we behave; how we choose to spend our time, money, and talents; how we can receive by giving to others; and how we are enriched when we are with others who are doing the same. In some religious traditions there is also the opportunity for men to be solely with other men. Ideally, all-male sacred space leads to men expressing their deepest feelings in ways they rarely do in other all-male endeavors like watching sports, and would certainly never do with women present."

Clearly religious practice encourages men to discover and explore their emotional awareness. If your man isn't one for religion, he can perhaps look to something similar, but more secular, such as mindfulness meditation, to foster his health and well-being. This practice, which has been shown to have great stress-reduction effects, can also help to modify his behavior for the better. Jon Kabat-Zinn, Ph.D., the founding director of the Stress Reduction Clinic and the Center for Mindfulness in Medicine, Health Care, and Society at the University of Massachusetts Medical School has helped to bring "mindfulness" and mindfulness meditation into mainstream medicine with his scientific research. His work focuses on people coping with the daily pressures of modern living, as well as on people with chronic illness and those facing death. The practice of mindfulness recognizes and accepts things are constantly changing in ways that no one can stop, and it purports that if you try to hold things back—to resist change—your struggle will be to no avail and will only result in more suffering. Mindfulness is a way of being awake in the moment, resting in a kind of awareness that is so stable that one's mind and emotions are not thrown off by comings and goings, or by upsetting news. The goal is to remain grounded in the midst of turmoil, especially during manopause.[12]

Kabat-Zinn believes the path to this grounded existence is through meditation. And the practice of meditation appears to offer a plethora of benefits. A 2009 study conducted at the University of California in Los Angeles pointed out that specific regions in the brains of long-term meditators were larger and had more gray matter than the brains of individuals in a control group. Since our brains shrink as we age, this finding is of profound importance to a man, or anyone, who wants to stay mentally sharp as they travel through midlife and into old age. Eileen Lueders, Ph.D., bears this out when she says that "if practiced regularly and over years, meditation may slow down aging-related brain atrophy, perhaps by positively affecting the immune system."[13] And we all can agree that an improved immune system is a good thing.

----------------------------------------------------------------

**TIP:** If your man is interested in learning more about mindfulness, there are a multitude of resources available to him. Much scientific study has been done on its benefits, and there are increasing discussions every day about what mindfulness can do for us. Check out mindful.org and the website for Jon Kabat-Zinn's stress reduction clinic at www.umassmed.edu/content.aspx?id=41252.

----------------------------------------------------------------

## The Many Roads to Emotional Growth

There are many ways for your man to become more emotionally intelligent. The expression of his feelings is essential to growth, but other things, like learning to laugh at his own changes, and at the silliness of certain *man*dates he has abided by can also help. He could choose to lean on you for love and support as he accepts weaknesses when, in the past, he would try to muscle through them, or retreat from them. Your manopause man may also choose, when he is feeling threatened, to search out paths that lead toward calmness. Therapeutic massage and other forms of relaxation therapy are an option. Perhaps he will pursue a creative interest that he might have scoffed at in the past as inappropriate or useless. The option your manopause man chooses does not necessarily matter, but his emotional acceptance of change, both on conscious and subconscious levels, does. By walking down any number of paths, he can visualize change as a positive, forward movement toward growth.

Add to these some other, everyday ways for your manopause man to manage the internal stress that he may be feeling during these years of change. According to Robert Tan, M.D., in his book *The Andropause Mystery,* to help combat stress he should learn to love and reward himself; to organize and take control of his life; to exercise, relax, and eat healthily; and to generally learn to enjoy life. He should also try to spend more quality time with children and loving family members. The happy energy this engenders will rub off on him. He should reward himself with the things that feel good, while always being careful not to go overboard. The aftereffects of overindulging could cause unnecessary additional stresses.

And remember, it's okay—and actually healthy—for your man to cry. Not only can it help him psychologically, it is proven to be *biologically* better for him to cry. William Frey II, Ph.D., of the University of Minnesota, is a biochemist and a student of "psychogenic lacrimation," the study of emotionally induced tears. His studies have demonstrated that these tears, the ones you *don't* get from cutting onions, serve an excretory function, ridding the body of toxins which accumulate under stress. By excreting these chemicals through emotional tears, Dr. Frey explains, the body is cleansing itself.[14]

Conversely, what happens when you hold back tears? Can this damage the body? Dr. Frey suggests it can, and that it may be the reason men develop more stress-related diseases than women do. At the Marquette University College of Nursing, Margaret Crepeau, Ph.D., found that people with stress-related disorders—ulcers and colitis, for example—were more likely than healthy people to view crying as a sign of weakness or a loss of control. These ill people also reported that they cried less often, which would seem to indicate that it is better for people to shed tears than to hold them in.[15] Keep in mind that people are the only animals known to shed emotional tears, and that crying somehow enhanced their survival. So let's stop saying to our boys, "Keep a stiff upper lip, don't cry." From now on, let's encourage our boys and our men to stay healthy by shedding tears, even if it doesn't fall in line with the *man*dates.

### Strengthening His New Emotions: Male Friendships

Spirituality prepares your man for emotional openness; friendship lets him practice it. Your man's human desire to delve deeper into his newfound awareness should not stop with you and his family. The relationship your manopause man has with his male friends needs to strengthen as well. But the *man*dates discourage men from pursuing male relationships. This, coupled with the notion that men can never show weakness, forces them to stay clear of strong bonding with other men, and to avoid revealing their vulnerabilities to them. These self-imposed limitations become especially problematic during the manopause years, when men crave connection and support.

Rabbi Steven Z. Leder highlighted the problem when he wrote to us, "Men almost never talk to other men about feelings, because doing so means unlearning a lifetime of defensive and aggressive posturing—the silent sizing up of the other, the camouflaging of spirit and soul bequeathed to us by generations of men who went to work and went to war and didn't want to talk about it."[16]

This male legacy is extremely unfortunate. Men should not be denied the comfort of bonding with others who are going through similar changes. They should be made to feel comfortable sharing relatable feelings and experiences in an attempt to help their fellow men move more easily through this time. When they are troubled or confused, they should be able to find out whether the same things are happening to their friends, things such as bouts of irritability, frustration, even anger or depression, and if so, how they are dealing with them.

Male friends are the ones who can bust your manopause man when his behavior is pushing too far over the line, or tell him things he might resent hearing from you. Open and honest communication with other men helps men become more at ease with being vulnerable, which will make them more comfortable seeking answers. Once men understand that their friends are experiencing the same things they are, they will feel stronger, less burdened, less alone, and eventually, as their male bonds strengthen, more empowered.

The benefits of friendship, as reported by columnist Sue Shellenbarger in *The Wall Street Journal* in November of 2010, are enormous. Her article, "Beyond Facebook; the Benefits of Deeper Friendships," says research published in *The Journal of Health and Social Behavior* linked social and emotional support for men with better health and lower rates of disability, depression, and anxiety. The report tells us that, "A sense of being loved, cared for, and listened to fosters a sense of meaning and purpose and reduces stress-induced wear and tear on the body, lowering the heart rate, blood pressure, and stress hormones."[17] So encourage your manopause man to get together with his friends more often. If your manopause man has never felt comfortable bonding closely with male friends, maybe you can encourage him to invite some to get-togethers, and then offer to help him with the arrangements once he does. These could be card nights, football parties, or even lunches. Or if he's not comfortable on his own, you can ease him into getting together by hosting some events where you invite men and women to dinner or a simple barbeque—any event where the initial spark of friendship can kindle.

### Your Contributions Are Key

We've outlined a number of things you can do to help your man in his emotional awakening, but there's one more step for you to undertake. It involves taking a look at yourself. Be honest. Are you contributing to your manopause man's emotional predicament? Are you uncomfortable with the idea of your man being emotional instead of invulnerable? Does the thought that he might cry threaten your sense of security? Do you think that a man who is emotionally open is "soft"? If any of these questions resonate with you, you could be thwarting your man's ability to feel and, in the process, limiting the quality of your communication and weakening your relationship. Now that you are educated about the cultural pressures the two of you are carrying, you need to be strong enough to encourage his new emotional openness, even if it temporarily disrupts your own level of comfort.

One of the many stumbling blocks men have with disclosing their vulnerabilities, especially during manopause, is the shame associated with the reveal. They worry that they will be judged—by their peers, their co-workers, and you. They need to work toward shedding these concerns. Help that along by being careful not to judge your manopause man or his feelings. Give him permission to be vulnerable and to admit weakness without embarrassment. Show acceptance as you help him to communicate what he is feeling on the inside, with the goal of making him feel more comfortable with what he is projecting on the outside. Never forget the important differences that can stand in the way of clear and effective communication. Work to bridge that communication gap, because if your manopause man can open up, he will feel and act much more empowered, and his mental outlook will become more positive.

And remember, praise the positive changes that your man's emotional openness is bringing about in his behavior. As Dudley Danoff, M.D., says in his book *Penis Power,* the real source of your man's power and strength emanates from his heart and soul, not his possessions. These inner qualities include self-confidence, the ability to express full potential, healthy self-esteem, positive thinking, and emotional balance.[18]

The more fully you support your man as he learns to express his feelings, the easier his adjustment will be to his new way of thinking about his manhood. Once your manopause man becomes honest about who he is, accepts change, and develops an emotional vocabulary to voice the feelings he can now define, he will possess a toolbox of emotional intelligence that he can use to rebuild the structure of his changing life. The rich palate of emotional intelligence will also provide him with a deeper understanding of life's many colors—with all its treasures and disappointments. You can make the process easier by being sensitive and empathetic. Living with an emotionally awakened and open manopause man will bring you levels of togetherness and joy you may never have thought you could have.

# EMOTIONS AND BEHAVIORS GO FROM **BAD TO WORSE**

During manopause, your man will go through many feelings, both positive and negative. If he hasn't honed his emotional intelligence and learned to deal with the feelings that manopause creates in him, negative emotions can go from bad to worse. Your man may experience an overall increase in anxiety, which can spin out of control and perhaps even send him into depression. And then his bad behaviors can take him even further down a path of unhealthy living, one that will impact both of you.

Depression, or "the black dog" as Winston Churchill referred to it, is one of the most powerful of all negative emotions. It can reveal itself through any number of bad behaviors, including withdrawal, aggression, or a combination of the two. When these bad behaviors go untreated, emotional or physical abuse, even violence, can be the ultimate result. Anyone can be the victim of that violence. In the worst-case scenario, anger can lead to murder, and depression can lead to suicide if left undiagnosed and untreated. The suicide rate for men in their 40s and 50s is three times higher than the national average. This isn't meant to scare you, but rather to shed light on the seriousness of identifying behavior that is problematic and taking the necessary action to treat it as quickly as possible.

## Depression in Manopause

According to the National Institutes of Mental Health, reported by the Mayo Clinic, depression affects about six million men in America each year.[1] During the teenage years and early 20s, depression occurs in twice as many young women as men. But by midlife, both sexes are equally affected.

The reason men catch up during midlife is most likely associated with a decline in testosterone, which is a natural antidepressant. It pumps fast and furiously into teenage boys, and continues into their 20s. At midlife, men don't just feel the decline of testosterone as it affects their physical abilities, it also rocks their mental state. As your manopause man becomes aware of his hormonal loss, he may possibly feel declining muscle strength and a lessened sexual function, and that can be reflected in a weakening of his overall self-image. Add to the formula the realization that life is at least half over and possibly going in a downhill direction, it's understandable that he is experiencing depression.

Sometimes the onset of depression can be traced to a specific event or setback. "Situational depression" occurs because someone is experiencing stress and grief as a result of not being able to adjust to a specific situation. It may be the result of the loss of a job or a financial reversal. Eva Ritvo, M.D., former vice chair of the Department of Psychiatry, Miller School of Medicine, and co-author of *The Concise Guide to Marriage and Family Therapy*, has seen, in her practice, an increase in depression in men during tough economic times. In an interview in April of 2011 she said, "Men's self-esteem is often tied to their earnings, and when they see a decrease in their income their mood and relationships may suffer." Perhaps it is the result of experiencing a traumatic event such as a disaster, crime, or accident. It may have come about after a personal trauma, such as the loss of a relationship, or the illness or death of a loved one. About ten percent of adults experience situational depression at some point in their lives. Whether or not men want to admit it, depression can hit them hard at midlife. If and when it does, it must be dealt with.

### What Are the Signs of Depression in Your Manopause Man?

He may experience increased nervousness from anxiety and fear, irritability, mood swings, decreased short-term memory, irregular sleep habits, indecisiveness, loss of interest, or loss of self-confidence. Add aggression and anger to the list, as well as unexpected violence or abusive behavior. Your man might start drinking more or using other mind-altering substances to mask his depression. And sadly, you might also notice depression manifesting physically, in problems with getting an erection—which only adds to the depression he already has. So take note if your man starts showing any of the symptoms listed above.

------------------------------------------------------------

**TIP:** If you would like a formal definition of the criteria for a major depressive episode, you can refer to *The Diagnostic and Statistical Manual of Mental Disorders IV*. In this book you can also read more about the symptoms of depression.

------------------------------------------------------------

It is important to be keenly aware of the symptoms of depression because, if not treated, there could be serious, even permanent, repercussions. Your manopause man can experience a substantial drop in daily performance and productivity—up to a 30 percent decline, reports the National Institute of Mental Health. Psychologist and author Dr. Bob Murray has discovered through his research that depression is the main cause of divorce for men at midlife, the time when divorce rates are already at their highest.[2]

## Retreat or Aggression

When depression hits, men generally respond to it by following one of two paths, or a combination of the two. Some depressed men are always in retreat—in retreat from sex and intimacy, in retreat from challenges, in retreat from communication and confrontation. If this is your manopause man, he will react to his helplessness by becoming withdrawn, by suppressing his feelings and by trying to keep people at a distance, and that includes you. Most likely his depression is making him feel like a manhood failure. He thinks he doesn't deserve to be loved or to have sex. And with his hormones dropping, he subconsciously fears being unable to succeed at sex if he does have it. By avoiding sex, he avoids failure. Depression is both the cause of his problem, and the perfect way out. It deadens him to his feelings of failure as a man, and lets him avoid the pain they carry with them—or so he hopes. A man who retreats does not want to communicate; he is convinced that a man should be able to fix his problems by himself. When he cannot, you may find him seeking refuge in his bed, where he will find no relief because his sleep patterns are disrupted. Or, he may seclude himself in his workshop, where he will find it hard to concentrate. Overall, his work, his family, and his social connections will suffer. He doesn't care; he just wants to be numb to it all, to be left alone, or to find refuge in the dark.

The other path men take is the road of anger and aggression. While the retreating man has occasional angry outbursts, or sometimes displays suppressed anger, the hostile male sufferer reacts to feelings of depression by acting out with consistent episodes of aggression.

When a man perceives a threat, and there are many he is faced with on a daily basis, a natural reaction is to experience anger. Being angry isn't always a bad thing, reports the Mayo Clinic. It can motivate your manopause man to take action to protect the people and things he cares about. Or, it can alert other people to recognize his feelings. Not to mention the fact that anger can feel good in the heat of the moment. The key is managing anger in a healthy way.[3]

If the threat your man feels is intense, the anger response can have strong physiological effects. It can be felt as it moves through his body as his heart races, his muscles tighten, and his head pounds. And these physiological effects may remain, magnifying feelings of lack of control, which in turn intensify the feelings of anger. That is when negative consequences can kick in. In a March 2009 article in the *Journal of the American College of Cardiology,* Yoichi Chida, M.D., Ph.D., reported that, "Anger and hostility were found to predict a 19 percent and 24 percent increase in Coronary Heart Disease (CHD) events among initially healthy people and those with pre-existing CHD, respectively." He added: "The harmful association of anger and hostility with CHD events in healthy people was greater in men than women. This suggests that the accumulation of stress responses in daily life might have a greater impact on future CHD in men."[4]

Most people do not walk around angry, ready to fight at the drop of a hat. Instead, a "triggering event" is the catalyst that releases accumulated negative feelings that have been held inside, turning them into an angry outburst. Keep in mind that aggression is the physical action taken in reaction to angry feelings. And during manopause, with sensitivities high, there are so many new triggering events. This is exactly what happened when Mary realized, too late, that she was in the wrong lane to make a left turn at the upcoming intersection. She looked quickly in her rearview mirror, and swerved sharply to get in the proper lane to make a turn. Unfortunately, she ended up blocking two lanes, causing the red sports car behind her to slam on the breaks. Up ahead, the light in the intersection turned yellow. When the light changed back to green, the car in front of the left lane did not move forward enough into the intersection to release the red sports car from its locked position behind her. The driver held down his horn, then got out and ran to the front car, banged on the trunk and screamed obscenities. Next he turned to Mary and repeated his diatribe.

What caused such over-the-top behavior? Could the fact that he wasn't in control of happenings around him have threatened the driver's manhood? Maybe he was on his way to an important meeting, the kind of meeting where a "hero" can't be late and must succeed?

Was it a result of his declining hormones? Or did the driver suffer from excessive anger problems? Maybe it was a combination of all of them.

The man who acts out is hurting. He is displacing his angry feelings onto someone or something else, in an effort to protect himself by self-correcting the anxiety in his brain. He can do this through attacking, criticizing, demeaning, blaming, or belittling. And when this happens, if the recipient of his attack doesn't respond in the way he wants, your man feels even more deeply that he isn't in control, which leads to a never-ending cycle of depression and anger.

The Mayo Clinic reports that the healthiest way for a man to handle anger is by being assertive and expressing his concerns and needs. These may vary depending upon whether the threat is just momentary, such as noisy teens outside his bedroom window, or long-standing, such as the daily condescending criticisms of a boss. Regardless of the variation, his means of expression should neither hurt nor attempt to control another. Releasing anger in this healthy way, through expression and communication, is the best way to live.[5]

Suppressing anger, the passive approach, can be dangerous in that it teaches a man to hold in his frustrations. Internalizing these feelings can cause him to scheme in an effort to retaliate. Or, it can give birth to internal negative feelings of sadness, disappointment, or frustration. Internalizing emotions has also been shown to cause pulmonary and heart disease. It is imperative to learn how to manage anger to maintain good health.

------------------------------------------------------------

**TIP:** If your manopause man is having an anger episode, there are steps you can take. When he blows up, remain calm. Do not incite him. It is his tantrum. Instead of withdrawing, explain that while you validate and understand his feelings, you don't condone his bad behavior. After the episode is over, ask him how he feels now that he vented his feelings. Try to learn what he was truly angry about. And if the episodes continue, do not fail to mention, at the right time, that you feel they are affecting your relationship.

------------------------------------------------------------

Are you wondering if your manopause man has crossed the line with his anger? You may be questioning what is normal. You need to analyze his actions. Is it typical behavior for him? Or is it a newer trend that needs further examination? And how severe does he seem? Is he displaying irritability and impatience, or is it full-blown anger?

If your manopause man is physically or emotionally harming you or anyone else, even with intimidation, he must get help to control his anger. If he is doing things that cause him feelings of regret after hurting those around him, this may be a sign that it is time to seek counseling for anger management.

*"Anger dwells only in the bosom of fools."*

## — Albert Einstein

Getting help is important, because his aggressive behavior can turn into violence. Before it gets to that point, you should ask yourself if you are contributing to his behavior by not speaking up when it initially surfaces. Fear can be a trap that holds you back from taking action because you worry about your partner's potential reaction. And empathy can cause you to avoid the discussion, too, for fear that *you* will hurt *him*. Of course you should be sensitive to his suffering. After all, you realize that many of his behaviors are grounded in the need to be in control, to have power, to mask weakness, and to display strength. But while it might be against your nature, and you may fear the repercussions, you need to take action to help him.

----

TIP: "Out-of-control anger is a learned behavior,"[6] the Mayo Clinic reports. In order to calm outbursts, the behavior has to be unlearned, possibly with the help of psychological professionals. Do some investigating into your manopause man's personal history with anger. How was he raised? How was anger dealt with in his home? Knowing his background may help you deal with your manopause man when he is angry and showing signs of aggressive behavior.

----

### Recognizing Depression, in Him and in You

Most depression builds slowly, so instead of comparing your manopause man's behavior to his actions a week earlier, you should reach back to the way he behaved months, even years ago. How does his energy level compare? His optimism? His resilience? If you make a long-term comparison, you will be able to see whether he has become depressed.

Depression is not a feeling that you can will away. It must be dealt with. Still, many men firmly believe they can—and will—conquer their mental demons on their own. By acknowledging and accepting that this is beyond them, they start down the path toward understanding that they need help to alter their behavior for the better. This is step one toward taking responsibility and working in the direction of a helpful solution.

And the same goes for you. Depression is contagious. If your man is experiencing it, there is a chance that it will grow in you, too. One thing about being a woman is that, while your man may not recognize or admit his depression, you are more open to acknowledging it is happening to you—even though your symptoms will probably be quite different from your man's.

Women tend to curl up in a ball, withdraw, and feel worthless. Men lash out. Women may seek help for the problem. Men don't as often, not with the *man*dates bearing down on them. Generally, men have a tendency to act out the disorder, while women are more prone to hold it in. While a man may create or initiate conflicts, a woman will do what she can to avoid them at any cost. She may also become anxious and overly fearful, while he feels suspicious and guarded. A woman may slow down while remaining nervous, but a man will become restless and agitated. Overall, men become aggressive, while women withdraw. A woman will experience guilt over her depression, while a man, hard-pressed to discuss what he's going through, will fall prey to painful feelings of shame.

### Getting Professional Help

Depression ranks far down on the list of topics men want to discuss, because it's often difficult for them to acknowledge that they are suffering, and there's even less of a chance they are going to admit they need help. Being an empathetic creature, you have probably tried to support your manopause man with kindness and patience, but unfortunately if he is truly depressed during manopause, it's possible that this won't be enough. He may need professional help.

Aside from your patience and understanding, one of the best things you can do for your man is to help him realize that accepting professional assistance is not shameful. He may perceive the mere idea of admitting that he needs help as a threat to his masculinity. Beyond being uncomfortable with the thought of exposing his feelings to a doctor, he may be afraid that he will be seen as "crazy." Or if he recognizes his down behavior and feels bad as a result, he may fear that acknowledging and talking it out will only compound the problem and make him feel worse. Unfortunately, undiagnosed depression doesn't just disappear, despite your manopause man's strong attempts to deny its existence. Your assistance and understanding are very important in helping your man realize this.

---

**TIP:** Have *you* ever used professional psychological help? One way to help your manopause man deal with his problems is by revealing fully and honestly the benefits you experienced. Being open about your own struggles and progress can help to remove the stigma he fears. Do your best to persuade him. If he doesn't open up, he may choose to defend against his fears with anger.

---

With the goal of acceptance in mind, ease in for a soft landing when talking to your man about the possibility of getting professional help. Always stress the importance of his health and your happiness as a couple. Explain that depression and anger-management counseling, done by a licensed mental health professional, will help him to identify his anger "triggers," and assist with his negative moods.

Remember how much courage it takes for your man to admit weakness and seek professional help. Give him all the encouragement he needs and deserves.

Who decides if your manopause man's depression might benefit from professional help? The answer is—you both do. Only the two of you can assess the gravity of the negative changes in his behavior. Does *he* acknowledge his depression? If not, point it out to him. Reassure him that you understand that he is suffering in some way. Explain that his behavior is dragging down your relationship and those around him. Trust your gut to tell you when you should be taking this step. Why should you and your manopause man remain in pain?

You may also be wondering why it's important to go to a mental health professional. After all, you are his most sacred confidant, right? Wrong. It is hard to share information with or disclose it to people we love, or with whom we are intimately involved. This is because, as Jane Beresford, Psy.D., a licensed psychologist specializing in psychological evaluation and psychotherapy explained to us, "The information that needs to be shared may not be congruent with the agenda." Your personal agenda, as his partner, may prevent him from relaying the entire picture. For example if he is feeling uneasy about a situation or another person, and that relationship impacts you, then you are not the person with whom to seek counsel. Your personal agenda will influence how you try to advise your manopause man. An obvious example occurs when your manopause man begins to have a wandering eye, but wants to curtail the feelings. The last place to discuss his struggle would be with you.

If your manopause man is afraid to tell you something for fear he may hurt your feelings, the help you can give him will be limited. To gain insight, he has to be able to give the listener a full description of what is on his mind. A mental health professional, who can look at things objectively, can help your man redirect his feelings and prevent them from growing out of control. The doctor, who is a stranger with no hidden agenda, has only one goal: to treat the patient.

There are two forms of professional assistance to consider for your manopause man's depression and the anger it can produce: psychotherapy, and treatment with prescription medications. Generally, the first step is seeking psychotherapy, which may, after your mental health-care professional has a full understanding of your partner's condition, be supplemented with antidepressant medications. Because this will be an important judgment call, you should be careful in how you choose the professional who will best understand your manopause man and his needs.

### Choosing a Mental Health Professional

Once your man has accepted that he should seek help, he should work to find the therapy that is right for him. Suggest that he begin his search by considering the various options: there are therapies done one-on-one, with partners, or in group settings. Once he decides which type of therapy to explore, he can ask his general practitioner or a trusted friend for recommendations. Or, he might contact professional organizations such as the National Alliance on Mental Illness (NAMI), the National Institute of Mental Health Public Inquiries (nimhinfo@nih.gov), or the American Psychoanalytic Association (www.apsa.org), where he can get a list of therapists in your geographic area who specialize in the problems of midlife men.

Offer to go to the first appointment with your man, but don't be offended if he wants to do it on his own. If you are not accompanying him to his appointment, you may want to help him prepare. He should be armed with a list of questions that will help him establish how his treatment will progress. This will help remove that element of the unknown, which inspires fear and puts men on edge. During the first appointment, your man should discuss whether the therapist will be approaching current problems and suggesting practical solutions, whether he or she will be delving deep into the past to discover the roots of problems, or using a combination of the two approaches. He should ask how often they will have appointments and whether there will be "homework" for him to do on his own. He should determine whether the therapy being suggested will be short- or long-term, and what the costs will be. He should also discuss the goals and results he is looking for. Treatment by a mental health professional can be very effective, but your man has to be comfortable with the person he's seeing. So think of the first appointment as an interview that will help determine if you've found the right therapist.

------------------------------------------------------------

**TIP:** Don't be surprised if your manopause man chooses a female therapist—many men feel more comfortable revealing themselves and their vulnerabilities to women. Male or female, it is his choice; he must feel at ease.

------------------------------------------------------------

Once in therapy, it is possible that the professional your manopause man consults may prescribe antidepressant medications, or refer him to a prescribing psychiatrist. National surveys conducted from 1996 to 2005 concluded that while the number of Americans using antidepressant medications doubled in less than ten years, increasing from 13 million to 27 million, the number of people who opted for psychotherapy declined.[7] This is unfortunate, since the ideal approach is to treat using both methods. But if your manopause man strongly feels he does not want to undergo psychotherapy while taking the medication, listen to him. Insisting on psychotherapy may turn him off on getting help altogether. Understand that appropriate medication, on its own, can positively affect what is going on in your manopause man's brain.

If he will not accept the idea of going to a mental health professional, his general practitioner can prescribe antidepressant medication, as long as he or she can monitor your manopause man. Keep in mind that prescribing and monitoring the effects of antidepressants is an extremely complex area of medicine. While having it done by his general practitioner can be your fallback position, it is always better to rely on the skills and judgment of a specialist in this field.

### Drugs to Treat Manopause Depression

Clinical depression is believed to be caused by a chemical abnormality in the brain. Your man's natural chemicals—neurotransmitters such as serotonin, norepinephrine, and dopamine—are out of balance. Antidepressant medications work to bring these natural chemicals back into balance in the brain.

Selective Serotonin Reuptake Inhibitors, better known as SSRIs, are the most popular antidepressant medications. Also widely used are Serotonin and Norepinephrine Reuptake Inhibitors, better known as SNRIs. Which of these families of drugs will be more appropriate to treat your manopause man depends on the specific chemical imbalance in his brain. This can be a "trial and error" exercise. It could take months to hit on exactly the right formula. But once that formula has been discovered, he may find great relief.

Granted, pharmaceuticals are not a perfect solution. There may be side effects when taking these drugs. The most publicized is the possibility of sexual dysfunction. Keep in mind that it is only a possibility. Side effects are one of the reasons your manopause man must be under a doctor's care to receive these drugs. This is particularly important when he wants to decrease his dose or stop taking them. They are not addicting, but can cause withdrawal symptoms if your manopause man is not weaned off correctly. The two of you should research the use and side effects of any of these drugs before he uses them.

### Natural Helpers

In addition to the options provided by prescription drugs, there are a number of natural options to be considered. Some experts have suggested that the herb St. John's Wort is an effective treatment for depression, with fewer side effects than prescription medications. However, whether this is valid is still unclear. Several large studies have shown variable answers on St. John's Wort's effectiveness, from no effect to effects equivalent to some prescription medications. Should your manopause man decide to try it, you should keep in mind that since it is not a prescription medication and not monitored by the FDA, the amount of the herb included in different products can vary, which may influence the results it provides.

Unlike St. John's Wort, the benefits of exercise are so markedly positive that most experts agree it is an essential ingredient in depression treatment. It is the greatest stress reliever, depression deflector, and all-around positive health provider for manopause men. In an interview, Dr. Eva Ritvo confirms this by pointing out that when regular exercisers are incapacitated, their lack of physical activity can lead to depression. She prescribes exercise for all of her patients and notes dramatic improvement not just in mood, but in an overall sense of health and well-being. "Sex drive improves, blood pressure is lowered, weight is normalized, and research has shown that during exercise you release a protein called brain-derived neurotrophic factor (BDNF) that actually makes you smarter. Couples may find that exercising together allows them to spend quality time together. The best exercise is the one that you find fun to do."

Unfortunately, for a man suffering from depression, even a small amount of exercise may seem like an impossible challenge. And when he finally gets started, the next challenge is keeping him motivated. This is where you can help. There are so many forms of physical activities to choose from. Help him figure out which ones are the most appealing to him. Be sensitive to the choices that make him the least self-conscious. Maybe a machine in the privacy of your home or brisk walking in your neighborhood would make him feel less exposed than going to a public gym. And encourage him, when he has the occasional setback, to stay focused on his long-term goals.

Some other natural de-stressing treatments have also demonstrated benefits. Multiple studies have shown massage, yoga, self-hypnosis, meditation, and aromatherapy to be useful in producing positive moods and reducing mild depression. Jon Kabat-Zinn is an avid proponent of men learning different methods to de-stress—from exercise, to meditation, and more. As he tells us, "The more we can learn these lessons, the more we will not be in some sense running toward our death, but in a sense opening to our lives . . . All the scientific evidence is suggesting that when you choose life in the way I'm talking about, your brain changes in both form and function, your immune system changes, your body changes."[8] So, when your manopause man is feeling overwhelmed by his anxieties, encourage him to explore these alternative forms of stress reduction. Do it with him. Make it a shared experience.

## Moving Toward Emotional Health

*"A closed mind is like a closed book: just a block of wood."*

**— Chinese Proverb**

Depression grows from fear of change. In so many ways, change is the enemy of the man whose mind is locked in place. He doesn't realize that closed-minded behavior is a sign of weakness. Open-minded men are strong enough to accept criticism and, most likely, are willing to change. How ironic that the traditional man, who is trying so hard to appear strong, is actually the most weak and fearful. At this time of his life, your manopause man needs to understand that his masculinity is not in question, just his willingness to change.

Luckily, your manopause man's mind is *not* a block of wood. It has the ability to recognize the feelings washing over him and learn from them. But first, he has to learn to isolate and examine those feelings. Does he understand why he is having them? After he denies, blames, or digs in his heels, does he see his behavior as evidence of his unwillingness to accept change?

Rush Dozier, Jr., suggests that the best way for men to learn to adjust to reality is by actively shifting their attention away from the things that make them feel stuck, instead focusing on things that stir their passions and bring them pleasure. The more a man is satisfied that he has control, the more he will approach life with optimism and the better he will feel. Reaching this place isn't easy; it may require setting new goals. While his goals at midlife may be different from those he had when he was younger, keep in mind that they can be equally fulfilling. And by setting them, he is no longer stuck, but rather moving toward something *as* he is changing. This forward momentum can help to create a happier man, and this happiness will be reflected in his behavior.

Dozier goes on to explain that hopefulness needs a concrete foundation, a genuine subjective sense of optimism in order to take hold.[9] Your manopause man needs to work hard toward this true sense of hope, even happiness. This can be doubly challenging if he is naturally pessimistic, or stuck in the *man*dates. If this is your man, it is best to focus on his positive qualities, and there are so many at this stage in his life.

### Contribute to His Positive Feelings

Coming to grips with change can be a slow process. But to avoid depression, it must be done. Don't be discouraged. Patience and steadfastness are your best partners. Help your manopause man break his bad behavior patterns and let go of his defense mechanisms, since they lead him toward depression. After all, it's for you he wants to remain a hero. Make it clear the kind of hero you want—one with vast internal strength, newfound creativity, and emotional sensitivity.

Always remember to be conscious of the pressure points that society has imprinted on him. Show sensitivity to the manhood burden he carries every day, and communicate your awareness of the enormous feat it is for him to shed thousands of years of cultural beliefs. Remind him these are outdated beliefs created by populations who never lived to reach midlife. Never make him feel "less of a man" when you are guiding him. Your encouragement can be delivered in many ways: through kindness, humor, honesty, and intimacy.

Always remember the traditional male qualities and behaviors that are undeniably positive and absolutely ageless. A truly strong man will do things for others; sacrifice his personal needs for dependents; protect loved ones; try to solve other people's problems; maintain his integrity, steadfastness, and loyalty to others while hanging in until a difficult problem is solved; and remain calm and logical whenever danger looms. With these attributes, "a real man" can be very generous, strong, and noble at any age. Assure your manopause man that you have noticed these qualities in him, and appreciate them whenever you have the opportunity.

Throughout this process, also remember to have compassion for yourself—your man isn't the only one who is feeling insecure. You have spent a lifetime believing that you are safe when you are with a "strong" and "powerful" man who is in control. Perhaps, because of your own fears, you are inadvertently pushing him to remain the same. So think before you speak. Are you being sensitive to his feelings? Start presenting things in ways that are truly aimed at alleviating *his* pressures, not yours. When you find yourself going in a direction that is counterproductive, stop yourself, and start again. Take responsibility for your actions that enable or encourage your man's bad behavior.

And last, but not least, remember that happiness, the polar opposite of depression, is contagious. In a study performed by Nicholas A. Christakis, M.D., Ph.D., of Harvard University and James Fowler, Ph.D., and published in the *British Medical Journal,* it was discovered that if a person is happy, his or her spouse has an 8 percent better chance of being happy, too.[10] This may be because we all have mirror neurons in our brains that allow us to watch, and then imitate, the actions and emotions of others. Women have more of these mirror neurons than men do, so it is particularly easy for us to catch their emotions.

As you traverse this period of his life, radiate the positive feelings you would like your man to reflect back to you. If you are accepting the changes in your body and brain that midlife has brought on with equanimity, there's a better chance that he will accept his in that spirit, too. Show him with your words and actions that you are finding the changes in him to be positive, not a disappointment. Understand that you, too, can gain optimism by exercising control over your own attitude, and that optimism will spread and benefit both of you.

According to Martin Seligman, Ph.D., director of the Positive Psychology Center at the University of Pennsylvania, and author of *Authentic Happiness,* "The defining characteristic of pessimists is that they tend to believe that bad events will last a long time, will undermine everything they do, and are their own fault. The optimists, who are confronted with the same hard knocks of this world, think about misfortune in the opposite way. They tend to believe that defeat is just a temporary setback or a challenge, that its causes are just confined to this one case."[11]

It may take some doing to get to that place of optimism. We cannot lose sight of the fact that our culture is the enemy of manopause men who are suffering from depression. Its influence can be so powerful, that it can actually stand in the way of a man getting help for what he perceives as weakness, for fear of revealing himself to be less than "a man." Bad behavior and depression need to be recognized, discussed, and professionally treated. With your help and guidance, your manopause man can break through his mental roadblocks, conquer his fears, and rediscover himself.

# CHAPTER SEVEN

# TESTOSTERONE AND YOUR **MANOPAUSE** MAN

So now let's move from the emotional to the physical, and address a topic that most men either don't understand or are trying to ignore: lowering testosterone.

In your man's mind, testosterone is the fuel that drives him, the electricity that charges him, the juice that amps him up, the source of all of his strength. So what is he to do when his hormonal boat begins to rock on the river of midlife? Does he tap into his machismo and try to fight his way out of the rapids alone, denying dangers and relying on an imaginary reserve tank of sheer strength and determination? Does he throw his confusion and frustration back at you? Or, does he retreat in the opposite direction, withdrawing into his own personal cave?

Manhood pressures can deplete your man's sense of strength and power, particularly when he believes those "manly attributes" are rooted in a chemical that he has lost his ability to maintain. Few men realize that their true power lies in more than physical strength, contrary to the image that superheroes have conjured up in their minds since childhood.

Sexual stereotyping complicates things even further. Maybe, in your manopause man's mind, loss of hormones is a female experience. And the *man*dates are very clear: real men should avoid any hint of femininity or weakness. So if he is a traditional thinker, he may simply choose to avoid looking at his hormones.

By doing that, he may be missing out on some good news about lower testosterone levels. They give a man so many of the qualities we have spent the first half of our lives praying he would somehow develop. As his male hormones decline, your man may feel a more loving connection with you, your family, and your friends. He may develop the patience to sit and talk with you, the ability to bond with your children in a way he never could before, and the desire to make sensuous love, instead of racing to a climax. Obstacles that are standing in the way of his communicative abilities can decrease, making him an easier partner to converse with and to understand. With your help he may become less fearful of showing vulnerabilities, and more comfortable with displaying a host of sensitive emotions. And surprisingly, he may get in tune with his creative side as it begins to blossom. Wouldn't it be wonderful if all manopause men went down this path? Happily, most can, if they learn to understand, accept, and deal with hormonal changes in a healthy way.

----------------------------------------------------------------

**TIP:** If you want your man to thrive hormonally, feed him well. Robert Tan, M.D., author of *The Andropause Mystery* points out that research has shown foods high in protein and low in carbohydrates cause the greatest sustained levels of testosterone and growth hormone. He should be eating plenty of fresh fruit and vegetables, moderate amounts of protein, and minimal amounts of carbohydrates.[1]

----------------------------------------------------------------

### Solutions to Falling Testosterone Are Waiting

At this point, depending on your man's observance of the *man*-dates, he may choose to run from a hormonal loss that will most probably catch up with him. This is why you need to learn about changes in testosterone, what happens as it declines in midlife, and how that affects your man. Our culture accepts menopause and women's changing hormones. Perhaps you or your friends have used hormone replacement therapy to ease the way through this life transition. Perhaps not. But you are aware that this is an option; and we want you to know that this option is equally available to men. The first step, of course, is finding out whether your manopause man is an appropriate candidate.

That sounds simple enough, and it would be, if your partner were not a man. Hormone purgatory is the last place your hero wants to be. Because of his cultural conditioning, he thinks he has sprung a leak and his manhood is seeping out, never to return. And like the prototypical male, he can't and won't talk about it. It is best to deny, suppress his feelings, or man up and forget about it with the hope that what he is experiencing will disappear as mysteriously as it appeared. Unfortunately, it won't.

### Diagnosing Testosterone Deficiency

Because of our cultural conditioning, when men go to visit their doctors, they tend to pussyfoot around the testosterone conversation. Instead of getting to the point and saying, "Doc, I may have a hormone problem," they throw out vague symptoms in the hopes that their doctor will put together the pieces and voice the unspeakable. With doctors who are knowledgeable in the area of male hormones, this will work. With others, especially general practitioners, it may not.

A doctor who has not been trained to recognize the signs of low testosterone may listen to symptoms like, "I don't have the energy I used to. I'm always tired," "I'm feeling low all the time, not like myself," "I haven't been sleeping so well. Can you give me something?"

And he may respond by prescribing antidepressants, sleeping pills, changes in diet, or just telling his patient that this is a part of life to which he should adjust.

John Morley, M.D., an internationally known expert on male menopause, and the acting director of the division of endocrinology at Saint Louis University School of Medicine, is one of those doctors who *is* familiar with the symptoms of low testosterone. He has put together a simple ten-question screening test for physicians to use with their patients. If you think your manopause man will have trouble voicing his fears, you may want to go over it with him before he sees his doctor. Does he have a decrease in libido? Is he experiencing a lack of energy? Does he have a decrease in strength or endurance? Has he lost height? Has he noticed a decreased "enjoyment of life"? Is he sad or grumpy? Are his erections less strong? Has he noticed any decline in his ability to play sports? Is he falling asleep after dinner? Has there been a recent deterioration in his work performance?[2] If your partner answers "yes" to either the question about libido or erections, or at least three of the other questions, he may have a low testosterone level. And establishing that ahead of time may help him quash his *man*date-induced hesitations so he can more comfortably discuss it with his doctor when he is sitting in that exam room.

If he still can't voice it, but his doctor is knowledgeable, he will ferret out clues during a lifestyle interview. And then, he will look for visual clues: the amount of a man's body hair and where it is located, whether he has any breast enlargement, the size and density of his testes, as well as his general body shape and muscle tone. If these seem to point in the direction of low testosterone, he will proceed with more definitive tests, beginning with blood tests.

Most men don't know that their testosterone levels fluctuate constantly. This happens seasonally, daily, even within every hour. They are higher in the fall and lower in the spring. They peak in the morning, then fluctuate during the day, as often as every 15 minutes. In fact, daily testosterone level swings can be as high as 50 percent. This means that your manopause man's testosterone levels should be checked more than once, probably three times. These tests should be given in the morning, when levels are at their highest, usually at 15- to 20-minute intervals, and then averaged.

## The Two Types of Testosterone

To further complicate matters, men have two different types of testosterone: bound testosterone and free testosterone. When the two types are combined, their sum equals a man's total testosterone level. Throughout men's lives, some portion of their testosterone adheres to a protein called sex hormone–binding globulin (SHBG). And once it does, it's no longer freely circulating, making it less available to work its magic on the target organs that testosterone was created to help. As a man ages, his SHBG increases, the amount of testosterone that remains unbound decreases, and he is left with less metabolically active free testosterone.

While there is some debate on this point, experts generally feel that the amount of *free* testosterone a man has is much more relevant to his well-being than his level of *total* testosterone. In one study of men over 55, only 20 percent were deficient in total testosterone, but 50 percent were deficient in free testosterone. In another study of men with symptoms of testosterone deficiency, only 13 percent had abnormally low levels of total testosterone, but 75 percent had low levels of free testosterone. So be sure that your manopause man's doctor checks for both, since a man whose level of total testosterone is normal can still show symptoms of testosterone deficiency if his levels of free testosterone are too low.

## Testosterone Testing

As we learned in Chapter 2, there is no "normal" when it comes to testosterone levels. But broadly speaking, a man's total testosterone should range from 300 to 1,200 nanograms per deciliter of blood to be considered normal. Levels below 250 are generally considered appropriate for testosterone replacement therapy. Between 250 and

400 nanograms, men are borderline, and the evidence of testosterone therapy's benefits is less clear.

Your partner's ratio of testosterone to estrogen should also be checked. A man in his 20s might have 50 times as much testosterone as estrogen. But as men age, their testosterone can drop, as their estrogen levels rise. In fact, high estrogen levels can actually cause a drop in testosterone. A few of the things that can trigger the rise in estrogen in men are increased body fat, smoking, excessive use of alcohol or recreational drugs, and some medications.

### Treating Testosterone Deficiency

A man who has decided to use testosterone replacement therapy has several choices, including transdermal patches or gels, and injections. All of these therapies require a man to have regular testing of his cholesterol and levels of prostate-specific antigen (PSA)—high levels of which can indicate prostate problems such as cancer. He should also have frequent blood tests to monitor his testosterone levels.

## Patches and Gels

There are a number of advantages to patches and gels. Because they are applied daily, they provide a uniform delivery of testosterone, with fewer highs and lows than injections. This means that they more closely simulate a man's normal testosterone pattern. They don't require doctor's visits to apply, and they are easy to use. They are also less likely to increase PSA levels in the prostate than injections. However, they are more costly than injections, and can sometimes cause skin irritations. They can have a musty smell, and if the gels aren't allowed to completely dry, they can be transferred to a man's female partner.

## Injections

A man who is receiving testosterone through injections needs to go to his doctor every two to four weeks to have them administered. Because the fluid is thick, a large needle is used, which can be uncomfortable.

Unlike a man's natural testosterone rhythm, injections produce a very high level of testosterone in week one, which gradually diminishes until it is time for the next injection. In other words, a man's testosterone level will begin unnaturally high, and then it will fall until it is unnaturally low. This can result in mood swings. The high testosterone level can lead to anger, irritability, or even violence, and some men report that in the first few days after their injection, they have difficulty concentrating, and they are impulsive and edgy. There is also the possibility that when the shot is administered, and extra testosterone is in the system, it can convert to estrogen, which is certainly not the intended result.

### *To Treat, or Not to Treat, That Is the Question*

The U.S. Food and Drug Administration has estimated that of the four to five million American men who suffer from low testosterone levels, only about 5 percent are being treated for the condition.[3] But certainly the trend is increasingly moving toward testosterone supplementation. With so many prescriptions being written, is testosterone supplementation necessary and safe? How should you feel if your manopause man decides to engage in testosterone supplementation? Opinions on its use differ radically within the medical community. On one side stand doctors who are certain that testosterone supplementation can treat what they view as an endocrine system dysfunction. They laud a list of wonderful pluses for the men who use it. They are facing off with doctors who firmly believe that falling testosterone levels are just a natural phenomenon of aging, not a medical problem that cries out for treatment. They counter with an inventory of problems, both serious and not so serious, that supplementation could potentially trigger.

## Yes, He Should

Doctors on the pro side feel that testosterone deficiency in midlife and onward needs to be recognized as a medical condition that should be dealt with before it affects men's health and their relations with their partners and their families, or their rapport with their co-workers, and the world at large. They argue that a man's testosterone deficiency is not set in stone. Just the opposite: it is reversible. And, they go on to point out, there is no evidence to establish that older men need less testosterone than younger men. In fact, some studies have suggested that receptors for testosterone, and other androgens, are both created and kept healthy by receiving adequate amounts of testosterone. If testosterone is reduced, the smaller amount of the hormone that is left will have a doubly hard challenge being effective, since those receptors will not be as numerous or as "receptive" to its effects. They suggest men should cut this possibility off at the pass. Their position is bolstered by the very rapid response most men have to testosterone replacement, with many of them or their partners noticing its effects within days.

What effects will they notice? A number of studies have reported that testosterone supplementation causes a man's lean muscle mass to increase, while his body fat decreases. And it can make his general strength, as well as the strength of his grip, improve. There have even been studies that have shown men using a testosterone patch for as little as nine months had a decline in abdominal fat. One reason for this might be the increase in a man's metabolic rate that seems to occur with testosterone replacement therapy. Supplementation also seems to aid in the return of a man's secondary male characteristics. Men using it report an increase in body and facial hair, as well as a thickening of their skin.

A less visible change takes place in men's bones. While there is much less discussion of osteoporosis in men than there is in women, it is a problem for them, too. While decreased bone density seems to surface around ten years later in men than it does for us, the ones who suffer from it have an increased risk of debilitating bone fractures, just as we do. Testosterone therapy has been shown to increase both bone density and mass, and to help prevent bone loss by slowing resorption of calcium.

Some of the more interesting research on testosterone and men's health was done by Molly Shores, M.D., of the University of Washington, who was the lead author of a study showing that men with low testosterone levels are more likely to die within a specified timeframe than their counterparts with normal levels. In fact, men with low testosterone were at an 88 percent greater risk than men with normal testosterone. And men whose levels hovered between normal and low were at a 38 percent greater risk.[4]

This is because of a number of different testosterone-contingent health risks. Some research shows that testosterone helps to protect against heart disease and stroke. And without it, a man's glucose tolerance is impaired, opening him to the possibility of diabetes. And because it reduces body fat, testosterone ratchets down his risk for coronary artery disease.

But to some men, there are things that are far more debilitating than a loss of muscle mass or bone density, or even the possibility of a heart attack or stroke. A drop in testosterone can hit your manopause man where it hurts the most: in his image of himself as a vital and richly sexual being. For most men, if their penis is down, so are their spirits. If your partner falls into that category, hormone therapy can be a welcome aid. A number of studies have reported that for men with low testosterone levels, replacement can boost libido and can put the *drive* back into *sex drive*. This could be good news for both of you. With increased testosterone, sexual thoughts and fantasies seem to multiply and intensify. A feeling of need and an appetite for sexual gratification surface more frequently and forcefully. And these urges can begin to occur within days of a shot, or weeks of beginning to use patches. Part of this may be due to cognitive changes that have been reported to occur in a man's brain when his testosterone levels are somewhat restored. His vision and hearing become more acute. So looking at his partner and hearing the sounds she makes as they have sex is more stimulating to him. His sense of touch is more sensitive, and the sensations he gets from sexual contact are stronger. And with all of this, his partner begins to feel more desired. It doesn't stop there. Even masturbation is enhanced with new surges of excitement.

And this is not all in his mind. A study by Lisa Tenover, M.D., Ph.D., clinical professor of medicine at Stanford University and expert in androgen therapy, showed that when men with low testosterone received hormone supplementation, their weekly and nocturnal erections increased and their sexual function was enhanced.[5] If a low testosterone level was the culprit, boosting it can help a man to achieve and sustain erections, and become more sexually active. Penises become more sensitive to physical stimulation. Erections become larger, firmer, and more reliable. Orgasms are more intense. And seeing these improvements in their sexual function allows some men to open up and talk about their former performance problems.

It is no surprise that this turn of events affects men's moods. And beyond a sexual ego boost, it appears that testosterone supplementation can have an even more direct effect on their sense of well-being. Men who receive testosterone, especially those who are getting shots, will tell you that almost immediately after testosterone enters their systems, they feel a general boost in their energy level and an improvement in their frame of mind. Beyond being an aphrodisiac, testosterone appears to be something of an antidepressant. Men who are receiving it, not to mention their mates, report that their irritability and depression decreases, while their cognitive abilities, mental acuity, and memories improve. An increase in their visual and spatial skills is particularly striking. In short, they are feeling like themselves again, ready to tackle work, more eager to compete, showing more endurance, able to handle disappointment more easily, and open to gleaning more satisfaction from every aspect of their lives.

Studies point to the possibility that even some cases of depression may be relieved through testosterone therapy. The University of Washington, School of Medicine reported a study conducted by Molly Shores, M.D., and her colleagues. They examined the relationship between testosterone levels and diagnosed depression of 278 men who were 44 years of age and older, over a two-year period. They found that 21.7 percent of the men with testosterone deficiency were diagnosed with depression, compared to only 7.1 percent of the men without the deficiency. Men with low testosterone levels were 4.2 times more likely to be diagnosed with depression.[6] To further demonstrate the point, experts such as Elizabeth Barrett-Connor, M.D., chair of the Department of Community and Family Medicine at the University of California, San Diego, have shown that when men have low testosterone, they score higher on the Beck Depression Inventory test, bolstering the charge that low testosterone increases depression.[7]

## No, He Shouldn't

Before we get too carried away, we should let the other side weigh in. While some doctors are impassioned cheerleaders for testosterone therapy, there are many doctors who are adamantly opposed.

They argue that decreasing testosterone isn't a *deficiency*, it is simply a lower level that is appropriate to a manopause man's age; that growing older is a stage of life that should be accepted, even relished, instead of being resisted. And to bolster their argument, they suggest that a drop in testosterone levels may be nature's way of protecting men from the rapid cell growth that can fuel prostate cancer and cardiovascular disease. They also point out that advertisements for testosterone testing and supplementation are underwritten by drug companies, which have a vested interest in their use. Very few doctors argue against giving testosterone therapy to men who are clinically deficient. But a large number feel that for men who are within the normal range for their age or just below it, the jury is still out.

One reason for their doubts is that testosterone levels are quixotic. They can vary with a man's psychological state. Is he married? Is he single? Does he have children at home or not? Did he win his golf game today? Does he feel as if he's on top of the competition at work? All of these psychological factors can influence a man's testosterone levels, on an hourly, daily, or longer-term basis, and this can skew the testing that establishes them.

Hormone studies for men lag behind those for women. There have been a number of small studies over the years that have had different, and confusing, results. But there is yet to be a long-term, placebo-controlled study of testosterone replacement. The National Institutes of Health has created a task force to determine the risks and benefits of testosterone therapy, but that study hasn't yet been completed. However, in 2003, when the Institute of Medicine reviewed evidence from then-current studies, it recommended that treatment was only appropriate for men who produce little or no testosterone until the long-term effects on otherwise healthy men are known.[8]

While long-term studies may still be lacking, doctors who campaign against testosterone replacement have suggested doubts about its true value. They point to the fact that the small studies that *have* been done have had confusing, even diametrically opposed, results. And they explain that while testosterone may increase muscle mass, there are doubts as to whether it simultaneously increases strength, makes normal activities easier to perform physically, or lessens the chance of falls and fractures or other health-related concerns. Most telling is the fact that no studies to date have proven that restored testosterone levels will help otherwise healthy men to get healthier or live longer.

Furthermore, while many physicians have put forth extensive anecdotal evidence stating patients are more energetic and contented with treatment, the data is not conclusive. While some men report physical enhancement, including anecdotal evidence of rejuvenated sexuality, boosted morale, and unhappiness being replaced with self-confidence and pleasure, there is no indisputable scientific evidence to prove that in general, men are happier when testosterone replacement is used to treat a deficiency.

Naysayers have also catalogued a range of problems that can be traced to testosterone supplementation. Skin rashes occur in a very small percentage of men who are using testosterone patches—less than 1 percent, according to a study by Judith Rabkin, Ph.D., an expert on the effects of testosterone replacement therapy. And it can also cause acne in 8 percent of men who receive it. And excess testosterone can contribute to baldness in about 6 percent of the men who use it. What else can go wrong? It can make some men irritable, and while it seems to improve their spatial abilities, it does not seem to help with either memory or verbal abilities. Excess testosterone can lead to a man having excess estrogen, which can cause breast enlargement and tenderness. For men who have sleep apnea, testosterone therapy can make their condition worse. And men who have used oral testosterone for long periods of time, or who have injected excessive amounts, have been known to suffer liver damage.[9]

As to the idea that testosterone therapy is a sexual "cure-all," psychiatrist and sex researcher Helen Singer Kaplan, M.D., says that, "No physician can tell if a lack of desire is due to psychological inhibition or hormone deficiency."[10] Perhaps the key word here is *desire*. If your partner, for whatever reason, is not interested, evidence seems to point to the possibility that testosterone will not help him turn that corner. Testosterone doesn't necessarily cure erectile dysfunction, which can stem from many psychological and physical causes. And it doesn't seem to have a huge effect on men who are on the borderline of low testosterone.

Men who supplement with too much testosterone can see their natural production of the hormone plummet, as the glands that are normally responsible for producing it sense that there is enough testosterone in their man's system for them to kick back and stop working. If that happens, a man who was producing some testosterone on his own may find himself producing little or none. And since most of a man's testosterone is produced by his testicles, when this happens, they shrink—sometimes even atrophy—at which point sperm production can grind to a halt. Is this a common side effect? According to Dr. Rabkin's study, 8 percent of men on testosterone therapy have decreased testicular size, and 20 percent have reduced ejaculate.[11]

If a man stops testosterone replacement therapy, will he begin manufacturing his own testosterone again? Maybe yes, maybe no; it varies. Some doctors warn that a man with a borderline low testosterone level who begins supplementation could possibly commit himself to a lifetime of hormone therapy. This is one of the reasons why, for men on testosterone therapy, regular blood tests are so very important. They can flag a dangerous situation.

## Prostate Cancer

The biggest point of contention for those who are against hormone replacement therapy deals with prostate cancer. Your manopause man's prostate gland has spent its life making the liquid portion of his semen. It surrounds his urethra as it leaves his bladder, and when it enlarges, which tends to happen with age, it can cause him all sorts of problems. One of the major topics of debate when it comes to testosterone supplementation is whether adding additional male hormone raises a man's risk for cancer of the prostate. In fact, in 1966 Charles B. Huggins, M.D., won the Nobel Prize for his research showing that if men with prostate cancer were castrated, which would rid them of almost all their testosterone production, their survival was extended—a graphic example of the cure being as bad as, or *worse* than, the disease.

To say that an enlarged prostate is common for men at midlife is an understatement. It might be more accurate to say that as men age, *not* getting an enlarged prostate is a lovely surprise. Most of the time, an enlarged prostate is benign. But sometimes, it is cancerous. How often? Prostate cancer is one of most frequently diagnosed cancers in the United States. About a third of men over 50 have atypical cells in their prostate which simply haven't grown yet. And because most types of prostate cancer are extremely slow to develop, much of the time they will never become a life-threatening problem. But, not surprisingly, given Dr. Huggins's research on totally withdrawing testosterone, doctors have continued to ask whether testosterone replacement therapy might contribute to prostate cancer's onset or its development.

As of right now, there is no clinical evidence that testosterone replacement increases the risk of prostate cancer developing in a man who does not already have it. One short-term study did not show a difference in the testosterone levels of men who did, and did not, develop prostate cancer. The men who developed it were simply, on average, older. In fact, some studies have suggested that testosterone replacement therapy might prevent prostate cancer by maintaining a youthful androgen/estrogen level. But whether testosterone supplementation makes existing cancer cells multiply in a man who already has them is another question entirely.

The main argument urologists have against testosterone replacement is that increased hormone levels can cause benign growth, leading to an enlarged prostate. It may also activate abnormal cells in the prostate and fuel their growth into full-blown prostate cancer. But research can be confusing. To date, there have not been any long-term studies that have borne this out. Still, there is a suggestion that existing cancers, which normally would be slow growing and not life-threatening, may grow more quickly in the presence of increased testosterone. It is important to keep in mind that within the general male population, as reported by *The New York Times Magazine* in October of 2011, "about 30 percent of men in their 40s have prostate cancer, 40 percent of men in their 50s and so on, right up to 70 percent of men in their 80s."[12] Looking at those statistics, it's clear that when it comes to the possibility of prostate cancer, testosterone therapy should be considered carefully.

Should your manopause man, after giving it consideration, still be interested in trying testosterone replacement therapy, what precautions should he take? First, he should eliminate the possibility of a preexisting cancer. One fairly effective way to do that is through testing for PSA, a blood test that detects about 70 percent of prostatic cancers. And, of course, his urologist should give him a digital rectal exam. Generally, if PSA-level tests are negative, he is a good candidate for replacement therapy. But he should be consistently monitored, with PSA tests every six months and rectal exams annually.

## Heart Health

Next to its possible effects on the prostate, the greatest area of debate when it comes to testosterone therapy is your man's heart. For many years, men were cautioned against testosterone therapy based on its possible negative effects on the heart and circulatory system. Animal studies showed that testosterone therapy altered the way fat is metabolized, decreasing good cholesterol and increasing bad cholesterol, and raising the risk for high blood pressure and coronary artery disease in the process. Another area of concern was water retention, something that is particularly problematic for men with preexisting heart, kidney, or liver disease. A final worry was that testosterone supplementation can prompt the body to make too many red blood cells, thickening the blood and increasing a man's risk of heart attacks and strokes.

Doctors who are in favor of testosterone supplementation point out that these risks can be monitored. And they go on to argue that some of them are not even real. While some studies have shown that testosterone narrows the arteries in the heart, others have demonstrated the exact opposite, that it can open coronary arteries. For some time, researchers started from the premise that since men have the greatest amount of testosterone and they also have the most frequent heart attacks, it was testosterone that was causing them. More recent studies seem to be disproving this logic. Some published studies suggest that high testosterone increases the risk of coronary disease, others show the opposite finding, and still others don't find any relationship between the two. Like all debates regarding testosterone supplementation, it is complicated.

### The Natural Way

Maybe, after thinking it over, you and your manopause man are still on the fence about testosterone supplementation. That's all right. There are other things he can do, with your encouragement, to minimize the effects of his hormonal changes. A healthy diet, exercise, and lifestyle can all lessen the symptoms of manopause. Some believe DHEA (dehydroepiandrosterone) helps as well.

## Diet and Exercise

There is a direct relationship between testosterone and muscle mass, and there is also some evidence that physical activity can increase testosterone levels. Not to mention the fact that testosterone can help to combat depression, irritability, and anxiety, all of which may dog men during this period of change. So exercise is an obvious "should do." Diet is important, too. Your manopause man's eating habits should be moderated. "Bad fats," the partially and fully hydrogenated ones, can impair hormone balance by converting circulating testosterone into estrogen. Sugar can do the same thing, by making your manopause man put on weight. Since fat cells contain aromatase, an enzyme that converts testosterone to estrogen, being as little as ten pounds overweight can raise his levels of this "female hormone." However, your man will have to walk a fine line. Since testosterone is synthesized from cholesterol, he needs *some* fat to produce it. A study of 36 middle-aged men showed that switching to a strict, low-fat diet for eight weeks reduced circulating testosterone levels by an average of 12 percent. Other studies have demonstrated that overly intense exercise can also lead to lowered testosterone. In the world of diet and physical fitness the key to maintaining testosterone is moderation.

------------------------------------------------------------

**TIP:** To boost your man's levels of testosterone, keep track of his exercise pattern. Moderate aerobic exercise combined with weight training for 20 to 30 minutes several times a week encourages testosterone production. Endurance training for more than 60 minutes, on the other hand, can lead to lowered testosterone. Yes, there is too much of a good thing!

------------------------------------------------------------

## DHEA

Maybe the two of you will decide to go to your local health-food store for recommendations. If so, your manopause man may very well be pointed toward dehydroepiandrosterone (DHEA). On the surface, this makes sense. Like testosterone, DHEA is a steroid that is naturally secreted by the body. And like testosterone, it declines as men age. But unlike testosterone supplementation, it doesn't require a doctor's prescription.

DHEA is at its peak during childhood and puberty, when a man's body goes through its greatest growth spurts, but by the age of 60 it may have dropped to 5 percent of those maximum levels. There is certainly some intuitive logic to a man taking DHEA if he suspects he has a testosterone deficiency. DHEA is both an androgen receptor, and a precursor to the production of testosterone. In other words, it is a substance that helps the organs that testosterone will be acting on to receive and use it, and it is a substance from which testosterone is synthesized. So as a man's levels of DHEA drop, that plunge can magnify a man's loss of testosterone and the effects he is feeling, in two different ways.

There is much debate as to whether taking DHEA actually increases a man's sense of well-being, his muscle mass, or his levels of testosterone. Many experts argue that at best, it has a placebo effect, and Howard Liebowitz, M.D., of Liebowitz Longevity Medicine, offers that there are no over-the-counter remedies to replace a man's testosterone.[13] Some small clinical trials have indicated that supplementation with DHEA has an antidepressant effect; others have found that it worsens mood. Many men use it to build muscle and enhance athletic performance, but no scientific trial has shown a statistically significant effect on lean body mass or testosterone levels.

On the plus side, some studies have shown that a high level of DHEA correlates with a lower risk of cardiovascular disease and greater longevity in men. But be forewarned. In 2011, the Mayo Clinic reported that no studies on the long-term effects of DHEA have been conducted, and that it can theoretically increase a man's risk of prostate cancer.[14] The bottom line is that DHEA supplements have not been approved for medical use by the FDA, and we don't know about safety in the long term. The recommendation is that if your manopause man's physician agrees that he should begin supplementing his diet with DHEA, he needs to have the same continuous health monitoring that he would undergo with testosterone supplementation.

### Testosterone Loss Can Be a Gain

To most men, testosterone means strength, and the need to perform feats of strength is inborn. But as men mature, and testosterone levels lower, it becomes increasingly difficult to prove their strength with physical prowess. The real question to ask is whether, in today's culture, physical abilities are sufficient to satisfy a man's need to display strength at any age. The answer is no; they are not enough. The *man*dates dictate that men must be aggressive, daring, and strong. If your manopause man wants to live a long, happy, and fulfilled existence, the *man*dates must be readjusted to include other types of strength.

*"The ultimate measure of a man is not where he stands in moments of comfort and convenience, but where he stands at times of challenge and controversy."*

**— Martin Luther King, Jr.**

Life experience is essential to gaining insight, knowledge, and judgment. Suffering, hardship, loss, and disappointment are some of the many experiences a man endures along the way. From them, wisdom can be gained. By accepting his physical weaknesses, inner strength is developed. But thanks to our cultural conditioning, this is hard for many manopause men to see. The man who can admit flaws and vulnerability is the man of true power.

We need to accept that along with the gift of longer life and the insight that it brings, come changes in hormones, and therefore challenges that our ancestors never experienced. Happily, we now have ways to mitigate the negative fallout of decreasing hormone levels, while enjoying the mellower, fuller, and more emotional men that result.

Testosterone loss aside, over a lifetime, the virtues of King Solomon—wisdom, wealth, and respect—are far more durable than those of Hercules. Keep in mind that Hercules was mythical—part god, part human—while King Solomon was a real man. The merits of King Solomon offer a deeper and more powerful strength, one that can never be taken away or overpowered. Once this more complex definition of power is understood by our culture, those who attain wisdom, knowledge, judgment, sagacity, discernment, and insight will be considered the mightiest of them all. Testosterone loss is a complicated area, and the pathway through it is individual to each man. There are men who may never notice a dramatic change; others will. When this happens, in some cases, you will need professional advice to find your way. But armed with the right questions to ask, and with some knowledge of the possible side effects of various treatment approaches, you and your manopause man have enough facts to find the answers that are right for him.

# CHAPTER EIGHT

# MANOPAUSE SEX, HIS PENIS, AND YOUR RELATIONSHIP

A love relationship is the ultimate fusing of two people, and sex is one of the most significant glues that holds it together. If sex begins to wane, a relationship can start an inexorable decline. There is no reason such an unfortunate thing needs to happen at midlife. Manopause sex can be more satisfying than ever, and in the process, it can foster strong bonds that will prove unbreakable.

Still, while a healthy sexual relationship may be vital to both you and your partner, there's no escaping the fact that biology makes his physical performance key to your coupling. The pressure is on. In the sexual arena, men are all too aware of how important the penis is.

In fact, there is no marker more definitive on a man's journey through manhood and masculinity than his penis and its performance. For men, penis pressure is the *ultimate* pressure. They have been socialized to worry about how often they have sex, how long, and how hard. These lifelong worries are often self-imposed. And yet, despite these fears, men also have a belief that their penis should, eternally and without fail, rise to the occasion when summoned.

Manopause men who look in the mirror daily are all too well aware that hairlines and jawlines are changing. But most still assume their penises exist in suspended animation, staying forever the way they were at 17. And all too often we, as their partners, assume the same thing. At 17, the penis controls the man. At 50, the man might just need to learn how to control his penis. While it may take some time and effort for your manopause man to learn to express his feelings verbally, his penis shows how it, and he, are truly feeling without any coaxing. Some manopause men spend their lives dogged by an underlying fear that their penis may not cooperate at crucial times, and their self-image is inextricably tied to their sexual abilities. As J. Francois Eid, M.D., a New York urologist who specializes in erectile dysfunction, explains, "If a man loses his potency, he loses a part of his identity."[1] Since boyhood, men are led to believe they have to be potent and aggressive studs, obsessed with just one thing: being perpetually ready for sex and tireless when engaged in the act. Living up to that image and winning the masculinity competition as he boasts to his friends about his exploits have been ways for young men to reassure themselves about their masculinity ever since Homo erectus developed sophisticated vocal cords and the power of speech. It is no wonder men dig in their heels and refuse to acknowledge that they are changing sexually. But subconsciously, deep down, they fear they are.

Is this paranoia theirs alone? Not really. Sitting at lunch with girlfriends, we would be quicker to tell them our husband had been diagnosed with cancer, than that he couldn't get an erection. One part of that reluctance might be because we fear his lack of an erection means we aren't appealing enough. Or maybe we're afraid it means our man isn't as "manly" as he used to be, and that reflects badly on us and our femininity and status. One thing is for sure, we want our men to perform sexually. And they can feel that pressure.

### The Big Fear

In your manopause man's mind, threats to his sexual performance, no matter how slight, may seem massive. If your partner doesn't seem worried, don't be fooled. Men are not about to talk about the prospect of their sexual abilities dwindling. They are not even going to acknowledge the slim possibility. So they don't discuss it. They don't compare notes with their friends. They do everything they can to put it out of their mind. But keeping this fear in the dark makes it potentially self-fulfilling. Happily, given a healthy lifestyle, and appropriate medical support, in most cases, these fears can be diminished.

Unlike our partners, we are inquisitive. We not only see the big picture, we explore all the details and nuances that fill it in. In the case of your partner and his potential midlife sexual changes, you will be doing a service for yourself, as well as for him, if you take the time to learn the intricacies of what might possibly happen sexually as he passes through his 40s, 50s, and 60s. There is good news ahead, as well as fixes for many of the problems that may arise.

### A Reality Check

With apologies to Mark Twain, the rumors of "sexual death" in midlife are greatly exaggerated. A vast number of men traverse these decades with little, or no, notice of change. But because of hormonal decline, and other midlife mental and physical stresses, that is not always the case. Much depends on the man. The level of sexual desire a man feels in his 20s is probably an indication of his lifetime level of sexual desire. If your manopause man "loved love" in his 20s, he will probably continue to want frequent, and satisfying, sex later in life. In truth, the largest decline in sexual activity takes place after one year of marriage, which is, most often, in our 20s. In the 2009 "Sex in America" survey, women with the lowest frequency of orgasm were between the ages of 18 and 24, certainly not an argument in favor of the skill of the younger man.[2] Assuming that a satisfactory sex life is an important aspect of marriage, consider this: more than one-fifth of marriages break up within five years. The median age for a first divorce is 30.5 for males and 29 for females. These are all statistics in favor of manopause sex.

Granted, the number of times you have sex may decline as you age, but is that the whole story? Think back to your 20s. His erection lasted a frantic 20 minutes, if you were lucky. Now, look forward to midlife. Sex? Possibly a hedonistic hour of physical and communicative exploration, on those wonderful occasions when hectic lives allow it. What a challenge for the very young, having to have sex three times as often, just to spend as much intimate time together. And there's more good news about your manopause man. Generally, men who enjoyed sex in their earlier years will still relish and need it as they age. Which means there is nothing to worry about, right?

Wrong. Manopause men, particularly traditional ones, can get rattled at any hint of alteration in their erotic lives. Let's face facts: change is inevitable. It is important for us, and for our partners, to understand how to define "normal" change, in order to keep unnecessary worry from creating an erectile dysfunction problem where one doesn't exist. So let's jump right in and start this sexual exploration.

## Sex Is Good for Him

*"Men do not quit playing because they grow old;*
*they grow old because they quit playing."*

**— Oliver Wendell Holmes**

It had a ring of truth when Holmes said it, and now we know why. Science has confirmed that while men may start their amorous adventures living for sex, as they age, having sex may very well help them live. As Daniel G. Amen, M.D., explains in *Sex on the Brain*, there's a wealth of research connecting healthy sexual activity and longevity. A study of 1,000 men ages 45 to 59 conducted at Queen's University in Belfast, Ireland, demonstrated that men with a low frequency of sex, less than one time per month, died at twice the rate of men with a high frequency, two or more times per week.[3] The high-frequency men had fewer sick days, maybe because orgasms boost infection-fighting cells by 30 percent. And they had less anxiety, since physical touch boosts levels of oxytocin and lowers levels of cortisol, the hormone of chronic stress. And if that's not enough, other studies have shown that regular sex can improve men's cardiovascular function and raise their pain threshold. Humans crave touch from the time they are born. Erotic touch is a very important part of that yearning, and a very necessary aspect of staying healthy.

Use it or lose it? That's true, too. Help your manopause man maintain a healthy sex life, and you will be helping him preserve the arteries and muscles that make it possible for him to get an erection. And in the process, you will help him nurture a sound mental outlook on life. Knowledge is the first step.

### What You May Not Know, Can Hurt You

Certain aspects of your manopause man's sexual life may alter, both in intensity and duration. Often, when men have not been apprised of this reality, and those inevitable changes begin to creep in, they conclude there is something wrong with them as men. They feel that, despite their best efforts to embody the *man*dates and remain impregnable in every way, they are weak and unworthy. Worse yet, they feel that they are the only one this is happening to. And having been so deeply inculcated with traditional male values, this can take an immense toll, both on your man's psyche and on your relationship.

At the same time, because you are not getting the same sexual reactions from your partner that you have become accustomed to, you may fear that he has lost interest in you. Could it be your fault? Your mind works overtime. Maybe you aren't attractive to him anymore. Maybe he is bored with you. Maybe your relationship is stale because you have failed to bring enough to it. Sometimes, as women, our rich emotions and vivid imaginations work against us, conjuring up complicated answers to simple questions. Questions we would be able to answer easily if we just understood the physical and mental changes a man experiences at midlife.

## Mental Arousal

While women connect love and emotions to sex, men are almost singularly focused on the physical act. "The part of the brain that is devoted to sexual drive is two and a half times larger in men then in women,"[4] says Louann Brizendine, M.D. It's no wonder men are thinking, and wanting to act on, their sexual thoughts far more often than women. This discrepancy may be hard for women to grasp since we are much more attuned to emotions. But as men enter their middle years, those teenage days of a surreptitious look at *Playboy* producing an erection may become a memory. Blame it, at least partially, on the brain. As men age, their cortex's response to sensory stimuli decreases. Granted, that centerfold still looks as interesting as it used to. But the automatic physical arousal that it once triggered may not be there. And if it is, it may take longer to appear. So do not leap to blame yourself if your partner is no longer physically aroused at the mere sight of you. To some extent, you can blame it on his brain.

## Physical Reactions

As men age, the nerves in the penis age right along with them. This is particularly true with men who have impaired circulation caused by blood pressure problems, smoking, drinking, or other health issues. When nerves are damaged, the penis's tactile sensitivity slips, too, making it less responsive to physical stimulation. Men in their 20s and 30s can become erect within seconds at the mere touch of a fingertip. Men in their 40s and 50s may require more direct physical stimulation of their genitalia. And in order to get, and maintain, an erection, your manopause man may need not only longer periods of stimulation, but also firmer stimulation. This is a normal physiologic change. Chances are your partner is not able to run the 100-yard dash at his high school time, either.

So, you become more physically forward, only to have your partner prove resistant. What does that mean? Cultural conditioning may be kicking in. Some *man*date observers believe, in their heart of hearts, that it is not masculine to have a woman help them get an erection; that ceding control in this area may lead her to think that she can be in charge in other parts of their lives. On the flip side, some women are equally troubled if their mate isn't "man enough" to produce his own erection. It undercuts the sense of security they get from being with a "strong" and "powerful" partner. This is one of those instances when we may be handicapping our men with our own insecurities.

Because men are so goal-oriented, they are constantly striving to be on top in every way, including competing with their teenage selves. Even if your man's intellect does understand, it can be hard for his psyche—hard for a man who is accustomed to being the aggressive partner in sex to find himself suddenly dependent on his partner. This is a possibility to consider. He may have to start from scratch and learn a whole new set of rules. And if this happens, you need to think about what this loss of sexual spontaneity means to your manopause man, and to offer emotional support along with your physical encouragement.

A delay in reaching an erection, the "excitement phase of sex," is often the first hint of sexual change that men notice during manopause. And unless they understand that it is the result of normal physical changes, it can bring on panic, and unfounded fears of impotence.

## Riding the RAMP

When a manopause man does have an erection, it may not be the same as the one he had when he was 20. In his mind, he may fear it's because his penis is smaller. It's not. It's just that he might have a bigger belly blocking his view. Still, the nature of your manopause man's erections can begin to change. His RAMP—Rigidity, Angle, Maintenance, and Plateau phase—may be changing.

**Rigidity:** From adolescence through the mid-20s, penises get rock hard, sometimes at the most embarrassing moments. But erections this rigid are not a given for men in their 40s and onward. One unfortunate side effect of this is a loss of sensitivity, since skin stretched tight over the head of an erect penis is more responsive to stimulation than the skin covering the glans of a semi-erect penis. Having an erection that is serviceable—capable of vaginal penetration and of pleasing their partner—is no comfort for many men. And their concern about this loss of rigidity can make things worse, since worry about sexual failure can easily become a self-fulfilling prophecy.

**Angle:** As men age, the upward angle of their erections often decreases. This can be even more unnerving to your partner when he realizes the size of his testicles is also decreasing. Why are things suddenly trending downward? The suspensory ligament, which attaches the penis to the pelvic bone, elongates as it ages. And, at a certain point, the *levator ani,* the muscles of the pelvic sling that support the penis, lose some strength. You should let your partner know that angle is one thing that men can work on by doing Kegel exercises to improve muscle tone.

**Maintenance:** It's a fact of life. The older a man is, the harder it may be for him to maintain his erection. Consider this an opportunity to display your erotic wiles, as you help him to reinvigorate it. Happily, this diversion can be every bit as interesting as intercourse itself. You will find that one of the pleasures of sex with a manopause man can be the ups and downs of the sex act itself, with peaks of pleasure interspersed with periods of sensual, stimulating, and arousing play. And isn't more foreplay what you always wanted?

**Plateau phase:** The plateau phase is on the list of things that are going to get better in your sex life as your man enters manopause. This is the time between erection and orgasm. As a man ages, his plateau phase generally lengthens. This means that the older man has greater control, more time to satisfy his partner, and more time to savor sex himself.

## Orgasm like Never Before

Orgasm may be slightly different for your man over the 25-year span of manopause. Ultimately, the duration of ejaculation decreases to about three seconds—in youth, it ranges from four to eight seconds. The force with which semen is expelled often decreases from 12 to 24 inches, to 2 to 12 inches. And the intensity of orgasm may decrease, as there are fewer muscular contractions, from the prostate to the urethra, during ejaculation. Less semen is ejaculated, dropping from around a teaspoon to less than half a teaspoon. The semen is thinner and less viscous, and the penis will lose rigidity and the testicles descend more quickly after ejaculation than they did before. Plus, the refractory period, the time between ejaculation and the next possible erection, may lengthen to hours, or even a day.

If you don't understand that these are perfectly natural changes, they may be confusing to you. But once you realize how totally typical they are, does it really matter how long your partner's ejaculation endures? Or how much semen he has? Why quibble over details, when what you are really interested in is the experience as a whole?

Among the many myths of manhood, especially young manhood, is the one that says sex must lead to orgasm. But for some men, as they age, having an orgasm every time they have intercourse is no longer absolutely required. As men mellow, there can be less mental and physical tension built up during sex, and less need for relief. In fact, many manopause men have reported that when they do not have an orgasm every time they have sex, their next experience makes up for it by being even more earthshaking and powerful. Also, premature ejaculation, the secret shame of so many younger men, is often cured with age, as less penile sensitivity translates to more staying power.

If you want to help your partner have happy orgasms, he has to clear his mind. Having an orgasm requires focus, both physical and mental. Anything that breaks his concentration can interfere. A fear of being interrupted by children, for example. Other potential roadblocks include alcohol or sedatives, particularly barbiturates; or antidepressants, which can prevent or delay orgasm in up to 30 percent of men.

Even if you do everything right, an ejaculation just may not happen. Not every time. But don't think that because he has not ejaculated, he hasn't had an orgasm. Interestingly enough, the definitions are not the same. An orgasm is the mental release of his sexual excitement, while an ejaculation is a physical discharge of semen. He can actually have one without the other. As Dudley Danoff, M.D., urologist and author of *Penis Power,* explains, "Ejaculation is not to be confused with orgasm, even though the two usually, but not always, go together. Orgasm refers to the intense feeling of pleasure and release felt at the climax of sexual excitement. Orgasm is mainly neurological in nature. It is an electrochemical event centered in areas of the brain that govern pleasure; ejaculation is discharge of semen through the penis."[5]

## Mortality and Erections

As we have explained, a newly emerging sense of mortality could be at the heart of any man's thinking at this time of life. Even without being aware of it, most men see sex as an affirmation that they are alive. How can the grave be waiting, as long as they are vigorous and potent? But if they sense that sex is slipping away, what is left?

Some men reassure themselves with the myth of eternal virility. And ultimately, isn't sex about procreation? So while the media celebrates the beauty and sexuality of younger men, these aging males point to even older men, like Charlie Chaplin, who were still able to father children well into their 70s. But now, even that bubble has been burst. Researchers at the University of Queensland analyzed over 33,000 American children and discovered that those fathered by older men have, on average, lower scores on tests of intelligence than those born to younger dads. Worse yet, albeit there was only a difference of a few IQ points between children born to 20- and 50-year-olds, the older a man was when his child was conceived, the lower the child was likely to score.[6] And other studies, in Britain and Sweden, have shown a correlation between the age of the father and the incidence of schizophrenia and bipolar disorder in children. Manopause men have to face the fact that not only is there no fountain of youth for them, their sperm have an expiration date, too.

From the culturally traditional point of view, the midlife passage can be a true challenge. Men are pressured from birth to be bulletproof warriors. So it goes against everything they believe in to put the powerful feelings that are stirred by sexual conquests, those reassuring feelings of them being in control of the world, to some extent behind them. But sometimes, that lack of control becomes impossible to ignore.

### The Penis Tells the Tale

Dr. Mehmet Oz suggests that the penis should be thought of as the male body's "dipstick"—a measure of his overall physical health. The wear and tear on your manopause man's body as a whole will be reflected in his penis. Its behavior can give you clues about his arterial health, the condition of his endocrine system, his mental health, and the care with which he is maintaining himself. A man with penile problems is usually a man with other physical problems that the penis just hints at. But remember, like everything else dealing with manopause, penile problems are complicated.

Sometimes it is hard to separate cause from effect. Does a penile problem cause destructive habits, or do destructive habits cause a penile problem? It may take some careful analysis to determine which came first: your man's sexual difficulties, or the physical and mental conditions that could be behind them. As Myron Murdock, M.D., director of the Impotence Institute of America in Maryland and instructor of urology at George Washington University Medical School explains, "Anywhere from 50 to 85 percent of patients have a real physical cause for their sexual difficulties." He goes on to point out that any male with sexual difficulties will have a secondary psychological impact—they go hand in hand.[7]

Sometimes, it is obvious what you are dealing with. Some men respond to their fears of mortality and changes at midlife with self-defeating behavior. They drink more than they should, smoke, do drugs, overeat, and throw in the no-longer-sweaty towel on exercise. If you see those behaviors in your partner, it's up to you to point out that he is embarking on a vicious cycle.

If your partner needs convincing, an article published in *The Journal of Sexual Medicine* in January 2009 should help. In an Italian study, men who either had or were at risk of developing erectile dysfunction made lifestyle changes such as exercise and a healthier diet. At the end of two years, 58 percent had normal erections.[8]

The good news is that we are all exercising more. In 2008 the International Health, Racquet, and Sportsclub Association, made up of 30,022 health clubs, stated that there were 10.5 million membership applications from 55-year-olds and older that year. This is an impressive number considering 20 years earlier, in 1987, there were only 1.5 million memberships.[9] Our cultural conditioning is beginning to move in the right direction.

In large part, this is influenced by the baby boomers. As the healthiest generation ever, this group has worked hard to extend their lives. Their unprecedented health consciousness has changed the world in ways far beyond what was anticipated. They have contained their fears about aging by trying to cure cancer, by encouraging quality health care, and by trying to develop and maintain a youthful existence in very important and creative ways. As Eva Ritvo, M.D., added in a recent conversation, "Although many criticize the baby boomers for their overzealousness, they are the healthiest group of adults yet. The benefits of their exercise, nutrition, and supplements are evidenced by the fact that men and women are remaining more active both at work, and after work, for many years longer than in the past."

## At the Heart of It

A penis comes to attention when it is engorged with blood. So it seems pretty obvious that when a man has arterial clogging, his penis flags just as quickly as his heart does. Perhaps even faster, since the small arteries that service the penis fill with plaque more rapidly than their larger coronary counterparts. It's no surprise that some studies suggest hypertensive men who are not treated—even men as young as 40—are three times as likely to have potency problems than men with normal blood pressure. Or that a Massachusetts study showed that high HDL, the good cholesterol, is associated with a smaller occurrence of impotence. In fact, for younger men, impotence can be a sign of impending heart problems. According to Ira Sharlip, M.D., clinical professor of urology at the University of California in San Francisco, "Erectile problems may show up about three years before a cardiovascular event such as a heart attack or stroke." One study of men with no diagnosed history of vascular disease, but with erectile problems due to poor blood flow to the penis, showed they were eight times more likely to suffer a heart attack and five times more likely to experience a stroke within 24 to 36 months from the onset of impotence.

So, to return to our cause-and-effect quandary, cardio problems can be a cause of erectile problems. And on the flip side, erectile problems can be a very strong indicator of undiagnosed health problems, which you need to encourage your manopause man to explore.

## Smoking, Alcohol, and Weight Gain

It's true that heart disease has genetic factors. But the more common path to impaired circulation includes bad diet, smoking, or drinking to excess. Indulge in more than one, and the risk of damage multiplies. Add smoking to heart disease and hypertension, and the chances of erectile dysfunction or impotence ratchet up considerably. So if you care about having a good sex life, you need to help your man bid adieu to Joe Camel.

Why is smoking so bad for your manopause man? Anything that causes a narrowing of blood vessels and reduces a man's supply of oxygen and blood makes it difficult for him to function sexually. Smoking injures blood vessels, including those tiny blood vessels in the penis that welcome the inrush of blood. Smoking also damages the smooth muscle inside the penis. And studies have shown that it decreases the chances of fathering a child. As Panayiotis M.

Zavos, Ph.D., professor of Reproductive Physiology and Andrology at the University of Kentucky in Lexington confirms, "Smoking has a direct, negative effect on the sexuality of a man on every level." One study, which graded sexual satisfaction on a scale of 1 to 10, showed smokers had a satisfaction level of 5.2, compared to 8.7 for nonsmoking couples, which may be why nonsmoking men are having sex twice as often as smokers.[10] It makes sense. If your partner smokes to the point of huffing and puffing when he exerts himself in everyday life, he is going to struggle with the demands of vigorous sex, as well.

On to the next vice—drinking. It's fun when you're young. But for a manopause man, it can contribute to depression, or it can be used to hide depression. It can also inhibit testosterone production. And over the long haul, it can increase the dilation of blood vessels, making it harder to contain blood in the penis and maintain an erection. Even worse, it can damage penile nerves, decreasing sensitivity. In fact, 10 to 15 years of chronic drinking can actually kill penile nerves, and once they're gone, it's almost impossible to get them back. Another way to constrict those all-important blood vessels is with cocaine or marijuana. According to Dudley Danoff, M.D., "Research shows that the negative effects of marijuana are similar to those of alcohol . . . There is good evidence that long-term marijuana smoking weakens overall fitness and reduces energy and motivation."[11] So discourage your manopause man from taking too many tokes.

Finally, here is a note on overeating. He shouldn't. Estrogen levels, which are counterproductive to male sexuality, can increase with obesity. And more often than not, a lack of exercise is a contributor to being overweight. This means that muscles may not be ready to exert themselves in an energetic sex act. Granted, you can't watch your manopause man 24 hours a day. So encourage the idea that broccoli and salmon and other healthy foods will lead you to good sex much more often than a double cheeseburger and fries.

## *The Big ED: Erectile Dysfunction*

The fact that we have all heard about erectile dysfunction, thanks in large part to television ads that tell our partners how to deal with it, does not mean that it will happen to your manopause man. It's probable that you and your man will continue to enjoy a healthy sex life for the entire length of your time together. Even if he is not the rock-hard stud he was at 20, his changes may be slow enough, or slight enough, that they never affect or impair your sex life. But you should be prepared for the possibility that his abilities are going to change to some degree. Why not be ready to deal with those changes appropriately by recognizing them when they occur, and by practicing preventative or remedial measures that will lead to you maintaining a totally satisfying sexual experience?

Put yourself in your manopause man's brain for just a moment. As Dan Kindlon, Ph.D., and Michael Thompson, Ph.D., tell us in *Raising Cain,* your man has been taught that in order to satisfy his partner he "has to do it right."[12] He has to be both a gentleman, and a hero. He has to get it up, and keep it up. He can't come too early, and he can't come too late. He should be a lusty lover, while his partner should remain the passive recipient.

For a man who has been brought up trusting in the *man*dates, erectile failure is a personal curse that is the cause of both shame and guilt. Convinced that he is failing to fulfill his natural gender role, the man with erectile difficulties can begin to feel like an incomplete person. Suddenly, he fears sex. What's his penis for, if it is just going to hang there? Is he becoming gay? How can he feel good about himself if he can't please his partner? As his confidence drops by the wayside, he begins to imagine what you are thinking about him. What are others saying about him behind his back? After all, with a problem this earth-shattering, how could they not know?

This fear of failure can become so overwhelming to a man that every time he prepares to have an erection, his anxiety causes his adrenaline to kick in. Any chance of having an erection is killed as his body prepares itself to possibly "flee from danger," thus ensuring the very thing he was so afraid of in the first place.

A man who used to think about sex morning, noon, and night now silently obsesses over his inability to get an erection. He sees sex on the television; in movies and ads. He forces himself to laugh about it as he listens to his friends' jokes. He carries the burden of his bad feelings about himself to every interaction he has, all day, every day. He approaches bedtime with trepidation. And when he does all of these things, he almost guarantees that the problem will get worse. Because, though a man can't force himself to have an erection, he can definitely think himself out of one. Especially when his manhood pressure is choking him.

## What Are the Chances?

Recent surveys indicate that around 15 percent of men have suffered in some way and at some time from erectile dysfunction.[13] One estimate predicts that 52 percent of healthy American men between the ages of 40 and 70 will have some degree of impotence at some point,[14] with two studies suggesting the largest percentage of onset occurs around the age of 60.[15] Precise timing aside, the likelihood increases with age. The National Institutes of Health puts the number of American men with erectile dysfunction at 20 million, although Leroy Nyberg, Jr., M.D., the director of the urology program at the NIH, believes that is a significant underestimate.[16] Before you panic, 40 percent of men over 65 are still enjoying sex several times a week.[17]

## Is It in His Head?

ED can be physical—a matter of wear and tear on a man's body leading to bad hydraulics. Or, it can be mentally based. Depression and anxiety can produce symptoms of "psychogenic impotence," a fancy name for impotence originating in the mind. And the reverse can also occur: declining hormones cause erectile problems that can aggravate depression and anxiety. A manopause man's problems may be due to illness or medications or hormonal shifts. Or, they could be due to depression brought on by relationship problems, issues at work, or other undeniable difficulties. Some professionals say the most frequent cause of erectile dysfunction in men over 50 is a mental block, most often a fear of failure. This can happen to men who are not aware of the normal physical changes their bodies are going through. But other experts disagree; when John Morley, M.D., tried to prove that impotence was largely a psychological problem, his study showed just the opposite. Ten percent of the erectile dysfunction he studied was psychological, the rest was physical.[18] Part of this gap might be bias. Most medical professionals are oriented toward technological fixes. On the flip side, by the time many men seek help for this sort of problem, it has already caused them to become depressed, even if depression was not the original source of the dysfunction.

Certain personality types are more apt to suffer from psychologically based erectile dysfunction than others. Chronic worriers and perfectionists are high on the list. Aggressive or controlling men, who hew particularly close to the *man*dates, can react poorly when they sense their dominance is waning. Narcissistic men, who require consistent praise, can fade when they realize their erections are not above and beyond. And, of course, men with diagnosed psychological conditions such as depression or bipolar disease are at risk.

If your manopause man is experiencing erectile problems, one place to start the exploration of what might be wrong is to find out if any of the medications he is taking are counterproductive. There are a number of prescription drugs that can contribute to erectile dysfunction. In fact, in some surveys, they have been tagged as the single most common cause of impotence. Prescription drugs can deaden libido, stop erections short, and interfere with ejaculation. If you and your manopause man aren't aware of which ones act on him in this way, it is time to check his medicine cabinet. Many of these drugs are so commonly prescribed that he may be taking a "penis depressor" without even knowing it.

What are some of the common offenders? Beta-blockers, which are used to combat hypertension, increase his chances for erectile problems, as do some antidepressants (especially the SSRIs), anticonvulsants, diuretics, antihistamines, ulcer medications, and cold and flu remedies. Alpha-blockers can also be a problem as they can cause a significant drop in blood pressure, which can interfere with erections. If you have doubts, you need to consult your doctor or pharmacist.

As the old joke goes, "anxiety" is the first time a man can't get it up twice. "Panic" is the second time he can't get it up once. The thought of losing one's "masculinity" is definitely anxiety provoking, and to most men, losing their erection is tantamount to losing their masculinity. As the invincible penises of teenage years become a memory, some men can be so overcome with self-consciousness and fear of failure that they lose sight of other aspects of sex, and they sacrifice the joys of love and affection. As June Reinisch, Ph.D., former director of the Kinsey Institute, explains, whenever a man loses the ability to have an erection for a period of time, whether it is because he is anxious or it is related to an illness or medications, he will usually stop having any physical contact. Instead of looking forward to sex, these men work themselves into what becomes a chronic erectile problem. As the prospect of a sexual encounter nears, panic creeps in, followed by avoidance. Sometimes, performance anxiety can turn into "spectatoring," as a man watches himself from outside, waiting to see if his penis will perform.[19]

As one thing builds on another, a man can fight back by withdrawing from sexual activity altogether, even from intimacies like hugging and kissing. Erotic thought is a thing of the past, replaced by chronic negativity. And once a man begins to live an asexual life, it builds on itself, making arousal more and more difficult. To make matters worse, if he does manage to get an erection, his worry can complicate the sex act, too, causing premature ejaculation or no ejaculation at all. So instead of getting satisfaction, he gets one more reason to devalue himself, a clear case of the hero beating himself up. This is a man who would need your empathy!

### The Laws of Libido

Beyond the physical aspects of getting an erection lie the Laws of Libido—the mental drive to have sex and orgasm that makes men want to get women into their beds. How will your manopause man's libido be affected by his midlife changes? There is no way to predict. Libido differs from man to man. Some have a lower level of libido throughout their lives; some have a consistently high sex drive. And while frequency of sex may drop as men age, their libido will usually stay relatively high or low, depending on their level of desire in their earlier years.

Libido is controlled by the limbic system in the brain, the same system that influences a man's eating, drinking, and emotions. Not surprisingly, if a man is depressed or suffering from low levels of testosterone, his libido will slide, as well. Sometimes, a lower libido will follow erectile difficulties. After all, why torture yourself by wanting what you can't have?

Conversely, a low libido can be the precursor to erectile dysfunction. Take a man who has a poor relationship with his wife. His lack of desire to have sex with her may cause him to have ED when he has no underlying physical problem. Because of the difficulties between them, he simply can't get an erection with her. He needs to pursue psychological treatment that will help him understand and possibly change his mental attitude, or marriage counseling to heal the problems in his relationship.

The intricate dance between the physical and mental aspects of erectile difficulties is one thing that complicates diagnosis when a man begins to suffer from sexual problems. It is hard to know whether his body or his mind is leading.

### The Mind Game: Depression and Sexual Problems

Even a man who passes his yearly physical with flying colors can struggle to have a functional erection, because good sex demands a healthy mind, as well as a healthy body—the two are intricately connected. If your partner has trouble functioning during the sex act, but wakes up with a nocturnal erection, chances are good that his problem is psychological. We all have "sexual scripts" embedded in our subconscious minds—ideas about sex that have been derived from our early experiences and the attitudes of the people who were around us as we were maturing. But it is the rare man who has long-standing difficulties due to lifelong guilt, negative feelings centered on sex, or other "script problems." It is more likely your manopause man has become trapped in a circular pattern of occasional ED causing depression, followed by depression aggravating his ED. This could be a short-term problem caused by situational depression. Or, if his depression is chronic, his penis problem could be, too.

Of course he wants to avoid this diagnosis. Wouldn't you? For far too long, it was felt that most impotence was psychological, a sign of falling short as a man. Today, however, we realize how much of it has physical causes. But normally, physical causes of erectile dysfunction develop gradually. If your manopause man's problems have come on quickly, it is more likely that they have a mental origin, possibly caused by some trigger event in his life. Maybe it is a physical problem that opens his eyes to the fact that his body is not bulletproof. Perhaps it is something like the death of a family member or friend, a negative career change, financial problems, or a shift in your relationship.

Whatever the cause, it is a common phenomenon. Men whose lives are changing as they age are stressed. And stress can kill the sex drive, even in younger men. It constricts the blood vessels that lead to an erection. Merely having erectile difficulties can cause men to become anxious and despondent, stirring feelings of weakness and worthlessness. These feelings are both the cause of his erectile dysfunction and can be an outgrowth of it.

Manopause men are often losing dominance in multiple areas of their lives: work, home, and relationships. As their status slides, so does their self-esteem, and often, their sex lives. Numbers differ, but it's estimated that anywhere from 50 to 90 percent of depressed men have decreased interest in sex. Looking at that from another direction, the Massachusetts Male Aging Study found depression was 1.8 times more common in men with erectile dysfunction.[20]

## What You Can Do about ED

When the family jewels aren't shining quite so brightly, we have to accept that because of our manopause men's cultural conditioning, it is up to us to help make them sparkle. Men need to learn that with sex, the destination can be less important than the sights, sounds, and touches experienced along the way. We need to focus on the intimacy and closeness that sex provides, to feel comfortable with this, and to help our men meet us in this new, and potentially exciting place.

Do not make the mistake of tamping down your own sexual reactions, in an effort to be sensitive to your partner. You will only cheat yourself. And, possibly, him. Men, especially those with good self-esteem, can find immense satisfaction in helping their partner come to orgasm.

If, on the other hand, an erectile problem is slowly creeping into the relationship between you and your manopause man, communication can require courage, tact, and sensitivity. Whether that comes naturally to you and to your partner will depend on how your relationship has developed over time. Do the two of you have a history of being flexible? Do either of you have a fear of intimacy? Is one of you passive-aggressive? Do you normally confront problems, or sidestep them? Whatever the imperfections in your style of engagement may be, midlife sexual problems have a way of magnifying them. Sometimes there is an unspoken agreement to simply avoid acknowledging the topic, and just live with unspoken tension in the air. You both deserve better. Whatever your pattern, it will probably repeat itself until one of you changes your approach to relating.

Sometimes, you will have to push past your own hurt and wounded feelings to do that. Remember, men often react to erectile difficulties by withdrawing from any show of affection, even minimal affection, for fear their partner will misinterpret this as a lead-in to sex. How many times can you hear your man say he's too tired, too busy, or too headachy before you respond with resentment, frustration, and self-doubt, jumping to the conclusion that he just does not find you attractive anymore?

If you are finding those feelings creeping into your mind-set, listen to your heart. It's time for an honest discussion. Sometimes, a couple can have problems for an extended period of time without mustering the courage to talk to each other about it. The importance of straight talk can't be underestimated. Expressing your own loneliness and frustration can present an opportunity for him to understand and empathize with you, instead of remaining trapped in his own head, to the exclusion of everything else.

Try brainstorming. Could your manopause man's erectile problems have been triggered by a specific event? Is the problem between him and sex, or him and you? If you had a sexual encounter where he was not able to have an erection, or maintain one that was adequate for intercourse, how did you respond? Were you silent, reassuring, or negative? Did you really understand the extent to which your reaction can set the tone for the future?

As women, it is hard for us to compute the body slam a potency problem can be to our manopause men. In fact, we can have intercourse without even being in the mood. There is no need for us to demonstrate fully erect genitals. Right out of the box, the culture makes men feel awkward about saying "no."

But as life goes on, and middle age encroaches, there are times when they aren't able to say "yes." This is when shame can begin to show up. A man who is afraid he won't be able to perform can be sapped of self-esteem and confidence. Because in his mind, sexual potency is tangible evidence of power. Without it, everything he stands for as a man is in jeopardy. His embarrassment may be so overwhelming in the face of this catastrophe that he tries to shift the blame to you, or to devalue your relationship. Is your partner withdrawing from sex, while nitpicking your flaws? Is he suddenly showing passive-aggressive behaviors, designed to tempt you to pull away from him? Is he pushing you to the point where you are now feeling sexually unresponsive, giving him yet another reason to point the finger at you?

Instead of letting his behavior be the jumping-off point for your worst fantasies, consider the possibility that these are defensive maneuvers. Better to risk the relationship, he imagines, then to talk about the problem. After all, talking about it could be dangerous. He could lose your respect, or be forced to face the possibility that it is his fault.

Here is where you can help. Take the word *fault* off the table. Let him know you understand how difficult it is for him to talk about the problem. Assure him there's no need for him to feel guilty about letting you down. And most of all show him your empathy. Understanding is the great goal of empathy. In this case, understanding the depth of fear and pain your manopause man experiences if he begins to question the infallibility of his sexual abilities, is essential. Let him know you appreciate how important this is to him as a man.

Of course the opposite of empathy is insensitivity. It is easy to be caring when a problem initially surfaces. But as time goes on, patience can wear thin, only to be replaced by frustration and worry. Do not leap into feelings of insecurity, thoughts that he may be having an affair, or that he may be contemplating ending your relationship unless you have something solid to bear this out. Some women even get so frustrated and angry about the quality of their sexual relationship, they imply their partners should not start something they can't finish—a sure way to reduce a man's ego to a speck the size of a pinhead. Catch yourself before your inner feelings get out of control. Is it your hormonal shift talking? If so, rein that in, while trying to remain your most authentic self. Communicate what is in your heart, while being sensitive to what is in his.

Also, try not to have this conversation directly following a failed sexual moment. Let enough time elapse so the immediate sting of the experience has started to ebb, and feelings of humiliation are not foremost in his brain. Maybe you can spend that time doing a little research on your own, so when you do talk, you can let him know that the changes he's experiencing may be quite natural at midlife, and that there are myriad ways to improve things.

Whatever you do, abstinence is not an answer. Do not think that you can protect your manopause man from the pain of sexual difficulties by simply avoiding sex. It could kill your relationship. Instead, you should use empathy and nonjudgmental communication, as you encourage your man to look at all types of professional help.

### Getting Professional Help

According to a National Institutes of Health estimate, approximately 20 million men under the age of 65 have sexual problems.

They affect one in four men between the ages of 40 and 60.[21] But you would be hard-pressed to know that by listening to men. Particularly, if you are their general practitioners, assuming they actually go to their doctors. Consider that if men have difficulty talking to their doctors about smoking, drinking, and blood pressure, fat chance they are going to open up about intimacy, virility, and sexuality.

----------------------------------------------------------------

**TIP:** Try to get your man to a sex therapist or knowledgeable doctor. Studies have shown that just communicating what is going on to a professional can improve symptoms, particularly if partners are committed to working on the problem together. The mere act of explaining his problems and fears can help relieve your partner's performance anxiety.

----------------------------------------------------------------

Hopefully, your partner's doctor is one of the enlightened physicians who *is* empathetic in his approach to understanding his patients' difficulties. But even if that is the case, when asked "What's the problem?", how many men with sexual difficulties are going to answer that honestly? Just as with testosterone loss, more often than not, because of their cultural conditioning and shame, men will give another reason for their appointment.

In an ideal world, we would all use a preventative approach to our physical problems, instead of trying a "fix-it" approach once the damage is done. Erectile difficulties are no exception. It is much easier to prevent erectile dysfunction than it is to repair it. Keep in mind, the longer your manopause man waits, whether he is in denial or he is putting the blame on you or elsewhere, the higher his chance for irreversible physical damage and unsuccessful fixes. Armed with this truth, you may have to take charge, help him muster his courage, and push him to seek help as soon as possible. In fact, most of the time, it is the woman who initiates a search for professional help. So do not be timid about encouraging your partner to see a doctor or sex counselor if you think that would be productive. And offer to go with him, if that's something he is comfortable with.

Let's assume that your manopause man is having sexual problems with a physical cause. The good news is that today, most of these physical problems can be compensated for medically. Pumps, injections, suppositories, and pills—each has its place. Your manopause man's choices depend on specifics. How severe is his problem? What is causing it? These answers will dictate his choices. The best advice will come from a doctor who specializes in erectile dysfunction, probably a urologist.

---

**TIP:** If you are not sure how to find a specialist, the Sexual Medicine Society of North America (www.smsna.org) or your internist is a good place to start for a referral.

---

### *The Power of a Magical Pill*

Far and away the most popular solution to erectile problems now comes in the form of a pill. The introduction, in 1998, of "the little blue pill" changed the world's view on sex for men at midlife and later. It liberated men who suffered from certain penile problems, and it changed the landscape of midlife marriage by giving the gift of "eternal youth" to our men. Before Viagra came to market, we called penis problems *impotence*. Post-Viagra they became *erectile dysfunctions,* a far more optimistic term that implies they are mere malfunctions, which can be easily fixed. Indeed, there is some truth to that notion.

We have come quite far in the years since Viagra first appeared. Some estimates put the market for erectile dysfunction treatments at over $6 billion a year.[22] Today, instead of viewing a prescription for Viagra as a cause for shame, many men see taking it as a potential adventure. When they unveiled their male miracle, Pfizer expected it to be used almost exclusively by men over 56, an age group they assumed was their logical target. Since then, the number of Viagra users under 45 has almost tripled, with younger men taking it as "an insurance policy."

What a relief for men to know they can have this sexual "manhood insurance" available with a prescription. It is no wonder so many of them are lining up to buy the little blue pill. It helps them maintain their heroic self-image, their strengths, and their unwavering physical prowess. If we know that our partner's manhood identity has truly suffered, as well as his self-esteem and feelings of self-worth, we should try to put aside our possible trepidations about his restored sexual prowess, and be empathetic as he attempts to reinvigorate himself and your sexual relationship. As his partner, you should look forward to an uplifting journey of mutual exploration.

Science has continued to make strides in understanding the physical and biochemical aspects of erections. So much so, that several pills—Viagra, Levitra, and Cialis—now compete for men's attention and loyalty. Happily, since there is some variation between them, if one does not correct the problem, another one might. All of these drugs work similarly in that they trigger a reaction that produces a neurotransmitter, causing blood vessels in the penis to expand. While they are comparable compounds, with very small molecular variations, there are differences in how quickly they take effect and how long their effects last. For example, Viagra and Levitra must be taken 30 to 60 minutes or longer before sex, and they remain effective for up to four hours. On the other hand, one form of Cialis, which you take 30 minutes or longer before sex, is effective for up to 36 hours. There is also a Cialis option specifically manufactured for daily use, which should help improve a man's ability to get and maintain an erection at all times. The newest drug in this family is Stendra, which was approved by the FDA in April 2012. In clinical trials, it was shown to work in as few as 15 minutes.

While these drugs each have different formulas, usages, and effectiveness, they also have varied side effects. So when you're choosing which to take, make sure your man discusses not just the desired lifestyle factors with his doctor. He must look at his overall personal health and what the possible side effects of each drug are, so he can make the best decision for him.

**TIP:** When your man is discussing the appropriate drug for him with his doctor, he should be sure to explore medical conditions for which each is contraindicated. This might include nitrate drugs he is taking for chest pain, or alpha-blockers for blood pressure or prostate problems. In addition to prescription medications, he should also be sure to tell his doctor about any herbal or dietary supplements he is taking.

Generally, erectile dysfunction drugs have a success rate of 60 to 80 percent, with a lower success rate for men whose penile tissue has been significantly damaged by causes as diverse as smoking, excess drinking, high cholesterol, artherosclerosis, or diabetes. A portion of these favorable success rates can be attributed to men's strong desire to have their sexual performance improve. In one early trial of Viagra, 78 percent of the men who were taking it reported stronger, firmer erections. But 28 percent of men taking a placebo reported precisely the same thing.[23] Obviously, the power of the male mind is strong. So if your manopause man cannot take Viagra for any reason, trying another new herb, diet, vitamin, or lifestyle change may give him a boost. All he has to do is believe in it.

It is important to note that ED drugs cannot give a man back his libido if his has waned. ED drugs may be able to improve blood flow and produce erections, but they cannot do those things unless men bring their own sexual desire to the table. If that passion is lacking, it may be because something is missing in your relationship. Or it could be because your manopause man has built up such a reservoir of shame, due to his perceived sexual shortcomings, that his anxiety is too strong for the drugs to be effective. Either of these possibilities calls for psychological counseling. Refer back to Chapter 6 for advice on how to find the right therapist for the job.

## Physical Side Effects

Life being what it is, we have to be ready to take the bad with the good, and sexual medications are no exception. Your manopause man may experience side effects such as headaches, flushing, indigestion, dizziness, nasal congestion, blurred vision, and diarrhea. In addition, Cialis can sometimes cause muscle aches and back pain, which usually resolve within 48 hours.

One reason side effects show up is that doctors sometimes prescribe the pill without doing a thorough patient screening. A man who is experiencing erectile problems very often also has an underlying condition—high blood pressure or cholesterol, diabetes, or prostate problems—that should be looked at carefully prior to taking these drugs. Men who ignore their underlying health problems by using ED drugs to mask the hints their penis is trying to send them about their overall health are running a risk. This is why you should discourage your manopause man from ordering ED drugs over the Internet, where questions are rarely asked. Your pocketbook can also be a consideration with Viagra and its counterparts. Unfortunately, at this point no generic, lower-cost versions of these drugs are on the market.

## Psychological Side Effects for Both Him and Her

Not all the side effects your manopause man may suffer are physical. There's also the problem of psychological dependence. Having seen his problems recede with the pop of a pill, a manopause man who uses erectile dysfunction drugs may believe he can't function without them. This is especially true if the source of his problem was psychological anxiety.

This can push a button in you. If your manopause man feels he needs a drug to have an erection, does that mean you don't turn him on any more? More likely, it means that he has physical problems, or that his own internal anxieties are getting in his way. Also big on a woman's insecurity checklist is the idea that once her man has reinvigorated erections, he is going to be tempted to try them out, maybe even show them off, to other partners. One way to forestall this is by having a close and communicative sexual relationship, which is something you should be working to maintain regardless of his ability to perform. Wouldn't it be a shame to deny him a satisfying sex life because of your fears?

The next psychological hurdle you may have to leap over is a change in the dynamics of your relationship. As long as your manopause man had erectile difficulties, he was somewhat dependent on you to help him achieve and maintain his erections. Once that is not the case, it can leave you feeling as if you are less important—even dispensable—to him. A variation of this theme is resentment against your partner for "curing" his problem without solving deeper issues that are troubling your relationship. Again, if those problems are lurking beneath the surface, the two of you should be exploring them and finding solutions. The ability to have an erection can gloss over deeper differences in the short run, but it's rarely a long-term solution to larger problems.

Another area your mind may be overworking if your manopause man begins taking erectile dysfunction drugs is the changes you perceive in your sexual style. Will he want to jump directly to intercourse, at the expense of foreplay? Not if you guide him correctly. You should also remember, an ED drug-assisted erection will last much longer than the ones he was having before trying the little blue pill. What if, having been handed this intriguing new toy, your reinvigorated partner expects "sex on demand"? If you find yourself in that situation, with your partner suddenly imposing a need for too-frequent sex, it may be his instinctive way of making up for what he feels were his previous failings, and his prior bad feelings about himself. Since this perception of having fallen short is in his own head, you can start by reassuring him it is not in yours, and build up the importance of the other manly attributes he has in your eyes. But what if he looks for "sex on demand" outside your relationship? What if he decides to show off his newly empowered penis to new partners?

While some men enjoy their enhanced ability with a long-term partner, others may choose a different path. Men whose partners are among the 20 to 45 percent of menopausal women who report a decrease in their sex drive may be particularly prone to choose this direction. These men may feel as though they have no one to share their new toy with, or at least not as often as they would like. As Jane Beresford, Psy.D., explained to us in an interview, "Some of my colleagues and I are seeing men who were previously in what they described as 'happy' or 'satisfying' relationships, but following 'the little blue pill' experience, they have revised their expectations of what constitutes a satisfying relationship, and have reconstructed it with an almost giddy focus on frequent sex and multiple sexual partners." For men like this, online dating sites have provided ample opportunity to seek partners without leaving the house or office, and with relative anonymity. Dr. Beresford continues, "Many men are seeking therapy for what appears to be a fairly critical conflict—'Do I remain in the stable family and relationship I've created with my familiar partner, or do I abandon my familiar partner, and possibly my family, for what feels like a sudden opportunity for diversity in sexual experiences with multiple nonfamiliar partners?'" Faced with this dilemma, and unwilling to make a commitment to either choice, more and more men are trying to do both. As a result, the number of men leading a double life appears to be on the rise. And, as Dr. Beresford explains, the only ones who know are their therapists, and occasionally, their physicians—the people who write the prescriptions.

The *man*dates tell men that they should be prepared to have sex wherever and whenever they see fit, and ED pills are their enabler. All too often, with this modus operandi, little or no emotional attachment is present. So while his penis is satisfied, the man as a whole is not. Manopause men need to understand that when they have sex without emotional attachment, they gratify an immediate need, but they run the risk of losing their chance to have a deeply meaningful and truthful life.

## Women and Sex

So your manopause man is having sexual problems, and you're doing all you can to make sure he gets the help he needs. But there's one other area that, as women, we should make sure to take into account. Since men are primarily visual—this is the way their brains are structured—to them appearance is important. Every man has his own idea of what is sexy and stimulating. And in the natural course of events, given that eyesight becomes more forgiving as the rest of us slowly age, those ideas change, too, accommodating our new, less-than-perfect bodies. But even the most loving partner has his limits, and that is not necessarily his fault.

So look in the mirror and be honest. Do you see any reason why your manopause man might be less interested in sex? Of course we all change by the time we reach midlife. But some of us change more than others, and the rate of your personal transformation is something you can affect. The typical man can be a couch potato, and still look attractive to other women because as women, we engage with all our senses. The typical woman has to fight harder to stay sexually appealing visually. Blame part of that on biology. Metabolic rates decrease around 2 percent per decade for all of us. But menopause also lowers metabolism an additional 2 percent. So as we approach that change, through no fault of our own, we find it harder to hold the line. Extra weight can change your feelings about *sex*, as well as his feelings about *you*. Being the sensitive creatures we are, females are very touchy about showing ourselves off when we do not look our best, and that reluctance, if read as a lack of interest, can quash our sex lives. Even if you are not retreating, there is the possibility that he is feeling cheated, but chooses not to communicate that to you.

## Menopause Meets Manopause

If you are also going through hormonal changes, either in the perimenopause or menopause stage, this can be another complicating factor in your sex relationship. As women approach, and at some point pass through menopause, their hormonal balance tilts slightly more in the direction of testosterone because of declining estrogen. Simultaneously, manopause men's testosterone is falling. For some men, this can mean thinking and dreaming about sex less often. For some of you, sex could be better than ever. The opposing hormonal swings of your manopause man and you are something you need to be aware of.

---

**TIP:** By keeping sexually active, you will discover some very nice surprises. Frequent sex boosts your arousal, your estrogen, and your lubrication—the lack of any of which can make sex more problematic for women at this time of life.

---

When sexual pleasure has been an integral part of your life, it is something you shouldn't lose. Instead of giving in to doubt and abstaining, use manopause as an opportunity to communicate openly and honestly with your man about things that may be feeding into your insecurity. Remember, it's a rare man who's attracted to a partner who is defensive or paranoid.

## The Manopause Man, Sexually Better than Ever

Here's the happy news: A man in his 40s and beyond has it within his power, if properly encouraged, to plot and prolong his performance, as well as to revel in the experience of doing so. Men who have bid adieu to their need for instant gratification make better lovers. They have the confidence that comes with experience. They have left behind the hormonal urges that say "Me, me, me!" They're finally ready to become more emotionally involved in the things that turn on "you, you, you." At last, they can be patient and tender. And do not discount the value of worldly wisdom. Years of practice may have suggested some increasingly sophisticated sexual techniques to your manopause man. Foreplay will no longer be a necessary inconvenience for him. He'll begin to realize that the tongue is good for more than verbally communicating his desire to get you into bed.

If he truly understood what a sexual turn-on his new staying power is for you, would he still be mourning the gradual fading of his teenage penis? He might be surprised to discover that there's a proven relationship between the time spent in foreplay and female orgasm. So do not hesitate to tell him how much you love taking time to experiment with positions that can stimulate both of you in brand-new ways. Explain how luxuriating in the kissing, touching, and fondling that are replacing the former mad dash leaves you glowing in a way you never did before.

Better yet, once the sex act is over, he will not be in as much of a rush to detach from you. No more launching himself from the bed while reaching for his pants. Your manopause man may linger, cuddling and spooning, talking and caressing—the very things you have always wanted. You can thank a lower testosterone level for this happy turn of events, since a high testosterone level suppresses oxytocin and vasopressin, brain chemicals that are a source of attachment and well-being.

Be sure to communicate that you would rather have a good lover than a good performer. Armed with this knowledge, your manopause man may find that he is now proud of his midlife attributes, and relishes foreplay as much as the main event. As you help your manopause man take pride in his lovemaking skills, you will be opening a door that will lead both of you to a whole new level of eroticism.

## Summing It All Up

*"If you have penis power, you are young no matter what your age may be. The strenuous use of your penis will sharpen your mind, exalt your soul, and keep you feeling vigorous."*

**— Dudley Seth Danoff, M.D., F.A.C.S.**

It is impossible to convey how devastating sexual failings are to men; they threaten the very core of their manhood. In the Middle Ages, there was a belief that impotence was a spell put on a man by witches. It's no less of a curse today. Society gives men performance anxiety from the time they are small boys. It teaches them to be ashamed of any weakness, and to be silent about their pain. And it pounds into them the idea that they should be ready to have sex and orgasm anytime, all the time.

If your manopause man insists on judging his midlife sexual pattern by the standards of his younger self, he is likely to be sorely disappointed and, quite possibly, depressed. The goal-oriented sex of teenagers is a performance that is short on feeling and tenderness. It cheats intimacy. At midlife, a man should want more than that. If he continues in his youthful pattern, he deprives his partner and himself of emotional bonding and a deep and authentic sexual connection.

Rabbi Shmuley Boteach, author of *The Kosher Sutra,* estimates that up to one-third of marriages are platonic.[24] Perhaps one reason for this is that once some uneasiness begins over sex, on the part of either partner, it can produce the sort of standoff where each partner waits for the other to make a move. And if neither does, the stalemate can grow from days into weeks, months, or even years. Sexual dysfunction is an animal that feeds on itself and grows. It spawns sex without joy and without deep value, or, at worst, kills it altogether. The longer it continues, the stranger it can feel to initiate sex once again, which is exactly why you have to be sexually active.

Henry Kissinger once said, "Power is the ultimate aphrodisiac." You, as a woman, have the ability to help your manopause man create a new definition of manhood, and to make him understand that at midlife, the ultimate aphrodisiac may be the freedom to revel in a new type and level of sexual expression. Your manopause man needs to learn that his true strength is founded in his ability to be honest with himself about the changes that are occurring to his body, and in his willingness to embrace new roads leading to sexual pleasure with you. Whether he will be able to accomplish that depends on the depth and quality of your intimate relationship, something we will be discussing next.

CHAPTER NINE

# INTIMACY WITH YOUR **MANOPAUSE** MAN

Intimacy is like music. If you are playing alone, the sounds you produce may be beautiful. But when you join a string quartet and harmonize with others, interweaving your individual artistry with their skills and feelings, the union gains boundless intricacy, stunning depth, and deeper, richer meaning. Through playing together, you can be inspired to become a virtuoso, and the group can transcend the sum of its parts. Cellist Yo-Yo Ma had this in mind when he spoke about collaboration, the musicians' version of intimacy:

> "It took me way beyond what I knew, into places of which I was totally scared, but as I became less frightened, I welcomed new ways of thinking and approaching something. It made me an infi-nitely richer person, and I think a better musician."

Imagine the contentment of a life like this, one where two people come together to create a union that is fulfilling for both! It's hard to imagine that anyone would turn down such a wondrous proposition, but many of us do. Or maybe it's not that we turn it down, it's that we forget it exists. Caught up in a daily whirl of family, work, and other commitments, we stop taking the time for intimacy with our mate. Whether you are with a partner of many decades, or are forming a new relationship with a manopause man, midlife is the perfect time to either renew bonds of unity or form new ones. It is never too late to cultivate your deeper connection. And it's a great time to explore intimacy because your manopause man's testosterone is lowering, his career may be shifting, and he now has more time for contemplation, exploration, and connection.

Yet for manopause men, intimacy can be frightening. Especially for those who are most traditional and have spent their lives hiding their vulnerabilities and feelings, attempting to be self-sufficient at all times. It requires them to reveal their deepest vulnerabilities and fears, and by doing so, it forces them to risk rejection at a time when they are already feeling somewhat unmoored. Their limited concept of the word *intimacy* is confined to sex—worse than that, to the emotional side of sex that is to be avoided at all costs. And yet, men need it every bit as much as we do.

Our need for intimacy is intertwined with our primal need to survive. If prehistoric men hadn't hewn together in close-knit groups, forming a mutually supportive band of brothers, they wouldn't have succeeded at hunting, and they would have starved. If they didn't connect and understand each other, even without words, if they didn't watch out for each other, if they didn't share common goals, they would have been snuffed out as quickly as the lone animals they managed to separate from herds. Intimate relationships are just as important today. We are born craving our parents' touch and their unspoken eye-to-eye contact. We struggle from day one to communicate our deepest needs to them. This hunger to be touched, loved, and understood expresses our profound desire to obtain intimacy— something we all yearn for. Intimacy is as necessary to us as the food we eat and the air we breathe.

Given how deeply we all lust after this close connection, it is surprising how rare it is that any of us attain pure intimacy. Maybe that's because so few of us comprehend our partner's true needs. And yet, those deepest human needs are universal. You will probably find yours, and your manopause man's, on this list of The Seven

Important Human Needs, which was compiled by Gary Smalley, world-renowned author and speaker on family relationships, in his book *Secrets to Lasting Love:* 1) the need to feel connected through talking or spending recreational time together as a couple, 2) the need to feel accepted and valued for who you are and what you do, 3) the need to feel that your mate is being honest and trustworthy, 4) the need to feel a mutual commitment that you and your mate will stay together and feel secure in love, 5) the need to feel that you are being included in most decisions that affect your life and marriage, 6) the need for verbal or physical tenderness, and 7) the need to feel that you are both maintaining a mutually vibrant spiritual relationship.[1] It isn't enough to simply understand what your partner's human needs are. To help him make it more smoothly through these tumultuous manopause years, you really have to make an effort to fulfill them, just as he should be trying to fulfill your needs. This is where intimacy comes into play.

### Understanding Intimacy

Contrary to popular opinion, intimacy isn't something you find only in the bedroom, as you shed your clothes and some of your inhibitions. Intimacy is a close bond two people form through experiencing life together—by understanding what the other is thinking and feeling as they travel along their road, and identifying with it. Helen Fisher, Ph.D., tells us it is "a deeply committed relationship based on honesty, trust, self-disclosure, respect, appreciation, interdependence, and togetherness."[2] Intimacy requires you to communicate openly and reveal your deepest vulnerabilities, desires, and fears. But intimacy involves more than talking. It involves every aspect of life.

According to Dr. Wayne Griffin and his team of therapists at the University of Florida Counseling & Wellness Center, intimacy can take many forms.[3] One form is cognitive, called *intellectual intimacy.* In this type of intimacy, two people exchange thoughts, share ideas, and enjoy the similarities and differences in their opinions. After listening to a political candidate speak, for example, you might spend an evening debating your totally at-odds reactions to his ideas. A second form of intimacy is *experiential intimacy*. This involves mutually shared activities—pastimes as diverse as hiking, digging in a garden, or reading in the same room. During experiential intimacy, people share their time and interests, and can often do so with few words exchanged. A third form of intimacy is *emotional intimacy,* in which two people can comfortably share their feelings and empathize with the feelings of the other person, trying to understand and be aware of their partner's emotional side. This could happen, for example, after the death of a relative, if you dig beyond surface reactions and express how you are really feeling about that person and your loss. A fourth form of intimacy is *sexual intimacy*. This is the stereotypical definition of intimacy that most people are familiar with. Ideally, this form of intimacy includes a broad range of sensual activity, and is much more than just sexual intercourse. To these, we would like to add a fifth type of intimacy. For many couples, *spiritual intimacy* is an experience of togetherness in which both partners are reassured that they are deeply connected by a shared faith.

## Developing Intimacy

Whether you are rekindling intimacy with your manopause man, or developing intimacy in a new relationship, the first step toward forming a deeper connection is one you will have to accomplish alone. Before you can become an intimate pair, each of you will have to know and be at ease with yourselves as separate individuals, unrelated to your relationship. If you haven't been bold enough to examine your deepest feelings, needs, and wants and accept them, how can you expect your partner to know and accept who you are? If you are not authentic and honest within yourself and about yourself, how can you expect him to trust you enough to reveal himself?

> *"The happiest people are the ones who are able to express and be their most authentic self in almost all situations in their life."*
>
> **— Louann Brizendine, M.D.**

Being your true self, being honest with your feelings and your actions, will unburden you. Take some time to think about what you want out of your life and your relationship. Knowing this will deepen your relationship with yourself and leave you available to have a more intimate relationship with your manopause man.

The second step of developing intimacy is communication. Being able to express your honest thoughts and feelings about yourself, your partner, and your relationship is an integral part of becoming closer. Look at your relationship and acknowledge, even if it is painful, where you and your man currently sit on the couples' communication scale. Are you being open in your communication, or are you treading water in the safest, yet least fulfilling, type of talk? Again we look to Gary Smalley, who tells us that there are five levels of intimate communication: 1) speaking in clichés, 2) sharing facts, 3) sharing opinions, 4) sharing feelings, and 5) sharing needs.[4] As your intimacy progresses, you will move from level one, the "starter level" of communication, to level five, which opens you to the greatest amount of intimacy you can experience.

It is easy to plant yourself, with a minimum of discomfort, on levels one and two. Clichés and facts are impersonal; you are putting nothing of yourself on the table for judgment. Conversely, you are gaining little in the way of love or comfort by doing this. Sharing opinions can be a little more risky. You might be venturing into areas of disagreement. But it isn't until you reach the levels of sharing feelings and needs that you are truly revealing yourself, and possibly putting yourself into jeopardy—something that may be frightening to your manopause man.

-------------------------------------------------------------

**TIP:** When you are sharing feelings, try to share those that are positive. At least once a day comment on how happy you are about some way in which your manopause man satisfied you, and encourage him to do the same for you.

-------------------------------------------------------------

If there is one rule to remember while communicating on more meaningful levels, it is that learning to talk intimately first requires learning to listen. Picture your partner as he starts to speak. Do you stay tuned in, giving what he is saying your full attention and acceptance? Or does your multitasking female brain veer off in different directions? Intimacy requires you to be attentive. It is based on understanding your partner's feelings, anxieties, and hopes. To do that, you must be fully present as he speaks. And you may have to do more. We've discussed the communication limitations your manopause man innately carries within him. Help him out. Instead of talking in generalized clichés and facts, with questions and responses you would have on levels one or two of communication, ask about specifics. Voice questions that require him to express his feelings, something he will only be able to do if he can trust you.

If there is a lack of trust, or if there are relationship or sexual problems developing or settling more firmly in, communication can become difficult, and soul-searching can become even more tenuous. If a couple has lived through decades of ineffectual, or worse yet, nonexistent communication, opening up to intimacy may trigger past grudges and wake up old insecurities. Frightening? Yes, but hardly worse than the alternatives: living in a constant state of nonfeeling, or losing your relationship altogether. The secret to navigating this intimacy obstacle course is making your approach nonjudgmental, sensitive, and loving. Unfortunately, there are times when that is hard to do.

When life throws up untold barriers to intimacy, be prepared to look at them rationally and figure out how to overcome them as they appear. These barriers may come in the form of the *man*dates, which discourage men from sharing or, perhaps, from even understanding what intimacy really is. There may be barriers to communication, which keep people from fully comprehending the profound feelings and urgent needs of their partner. And other barriers can be preexisting in a couple, with old wounds resurfacing when the partners begin to authentically express their inner feelings. All these bulwarks can block emotional, sexual, spiritual, experiential, and yes, even intellectual intimacy. And if you put off dealing with issues as they appear, they could kill intimacy altogether.

Always remember, developing intimacy takes time; it will not simply happen overnight. You will need to work your way from stage one to stage five of communication, as you share in all of the different types of intimate experiences. Communication is intrinsic to having an intimate relationship. All the time you spend in communion with one another will help you grow closer. Start from where you are today, and grow your relationship from there with the goal of open, honest communication and a healthy, robust, loving partnership.

### Five Sure Ways to Kill Intimacy

While ignoring problems as they arise often quells intimacy, there are a number of other *sure* ways to bring about its demise. The first intimacy killer is to want too much, too soon. Intimacy can't be forced. Impatience is its foe. Like a child who evolves slowly, learning new and wondrous things during every stage of development, intimacy needs room to grow and time to blossom fully. But rest assured, if you truly want intimacy, and work toward it, the baby steps you take today will turn into graceful, well-coordinated leaps and bounds with practice.

To avoid this intimacy killer, you should instigate your search for intimacy by first concentrating on the types of intimacy you and your partner feel most comfortable with. What is instinctively most satisfying and fulfilling may well depend on your gender. As Gary Smalley explains, intimacy can mean different things to women and men. To women, the most natural form of intimacy is talking face-to-face. Men, however, often regard intimacy as working or playing side-by-side. Sure, they might discuss a bad week at work, even troubles in their love lives. But rarely do they share their secret dreams and darkest fears without being prodded. Since intimacy comes more naturally to you as a woman, you may be wise, at least at first, to tip toward the types of intimacy that your partner is most open to. Knowing that talk is probably not his strong point, you might want to open your mutual door to intimacy by finding nonverbal ways to experience the world with him: the kinds of experiential intimacy that will allow you to learn more about each other through actions, instead of talk. For example, pitching a tent on a campground, if neither of you has done it before, can show you the way each partner's mind works, the mutually supportive skills you have as a pair, and how well the two of you can learn together and pull together to conquer an unfamiliar problem. During the process, even a glance, without words, can communicate exactly what you are thinking. For your man, this is a lesson in intimacy.

The second great intimacy killer is game playing. Balance-of-power games can be particularly common during this time of midlife changes for you and your manopause man. As his testosterone lowers, and your ratio of testosterone to estrogen rises, both of you may experiment with a certain amount of role shifting in your relationship. Certainly, as you are both changing, some adjustments may be warranted. But remember that if you resort to game playing in the process of reshaping your interaction, you will never be able to develop a truly intimate relationship, because you will be breaking the cardinal rule of being your most honest and authentic self.

Third on the list is blame. Accusation is a sure way to kill intimacy. When a relationship becomes less involving and fulfilling, fingers can start pointing; if not physically, mentally. Sometimes they point at our partners, and sometimes at us. Which way the fingers point may have a great deal to do with your couple dynamics. And keeping score is never a road toward coming closer as a couple. Being on the receiving end of blame can feed your insecurities, make you question yourself, and withdraw. And as hard as this may be for you, it can be an even tougher blow to a manopause man. Blame may make him feel as if he is falling short in your eyes, at a time when he is already convinced he is slipping lower in the world's esteem. Remind yourself that an honest discussion about relationship problems, and a consideration of possible solutions, is never pushed forward by blame. Intimacy requires that both you and your partner feel you can count on the other for support. Blame says you can't.

The fourth serious intimacy killer is putting your negative emotions in the driver's seat. The worst offender is anger. As we suggested in Chapter 6, anger is a many-headed hydra. And like the hydra of myth, when one head is cut off, two can grow back. Anger can be open, or it can be hidden. It can be the cause of relationship problems, or the result of them. It can be dealt with, or left to fester and grow. Resentments that have accumulated over decades of being together may be silently seething inside. This is even more common for traditional men, whose fear of communication leads them to tamp things down and hold them close to their gut. At the very least, negative feelings that are held in can take up space that should be filled by positive feelings, leaving them no room to grow. When ignored, unexpressed anger can be the death of your intimate relationship.

If your intimate relationship is slowly petering out at midlife, start by making an unexpressed-anger evaluation. Do you think resentments have built up over the life of your relationship? Could some of them be your fault? Have you been unkind to your partner over the years, and treated him with a lack of respect? Have you fallen into the sort of constant criticism that demoralizes a man? If your answers include any "yeses," it is time to start a dialogue as a first step toward developing the sort of intimacy that can cure this kind of standoff.

In the context of a midlife relationship, *expressed* anger serves different needs. Years of unresolved differences, piled on top of the stress your manopause man is already feeling about changes that are happening, both *in* him and *to* him, can finally bring long-smoldering anger to the surface. Teenage boys have a reputation for being surly and irritable as they are going through huge hormonal swings, and their lives are being turned upside down. Yet how many of us understand that our manopause men—who are also going through emotional ups and downs, plus hormonal and physical changes in their lives—can react by lashing out in a similar fashion? When your manopause man expresses anger, consider hormone changes as a contributing factor.

Remember what we said about anger being a many-headed hydra? One of its faces is confrontation. If you are truly seeking intimacy, this is nothing to be feared. Instead of looking at confrontation as a rupture in your coupling, think of it as a catalyst for positive change. For it is during moments of confrontation, when you may be speaking passionately and off-the-cuff, that your true feelings rise to the surface and come up for air. This is when you are your most authentic self. Only when your partner hears what you are really feeling, and when you are exposed to the hopes and needs he has been holding inside, can the two of you begin to approach intimacy.

---

**TIP:** Make sure to listen to the subtext of what your man says when he is angry—and examine the deeper meaning of your replies, as well. What underlying issues are behind the anger that is being voiced? What you "hear" between his words could provide valuable clues about what might be stifling your intimacy. Once the episode has subsided, consider the true content of the anger and decide whether any of it might have some basis in truth.

---

The fifth intimacy killer is betrayal of trust. We all need the freedom to confide our deepest secrets to a trusted partner without worry of judgment or betrayal. But by observing the *man*dates, and forcing distance and disconnection, manopause men can cut themselves off from needed support, just when cultural conditioning makes their lives the most challenging. Without the ability to open himself up, your manopause man will never be able to shed the armor he's girded himself with throughout his lifetime. Stuart Fischoff, Ph.D., a professor of psychology at California State University, Los Angeles, tells us that, "As a man becomes more vulnerable, he's going to need someone who is not going to use his weaknesses and frailties against him. Trust becomes a pivotal issue."[5]

So being in a trusting and open relationship is important not only to intimacy, but also to your man's overall walk through manopause, and betrayal of that trust is to be avoided at all costs. Just remember how you would feel if you confided your deepest needs and fears to your mate, only to have them used against you. For example, in a moment of intimacy you admit to your man that you are feeling insecure about your weight. Then later that week, when he is irritated at you during a dinner party, he embarrasses you by somewhat jokingly telling the table not to pass you the pasta; you need to lose a few pounds. When you shoot him a look, he points out that you said so yourself, publicly betraying your confession.

This sort of verbal betrayal of trust goes two ways. Women are inclined to share worries, problems, and concerns, even when it comes to our men's most intimate problems. Say you are having a cup of coffee with your girlfriends, or, perhaps, your mother. You've finally gotten your manopause man to open up to you about his personal difficulties and fears. You want their understanding, you want their advice, and you want them to calm your anxieties. Big warning! For a man to be open about his shortcomings is an extremely difficult roadblock for him to pass through. Once he has, for you to share his personal problems with outsiders could be thought of as a terrible violation of his privacy; a betrayal of his trust. If he is already feeling vulnerable, and he realizes you have passed this personal information on to others, humiliation will be piled on top of insecurity, which will only serve to stymie his communication with you, and quash whatever intimacy you have achieved.

------------------------------------------------

**TIP:** Betraying a trust can have serious consequences. Publicly revealing your manopause man's weaknesses and fears plays into his vulnerabilities. Privately, you can laugh and joke with him about both of your foibles. But laughing at him, even in a teasing way with your friends, is intolerable.

------------------------------------------------

The ultimate betrayal of trust is infidelity. Interestingly, there is a genetic component to fidelity, which can be seen in the structure of your man's vasopressin receptor gene. In a study done by the Karolinska Institutet in Sweden, researchers found that men with a particular variant of the vasopressin gene scored lower on bonding questions and were less likely to be married than men who did not have the variant. Also, men with two copies of the gene variant were twice as likely to report having had a relationship crisis with their marital spouse or partner in the last 12 months as men without the variant.[6]

While genetics may play some role, infidelity at midlife is often spawned by the fact that manopause men start to fear their mortality, feel less "manly," and need reassurance that they are still the heroes they once felt they were. What better proof of their drawing power than a new and preferably younger woman? To quote Groucho Marx, "A man is only as old as the woman he feels." Infidelity is particularly appealing to a manopause man who has resisted establishing true intimacy with his wife. It is reassuring for him to be talking to a different woman who does not know his flaws, and isn't prodding him to reveal them. But what appears to be an easy fix—avoiding intimacy by having an affair with another woman—may only make things more broken. How often does lying and deceiving make anyone happier? The betrayer cripples his authentic self by living with guilt, or in the very least, with a constant, underlying knowledge of his dishonesty. And the victim of the betrayal faces the nearly impossible task of mending bonds of trust that have been ripped apart.

A manopause man's decision to engage in infidelity usually stems from the fact that he is not completely satisfied within his relationship, and at its root, that dissatisfaction reflects the fact that he and his mate have either never developed true intimacy, or have stopped tending to it and helping it to thrive. If you are sensing this as a possibility in your relationship, consider whether you both have been truly honest with each other about your feelings and needs, and whether you are striving to be your authentic selves. Because doing that will open you up to the most wonderful intimacy of all.

### Sex Can Be the All-Encompassing Intimacy

The ultimate intimacy, sexual intimacy, can, at its best, encompass the full gamut of emotional, intellectual, spiritual, and experiential connections. But what if things are not at their best? The state of your union will reveal itself, for better or worse, between the sheets. You may have to work hard, using all your patience and understanding, both in and out of bed. But if the two of you can share vulnerabilities in the bedroom, and feel comfortable exploring your deepest and most authentic selves, the benefits will enhance the rest of your lives together.

To understand why midlife is a great time to develop intimacy through sex, you first have to understand that when it comes to sex, men and women are biologically very different creatures. Just consider the orgasm. His is external and very visible when it arrives; yours is internal and slightly mysterious. Women look to sex for closeness, while men look to sex for a sense of relief and of mastery. Women want to have sex with someone they already care about, as a way to make that love grow and solidify. They tend to connect sex with commitment. Men, on the other hand, do not feel this automatic bonding effect. Generally, for men, sex is more of a release of tension than an emotional connection.

Because of the biological and social changes that are happening to you and your manopause man, you have a perfect opportunity at midlife for these differences to merge, making sexual intimacy better than ever. Sex with a manopause man can be ripe, rich, full-flavored, sweet, juicy, and pure. While the wild sex of our younger years has its incredible highs, it also has its lows. Carnal and animalistic, it can be fun . . . for a while. But the best sex combines deep emotions and honesty with the physical—a pairing that can only be achieved with familiarity, understanding, maturity, and, most importantly, trust.

### Sexual Intimacy and Your Manopause Man

At midlife, the luckiest and most open-minded men are able to realize that while being locked in armor may protect you, going through life inside your own self-imposed barricade also blocks you from giving and receiving, both emotionally and sexually. When a man matures, and reluctantly recognizes his fragile edges, he is less likely to see women as objects, and more likely to acknowledge them as people, much like himself. It's then that he can learn to give of himself sexually in the best sense.

Why is this so important? When the respected psychotherapist Rollo May, Ph.D., explored the value of sexual love, he found that the abilities to give and to receive are essential to your full pleasure in the act. If you can't receive, your giving is nothing more than a domination of your partner. And, conversely, if you can't give, your receiving will leave you empty. On both of those counts, the young knight in his full and impenetrable armor is at a distinct disadvantage.

For those who are able to both give and receive, Dr. May explained that sex can be a wonderful form of life-giving renewal. Imparting pleasure to another enriches and fulfills you and expands your self-awareness. Climaxing together takes you beyond a sense of personal isolation and into a sense of union. And overcoming separateness frees you to revel as much in your mate's pleasure as you do in your own. This is the ultimate form of intimacy.

So help your manopause man to leave behind stereotypes that may be holding him back. Teach him, by example, the value of trust and tenderness. Help him understand that instead of making him less of a man, breaking with the *man*dates will let him relax into being himself, and allow him to enjoy the personal fulfillment of a truly intimate sexual relationship.

### A Midlife Shift of Power

In addition to helping him realize the *man*dates aren't strict rules that he must live by, you may also have to help your man reevaluate some specific rules associated with sex. There are certain sacrosanct sexual rules that most men live by—rules like the absolute standard of an orgasm every time he has sex or the expectation of a hard penis at the mere sight of a naked woman. But one of the hardest rules for your man to let go of often rears its head during midlife. This rule deals with male dominance, juxtaposed against female subordination. This is not only a universal erotic fantasy, but also one that is perfectly aligned with the *man*dates. Usually the more powerful partner is the one who initiates sex. And traditionally, that is the man.

When men enter manopause, there is sometimes a shift in this balance of power. As a man ages and he begins to doubt himself, his partner may feel she needs to be more assertive about what she wants sexually. Dealing with this shift can be tricky. Even if your man has started to reevaluate other rules about sex, this change may be hard for him to accept because in his mind, the implications are vast. He might be thinking that if he gives up control on the sexual front, he could forfeit your respect. If he believes he's falling short in the bedroom, your man may fear that you will look for sex elsewhere, causing his anxieties to grow. If they do, your manopause man may react with anger, which is often the refuge of a midlife man who is beginning to have sexual difficulties. Arguing is a wonderful way to eliminate the need to make love, and in the process, to remove the possibility of failure. Unfortunately, your man is maintaining his façade of control and power at the cost of your intimacy as a couple. And once that happens, *you* might respond in anger, which adds nothing to the development of intimacy.

Expressing old hurts or resenting unresolved differences in a relationship, a manopause man can withhold pleasure from his partner as a form of punishment. A man with a passive-aggressive personality may find this the perfect way to express his inner rage and hostility. By not giving himself to his partner, he gains control without having to challenge her openly.

------------------------------------------------------------

**TIP:** If your man expresses anger surrounding subjects dealing with sex, try not to snap back at him. Calmly let him know how much you love him and how much you value what he does for you in all aspects of your life. Remember, his anger grows out of uncertainty and anxiety. The best way to overcome it is to help him realize that he is still all the man you want.

------------------------------------------------------------

Is an angry fallout from changes in the balance of power always a death knell to sexual intimacy? Not necessarily. Anger can stir passion. That's how "make-up" sex got its reputation. It is aggressive and cleansing, a way to communicate your depth of caring and, on a very visceral level, to connect. The operative word when dealing with make-up sex is *occasional*. "Angry sex" should not happen often, and when it does, it needs to be the stimulus for honest and intimate discussions that resolve your underlying problems, and bring you closer together. Granted, that may not be easy for a manopause man, who is not accustomed to airing his hurts and insecurities, but it is the road to a better sexual relationship. And hopefully, as your partner gains in emotional awareness, and your relationship grows in intimacy, it is a skill he will be able to master.

Changes in the sexual balance of power are not always a negative. One of the great lessons of midlife is flexibility. As the genders' hormone levels change, the entire canvas of a loving sexual relationship can change with them. No longer should it be set in stone that sex has to be a certain way. This can be a door into a new level of intimacy. You can teach your manopause man to receive, as well as to give. You can help him understand that it is not necessary to be an alpha male in the outside world in order to have a sensual experience in the bedroom. If you have reassured your partner that you value him and his feelings, he can learn to take turns with you in initiating and guiding your sexual relationship. And when a man no longer perceives sex as merely evidence of his power, both partners gain the freedom to take it to deeper levels.

### Improved Sexual Intimacy Through Communication

Communicating about sex is one of those areas where your man may struggle. Generally, women want to feel close and intimate in order to give themselves over to sex, and one way to do that is by having open and meaningful communication. Men, on the other hand, think sex *is* intimacy, the only sort of intimacy they're traditionally encouraged to enjoy. They would rather express connection through their bodies than their words.

*"Among men, sex sometimes results in intimacy. Among women, intimacy sometimes results in sex."*

**— Barbara Cartland**

So your manopause man needs to adjust his thinking in order to enhance sexual intimacy. He cannot simply grab his metaphorical toolbox and quickly fix problems that come up in your sex life—even though he is more prone to do that than to engage in detailed discussions about why they may have cropped up. Because he has been taught since childhood to ignore his own emotional and intimacy needs, he's ill-equipped to express what he wants. And he's equally ill-equipped to deal with his partner as she expresses her emotional needs.

So it is up to you to help foster good communication in the sexual realm. You'll have to encourage your man to express what he wants. For example, most men are notoriously reluctant to tell women what turns them on. They are just plain embarrassed. And in their defense, some women do not want to hear it. Don't be one of them. When is the last time you asked your manopause man what he would like you to do to him? Remember, his tastes may be changing as he mellows. Don't be surprised if you have to coax this information from him.

Given the importance of sex to our lives, it is interesting to note that while most of us occupy a good deal of time sharing with our partners the many ways we want to spend our paychecks, parent our children, and enjoy our vacations, we devote little or no time to confiding what we would like from an erotic point of view. How foolish is that, when talk is the pathway to intimacy, and completely honest talk about sex is the road map to true satisfaction? Why do we sit, lips sealed, hoping some magical GPS will guide us to our goal, instead of expressing what would make us feel satisfied? Be honest. Are you being authentic with yourself in expressing your sexual desires? If not, it's time to start.

And keep the conversation going when the foreplay begins. The brain is stimulated by the sounds of excitement, so be open, reveal yourself in bed, and let your manopause man hear what you are feeling. It can take him to new heights and stir him to try new techniques. Remember, boredom is the death of good sex, and by midlife it can easily set in for your man, and for you. All of us crave variety. In midlife, your manopause man is becoming more ready to listen, so disclose your desires and get him to tell you his. Make this stage of life a time when you both become more secure and move beyond your inhibitions.

Another way to foster intimacy and sexual satisfaction is pre-planned sexual play. Knowing ahead of time that you will be together gives each of you the added titillation of anticipation. And the thought that each of you has found your intimate time together important enough to set aside a part of your day for it can make this sex even more pleasurable than a spontaneous act would be. Not that spontaneity should be forgotten—mixing up the typical week with your partner by surprising him at work with a visit, placing a sexually inviting card in his pocket, or surprising him with an overnight getaway can rejuvenate what may be falling into a mundane pattern. These subtle—or not so subtle—ways of expressing your desire for your man will not only enhance his confidence through these changing times, but also increase your levels of intimacy in all parts of your life.

## When Sexual Intimacy Has Waned

Often when things go wrong in a relationship, women jump to the conclusion that it is their fault. A blip in the sexual relationship is no exception. It is a dangerous leap from sensing that sexual fervor is slipping, to adopting a firm belief that your man doesn't love you anymore. Maybe you even assume your marriage is failing. Or worst of all, that he is seeing someone else. You get a new hairdo, you buy a new dress, you try a new perfume, and things between you are still stuck in neutral. Now you are sure he doesn't want you, which triggers worries about your future. Instead of thinking rationally about the fact that stress or distraction could be causing apparent sexual disinterest on his part, your worry consumes you. Even Viagra sets you off, when you decide that the only way he can have sex with you is to be medicated. The way to fight these fears is to retaliate with good, healthy communication. Don't let things spin out of control. Dive into his most intimate depths. Learn what he is thinking and feeling, and do it without delay.

The longer you are dispassionate toward each other, the harder it is to rekindle the flame of sexual intimacy. This is partially true because, after a time, initiating sex becomes awkward. Sometimes this happens because, in order to keep yourself from hurting, you may condition yourself not to feel. This can lead you to simply stop being interested. Sex doesn't happen in a vacuum. We approach each other carrying whatever psychological baggage has built up over the course of our years together. This is why recognizing underlying problems in your intimate relationship and dealing with them is so important during manopause.

Before you make any drastic assumptions or acute life changes, talk to your man. If he is so caught up in his *man*dates that he is not willing to let you penetrate his vulnerabilities or allow you to help him find his emotional side, you have three possible directions to go. You can break up the life you share, knowing he cannot grow with the aging process. You can remain stuck in a reality that will continue to be shattered daily by the conflicts that a traditional man bumps into during manopause. Or you can persist in trying to break through his armor. The answer, as always, is to be guided by your authentic self and to begin the process of working toward the resolution that is most true to who you are.

### Perfecting Your Connecting

Physical and emotional connections work together to perfect sexual intimacy. When both you and your manopause man have confidence in each other's concern for the other partner's well-being and desire to meet the other partner's human needs, you can totally reveal yourselves, without worry of losing love and respect. This trust allows for deep connection. As Mae West succinctly said, "Sex is emotion in motion." But too many partners are together, without being emotionally connected. An intimate relationship is built on common values and interests, and the sort of respect that takes years to accumulate. It is something to nurture and support. Its nonsexual side intensifies your sexual interaction, making it richer, and more inventive.

Having a healthy relationship is crucial for good sex. And having a healthy sex life is equally crucial for maintaining a solid relationship. As you move forward with your manopause man, you are approaching a moment of truth. His newly dawning sense of mortality could trigger a psychic alarm, even a crisis. But if you are a supportive partner, instead of pulling away, your man may find his eyes opening for the first time to how vitally important to him the intimate relationship he shares with you is.

Building on that sound relationship, you and your manopause man can be entering one of the most profoundly pleasurable periods of your lives. When you truly know each other intimately, you can share sensitivities and vulnerabilities, reveal your raw and honest selves, and communicate your deepest needs. Practice intimacy in every facet of your lives together, whether intellectual, experiential, emotional, sexual, or spiritual. Shared, honest intimacy can be your man's steady anchor in a sea of change, and it will serve to strengthen your bonds and your lovemaking. Once you understand each other's needs and desires, and are truly joined in intimacy, your union will be stronger than ever.

# CHAPTER TEN

# FAMILY MATTERS
# AT **MANOPAUSE**

One day he's Bill Cosby's Cliff Huxtable—wise, patient, and consistently working to put his family first. And then, without warning, your man turns into Archie Bunker—sniping at you and your children, and demanding that you all know who runs the show. A lot is changing. Not just in your manopause man, but in the family around him. When those shifts in the status quo come, they can make your man feel as if he is no longer fulfilling his cultural imperative.

The shifts can also trigger memories in him of unresolved pain and suffering from his past, as well as opening the wound of unattained goals. How your partner deals, at midlife, with those flashbacks to past events can spell the difference between a happy, functioning family and one that may fall into a state of simmering anxiety and antagonism. Armed with your own empathy, a new understanding of your manopause man's brain, his enhanced emotional intelligence, and your newfound shared communication skills, you can help your family unit maneuver through the obstacles of manopause.

*"One thing can safely be said: When it comes to trampling traditional family values, there's nothing more brutalizing than a middle-aged guy with a frustrated dream."*

**— Charles McNulty**

### In the Family of Man

From the dawn of time, cultures have taught men that they are the ones who are expected to hunt and provide, and then to stand at the mouth of the cave where their family dwells, ready to kill anything that threatens those who are dear to them. In order to do that, a man needed to keep careful watch over his mate and his progeny, maintain a close family unit, and prevent them from wandering away, quite possibly into danger, while he was busy doing his assigned job.

While this cultural conditioning may not be foremost in your modern day manopause man's mind, it is still lurking in its hidden recesses. But as he approaches midlife, it gets harder for a man to keep that cave door guarded, and to ensure that the ones he is trying to protect are willing to stay safely inside. A manopause man's children demand new freedoms, and sometimes his wife does, too. His authority seems challenged, as does his very conception of his place in the family unit, which, he has always assumed, he heads.

How a man handles this transition depends, to some extent, on his background. The things he observed in his own family as he was growing up will influence the way he reacts when the stresses of manopause set in. As will the expectations that *you* developed as *you* were growing up. The interplay between those two sets of assumptions will be one of the key factors shaping the dynamic of how you, your manopause man, and your family weather these occasionally confusing times. Your attitude may make the difference between your home becoming a battlefield, and your partner discovering fulfillment in learning to nurture you and his children in a new way.

210

### The Impact of Manopause on Your Children

If you doubt, even for an instant, the impact that manopause men wield over children, consider this statistic reported by Sean Maccaulay in *The Daily Beast* in 2009: "Since 1970, the number of first-time fathers over age 35 has doubled, according to the U.S. Census Bureau. That means a third of American men—the highest percentage in history—now have their first child at precisely the same time as they grapple with the existential abyss. Belated fathers have been further destabilized by a challenging job market and the biting credit crunch, which nix any chance of the classic ego-boosting spree."[1]

Given this trend toward later fatherhood, for many midlife men, manopause is hitting them at the same time their children are beginning to test their wings and try for new freedoms. Caught between the subconscious desire to protect his young, and the frightening realization that they are, probably for the first time, questioning his position and authority, how does a manopause man react? More than likely, he will hit back with "The Three C's": control, competition, and criticism. These are among the important points of contention between fathers and sons that Dan Kindlon, Ph.D., and Michael Thompson, Ph.D., cite in their book, *Raising Cain*.[2]

## Control

Almost every father is accustomed to being the "Leader of the Pack." In order to protect his children, he has had to exercise control over them since the day they were born. But now, they are suddenly becoming headstrong and secretive. His duty is to guide them, and in order to do that properly he needs to know and understand their every move. So why aren't they cooperating?

Manopause men can react to this perceived loss of control by exerting their authority randomly, on the spur of the moment. This can be bewildering to children, who don't realize that their father's power play has more to do with subconscious fears that have been triggered by one of their actions than by a careful consideration of whether it is logical for him to lash out at this specific moment. They do not understand that a man who feels he is losing control can be overly sensitive to even the smallest thing that seems to erode his children's respect for him and for his decisions.

That is why Jason was confused when, at 17, he found his perfect car. He had even done all the legwork, calling the seller, negotiating a better price, and having the used car checked out mechanically. He expected his father to be excited. After all, they had spent many years of their lives bonding over cars, talking about the ones that each of them would love to drive, debating the best colors, makes, and years. He was excited when he told his father what he had found, and eager to hear his reaction. When his father told him he had no intention of putting money into a car—especially *that* car, he was crushed. But his father claimed that Jason probably wouldn't take care of it, anyway.

Jason didn't understand that when he searched for the perfect car on his own, instead of seeking his father's advice, he was showing his father how little he was now needed and respected. And that when his father pictured Jason in that new car, a car he might have enjoyed when *he* was Jason's age, all he could see was his son driving away from him.

## Competition

As much as he may love his children, it can be incredibly hard for your manopause man, who is beginning to fear that his highest-achieving years are behind him and that mortality is hovering over him, to realize that his children now have all of their most-exciting "firsts" in front of them. His opportunities may be gradually narrowing, just as theirs are expanding. He is beginning to take blows to his self-confidence, as they are getting ready to move on and take chances in their lives.

A man who is accustomed to being head of the household won't want to relinquish that position easily. This is particularly true in father-son relationships, where a manopause man who is feeling insecure may be quick to put his growing son "in his place." One way to do this is physically. Your partner may begin to give your son playful punches on the arm that are just a little too hard. Or he may want to arm wrestle him into submission, even to the point of inflicting pain. Your instinct, when you tell him to stop, will be to suggest that he doesn't know his own strength. You also have to understand that subconsciously, your manopause man is trying to establish himself as being on top physically, before his son is too large and strong to be subdued by force. That is an internal fear you need to address with empathy and understanding.

## Criticism

"Father knows best" is a maxim that most men have taken to heart. When all else fails, and your manopause man feels he now isn't getting the respect he is sure he deserves after years of sacrificing, performing, and producing for his family, he may resort to criticism. On their face, many of the things he is saying may be justified. But the lasting effect of chronic judgments and disapproval is difficult for children, or even you, to shake off.

If your manopause man is falling into this pattern, he should be cautioned that the longer it persists, the harder it will be for him to restore an open and loving relationship—one in which his family feels free to show him their vulnerabilities. Criticism lingers long after the words have been uttered, particularly with growing and impressionable children.

### Men Fear Separation

At the bottom of most manopause men's family fears is a deep dread of separation, both from his wife and his progeny. As often as he may have told himself, during their growing years, that his goal was to prepare his children for independence, it is the rare man who can accept his children moving from home with perfect equanimity and no second thoughts. The driver's license he encouraged them to get, the part-time job that was to help them establish their sense of responsibility . . . suddenly these are things that are taking his children away from him.

Nicholas Evans summed up this push-pull feeling perfectly in *The Divide* when he said parents should "consider themselves the bows from which their sons and daughters were sent forth as living arrows. . . . But what no one ever told you was what happened to the bow once the arrows had gone. Was that it? Was that all? Did it just get propped up in a corner of the closet to gather dust?"[3]

The irony is that for many manopause men, they have reached a point in life where they are ready, and longing, to clear their calendars to be with their children, at the very time when those children are pulling away. The father that may have been "missing in action" while he was building his career and his reputation in the community, is now more available, just as his children are slipping out of his grasp. The son or daughter who would have treasured his company ten years before, now shifts in a chair, wondering how long they will have to listen before they can drive away to be with their own friends.

Helping your manopause man to weather this may prove to be a real challenge for you, since this is one instance where you may be experiencing precisely the same feelings and apprehensions that he is facing. What will your purpose in life be, when your children leave? And what will become of the relationship between you and your partner when that nest is empty? Will you look at each other and wonder what you're doing together? Once again, this is a time when open communication between the two of you, and a deep exploration of your doubts and fears, can help both of you regain a stable footing, and launch yourselves into a new direction in your lives together.

## Reliving a Father–Son Relationship

Some of the dynamics of any family are set in place long before that family is together. Old influences and wounds may be hidden, but stress, like the stress that your manopause man is experiencing during these years of change, can flush those old hurts out of their hiding places. What took place between your man and his father when he was growing up is one of the most important contributors to what will happen within your own family during his midlife. As Dan Kindlon, Ph.D., and Michael Thompson, Ph.D., explain, when a grown man cries in therapy, it's almost always about his father. His father may be hated or revered, dead or alive. The story may be one of his father's absence, his painful presence, or his limitations of spirit and feeling. The word love rarely comes up in the stories men tell, but that is what these stories are all about.[4]

If your manopause man's father was a workaholic, he may be responding by spending too much of his own life being self-indulgent and trying to reassure himself that he can remain free and playful. Or, if he had a father who was financially a low achiever, your mate may push himself toward success beyond a point that is healthy for him, or for your family.

------------------------------------------------------------

**TIP:** Talk to your man about his relationship with his father. This information could be very helpful when you need to evaluate what is happening in your own family.

------------------------------------------------------------

Even though our culture, and in particular the *man*dates, have taught them that expressing love openly and showing signs of physical affection might cause people to view them as "feminine," most manopause men want to be closer to their sons and better fathers than their own were. Somewhere deep inside they understand that their sons need the spiritual nourishment that only a father, and his male wisdom, can bring.

*"When you teach your son, you teach your son's son."*

**— The Talmud**

Yet all too often, as a father works to bond with a son moving toward manhood, he also passes on our culture's "manhood pressures." The dad who takes pride in being there for every one of his son's high school soccer games may also be making it clear that winning each of those games is all-important. Sending messages like these only intensifies his boy's future struggles. Or, a father may do the opposite, obeying the *man*dates by pulling into himself and remaining silent and distant, because of his own manopause journey, even as he sees his children slipping away from him. Sometimes the only emotion fathers are comfortable expressing is anger—anger that surfaces at inappropriate times and is out of proportion to the event that caused it. A teenager who carelessly drops his jacket on the floor should not be screamed at. But try telling that to a manopause man.

When you see this kind of eruption, consider the possibility that instead of chastising your manopause man for his behavior, you might try to talk about its underlying cause. Could it be the emotional distance that lay between him and his own father? Is it his fear that his children are preparing to leave the home and that he may have waited too long to try to bridge that very same gap with them? Remember though, you should wait until your man has calmed down to bring this up. As we learned, when men are in the fight-or-flight mind-set of anger, they are unable to constructively discuss what just happened. When you do talk about it, make sure to reassure your man that it is never too late, that whatever breach there is can still be closed. Help him find ways to connect on an emotional, vulnerable level. It may be as simple as finding and using words that reveal just how much he cherishes his son and their relationship. Happily, if he manages to do that, your manopause man may discover he feels more grounded in his transitioning family life.

## Living the Son–Father Relationship

Traditions are passed down from one generation to the next. If your manopause man is lucky enough to still be experiencing life with his own father, then he is not only dealing with passing forward traditions to his son and daughter, he is simultaneously being a recipient of them as well. What he sees in his own father can give him a mirror image of himself. But assuming he is trying to move away from the *man*dates of the former generation, understanding their source may do little to calm his anxiety, or help provide him with the patience he needs to divorce himself from them. It's no wonder there is often tension at extended family gatherings.

Every Thanksgiving Seth is of two minds, bringing his wife and children to his parents' for dinner. He thoroughly enjoys seeing the family together, showing off the kids to their grandparents, watching their interplay with their extended cousins, and knowing another year has successfully passed. But as everyone sits down to dinner, discomfort grows inside as his father, the "master of the family," maneuvers to be the center of attention. As a 50-year-old son, Seth feels belittled by his father, who speaks louder and interrupts a conversation when he is not the center of attention, then changes the subject to one he's an expert at. And he shares stories, the same stories the family has listened to many times in the past. Anxiety and anger build inside Seth, as he watches disproportionate homage being given to his father. He becomes quiet. His father comments that Seth should join the conversation, which irritates him even more. As Seth's father continues to lead the table, he is guiding the male grandchildren toward his *man*date philosophies. At times Seth interjects, positioning himself as the protector of his own son.

As usual, Seth returns home disappointed by the evening and angry at his father. His wife is more objective, empathetic, and aware of the "manhood pressure" that Seth, and to an even larger extent, his father, feel. She suggests Seth should try to put himself in his father's shoes. Seth's father has reached a phase of life when he, knowing he is no longer the primary provider and protector of his family, desperately clings to power. He feels his own dinner table is the only place where he has the ability to exert control.

With his wife's help, Seth gains the benefit of understanding what is going on beneath the surface of these family gatherings, and how his father is suffering from his own manhood fears. She reminds Seth that while he may not like the presentation, there are rich lessons in his father's stories and real value in the expertise he offers. She also compliments Seth. He did the right thing by not confronting his father. It showed compassion, respect, and understanding—qualities that should be reinforced in front of his son. His wife suggests that

Seth take a moment to discuss what he is thinking and feeling with his son in an attempt to push forward a more open-minded version of manhood thinking; one in which "winning" is a result of being sensitive to another man's insecurities and weaknesses.

## Holding On to Daddy's Girl

While manopause men frequently become competitive with sons, when it comes to their daughters, they are protective. With teenage daughters, they can become *overly* protective. It's no wonder—they understand exactly what is in the mind of the boys who hang around them. We know how important sex is to our men. So it is not surprising that our manopause men become terrified when they feel their sexual abilities beginning to slip, while testosterone-driven boys are knocking at the door in pursuit of their daughters. Those fears can surface at unexpected moments.

Fifteen-year-old Kimberly came out of her room, ready for her first high school dance. She was dressed in a teen girl's idea of sexy elegance. Her father met her at the base of the stairs. Instead of giving her the compliments she expected, he greeted her with a raised voice and a harsh tone. She was not going out looking "like that." She was to get back upstairs and change . . . now! Kimberly, frightened, fled. The father who normally loved her was attacking her.

Kimberly did not understand that her father's disapproval reflected the fears that were converging within him. Realizing his daughter, who had always sought his approval, was now looking for that attention from young men, triggered thoughts of his own mortality. Understanding all too well what boys are looking for, he also feared for her safety and well-being. And seeing her looking so mature sent him the message that his job as provider and protector would soon be coming to an end.

Even *he* was surprised by his angry outburst. Still, he was convinced that he was right. He wanted his sweet, innocent daughter back. He wanted to stop the changes that were taking over his life, and the life of the developing young woman who was once his little girl. His fears of losing control of her, and of no longer being her hero, were sending him into a spiral of anxiety and stress. And so he fell back on regressive behavior. After lashing out at her, he did feel in control, at least temporarily.

Kimberly's father would have caused much less damage to their relationship if he had adjusted to the fact that she was growing up, and he was aging. Instead of seeing her attempt to attract young men as a threat, he could have viewed it as the first step into another phase of the growth they would share as a father and daughter. In that frame of mind, he might have been able to suggest calmly that she find something less revealing to wear, and she may have perceived his behavior to be loving and protecting, instead of damaging and confusing.

Had Kimberly's father been emotionally aware, he might have been less vehemently protective, and more willing to trust her strength and self-sufficiency. Instead of locking her into a template of being polite and pretty, he would have encouraged her to explore who she is, and trust her own intelligence while doing that. Dr. Levant says that, "The more a man is capable of experiencing and expressing his own feelings, the more his children will learn from his example . . . and the more they will come to know and love him for the real human being he is."[5] It's the emotionally intelligent father who is able to empathize and communicate with his children, and who will reap the reward of having them confide in him, and listen to and trust his advice. These are the lucky men who will be able to establish close and trusting relationships with their children—so unlike the relationships that may have been thwarted with their own fathers.

## The Impact of Manopause on Us

If you are living with an irritable and moody manopause man, you may feel as if you are suddenly spending your time dodging bullets without warning. It can be difficult not to get edgy and upset yourself. Maybe you even find yourself firing back. If that is what you are doing, consider this change of perspective.

While it is easy to repay your partner's occasional unkindness with one of your own, it is equally possible to look at life through his eyes. Your manopause man may very well be feeling as if he is no longer necessary to you, or to your increasingly independent children. And since "provider and protector" has been his lifelong identity, he needs to be listened to and reassured that he is still a loved and valued person to all of you. Even if he is not the sole provider for your family, this is a traditional male image that means a great deal to him.

Try renewing your relationship with your manopause man within a different framework. While the euphoria of new love may not be as strong as it once was, the joy of deeply caring for one another can be stronger than ever. And there's no need to lose the sense of romanticism that made your early relationship feel so deeply satisfying. Part of that romanticism comes from being kind to one another. Have an honest conversation. During this time of great vulnerability, are you treating each other with the love you both deserve? If you are like most of us, the answer is no. On average, people apologize to strangers 22 percent of the time, and to their close family members just 7 percent of the time.[6]

Consider the possibility that if your manopause man is lashing out at you, it is because he is feeling insecure. Women, generally, have many layers of social support, from family to friends to co-workers. Men, more often than not, rely on their wife or partner for their sole source of intimate contact. So as your manopause man is beginning to feel less powerful, and increasingly fearful of losing your love and respect, he is also sensing that he is emotionally dependent on you. Somewhere inside he realizes that if you do decide he is now dispensable, he risks being cast adrift with no intimate ties whatsoever. Knowing this, you may want to take it upon yourself to initiate meaningful conversation with your manopause man, instead of nursing the resentments and hurt feelings his actions may have caused.

### Manopause Meets Menopause

As if life with your manopause man weren't complicated enough. If you are in your mid-40s or older, you may also be butting up against another common cause of polarization in a relationship. It is quite possible that you are either about to enter, or have already begun, your own perimenopause or menopause. If this is happening, you can find that you are changing in ways that are very much at odds with your man's gradual metamorphosis. Adjusting to the altered energy that each of you is giving off could make you feel as if you are stepping into an unfamiliar territory, wrapped up in a brand new set of challenges.

Because you are suffering through your own menopausal symptoms, things can get more complicated as you help your manopause man to traverse his passage. You may be fighting irritability and struggling to concentrate clearly after nights of your own mood swings, hot flashes, or depression. This means that, for a while, you may have to defer dealing with his problems, while resolving your own.

The world of work could be one point of contention in the manopause/menopause relationship. At precisely the juncture when your manopause man may be yearning to slow down his rigid push toward the professional top, your children may be preparing to leave home, and you may be in the process of considering ramping up a career of your own, or changing the one that you already have. Many experts believe that women over 50 commonly become more aggressive, managerial, and political. Focus is no longer diffused by childcare. Nurturing qualities can be redirected into a business orientation. Inconveniently, these newly blooming aspirations may be revving up at the same time manopause men's careers are winding down.

Be careful as you choose how to address this. Your manopause man's self-confidence is already on thin ice. As that ice breaks, he may interpret your excitement over your changing life as a fall into cold water, and jump to the conclusion that your new personality is, in reality, a rejection of him. If he does, he could respond by withdrawing from you, thrusting you into a "roommate relationship"—spiritually separate and lacking passion, connection, and caring. On the flip side, your feelings of anxiety, dissatisfaction, and resentment could turn *you* into an antagonist. In either scenario, not only will your emotional lives together suffer, your sexual connection can be damaged as well. In a worst-case scenario, your manopause man may even consider divorce.

### Divorce: The Ultimate Nonsolution for Men

Look around and you will see that divorce among midlife couples happens all the time. Manopause men, feeling discarded by their wives and no longer important to their children, may decide they would be better off on their own, or in a new relationship, instead of remaining in a relationship that isn't providing the support and understanding they crave.

In *The Divide,* Nicholas Evans writes: "The gist of it was that there were two types of men who absconded from their marriages: the naughty and the needy. The naughty absconder was a simple, dick-driven creature who just couldn't help himself. However much he might love his family, it always came second to his main object in life, namely, chasing women. The needy absconder was basically insecure and forever trying to prove to himself how much everybody loved him. His family was, in effect, one big love machine that needed his constant control and attention. When his kids grew older and got lives of their own and didn't need him so much, he suddenly got scared and felt old and useless. So he ran off to look for a new love machine somewhere else."[7] While Evans may have been voicing the feelings of manopause men everywhere, the truth is that frustration, awkwardness, and adjustments at this time of life can cause both sexes to seek outside relationships.

Manopause men rarely realize that they are the ones who will suffer most from the breakup of their families. Once a breakup occurs, the fear of losing touch with children, something that can easily happen to a divorced man over 50, can bring on a sense of personal failure that will cloud other aspects of his life. All too often, his children will blame themselves, or him, for his leaving, which makes their relationship with him even more complex and tentative. Experts say that men who remain connected and attentive to their children during the manopause years are the most deeply satisfied.

According to the 2010 Census, the highest rate of divorce is in couples between 45 and 64.[8] But happily, the divorce rate in America is at a three-year low. According to *The New York Times* in August of 2010, "the Centers for Disease Control and Prevention puts the current divorce rate at 3.5 per 1,000, down 8 percent in the last five years, 16 percent since 2000, and a staggering 34 percent since its peak in 1979. Roughly 20,000 fewer American couples are divorcing every year as compared with a decade ago."[9] Perhaps that is because, according to Michael McCullough, Ph.D., of Southern Methodist University, "The forgiveness instinct is every bit as wired in as the revenge instinct. It seems that our minds work very hard to get away from resentment, if we can."[10] Hopefully we are entering a new cultural era when, with societal changes swirling around us, we value our stable relationships more, and are willing to put aside discord and anger in order to preserve them. There is no time more important to consider this than during the manopause years.

## Family Time Fights with Technology

One nice thing about the cave that men used to guard was the size of its entrance. It was easy to see when someone or something was trying to get in to tear families apart. But things have changed. Now, the mouth of the cave is unimaginably large, and the forces that are intruding on the family unit are much more difficult for a manopause man to see and identify. It was hard enough to drive away a saber-toothed tiger. It's almost impossible for your man to defend against the ephemeral, invisible wave of electronic media that is threatening to engulf his loved ones, especially when he is one of the notable contributors to it. This is all coming at a time of life when he is questioning his priorities, and, possibly wondering where he would most like to be.

Families today are being inundated by digital data. *The New York Times* quoted Dawn Foster, an executive at Intel, saying in March of 2011 that "some 6,000 exabytes of digital data are now in existence. If they were burned on CDs, the stack would reach from here to the moon and beyond."[11] Most parents are apprehensive about the amount of time their children spend online. But how many of us worry about the time that parents, especially fathers, are spending online? Or about what that drain on their father's attention does to the cohesiveness of families? Pew Research recently reported that adults' online use doubled between 2004 and 2009, with them spending an average of 12 hours a week plugged in. And for the two-thirds of adults who are now sleeping with their cell phones next to their bed, it can be a 24-hour-a-day commitment.[12] As Dahna Boyd, a social scientist who works for Microsoft, points out, "Thanks to our ever-present messaging systems and devices, we never really have to disconnect."[13] And ironically, that "never having to disconnect" may be one of the most challenging roadblocks to real connection between our manopause men, us, and our children.

This means that just when a manopause man is struggling to find new ways to solidify connections with his family, he may also find himself being pulled away. Searching for reassurance that he is still important, he validates himself with electronic connections. Every time he hears the "ping" of a text coming in, or opens his e-mail and finds someone trying to connect with him on a social network, he can be reassured that even if things are falling off a bit, he is still very much wanted in the world. And these connections are easy to feel good about. Because if the "real-life" people around you are up-setting you in any way—if they get difficult or critical—it's easy to simply cut them off and move on. Electronic media is omnipresent, and relatively undemanding. And unlike face-to-face interaction with loved ones, it can be turned on and off at will.

Obviously, it would be nearly impossible for your manopause man, you, or your family members to function in a world of work and other commitments without being electronically connected and responsive. The problem arises when your man takes it be-yond work and habitually uses the Internet as the ultimate way to escape the difficult questions the reality of midlife is posing for him. On the Internet, if he is feeling irritable and unsatisfied, he can get instant stimulation that can, at least temporarily, block out his uncomfortable feelings and his subconscious thoughts of mor-tality. As long as he is connected, and people are reaching out to him, he can get immediate positive reinforcement. And as long as his cell phone and computer keep him in constant locomotion, he can feel active and involved.

The discouraging truth is that if your manopause man is constantly hooked into electronic media, this is at odds with him being truly involved in your marriage and family. During a time of life when being a fulfilled person is going to require human contact, reflection, and introspection, electronic media is his enemy. The constant stream of stimuli it feeds him can addict him to needing a life bursting with overstimulation. Impulsively responding to every text that comes in can develop a pattern that makes it hard for him to set priorities. And overtaxing his brain with constant responses to these "urgent" messages can erect a roadblock to the deep thought and self-examination that your manopause man needs as he makes his transition into midlife.

The most unfortunate fallout from your man's *over*connection to electronic media could be his *dis*connection from your family. In *Small, Beautifully Moving Parts,* an independent film released in 2011, Sarah Sparks asks, "Do you ever feel closer to the technology in your life, rather than the people in your life?"[14] Sarah's question is a valid one. The Internet delivers such an immediate and ongoing stream of information to evaluate, questions to answer, and feedback to our own comments, that real-life family interchanges can seem slow and tedious. Clifford I. Nass, Ph.D., a Stanford University professor, explains that the ultimate danger of heavy technology use is that it diminishes empathy by limiting how much people engage with one another. With his iPad in hand, your manopause man might be in the same room as you, and yet be mentally absent. "The way we become more human is by paying attention to each other," Professor Nass reminds us, "It shows how much you care."[15] And now we find our manopause men telling us, as they look at their smartphones, that they would like to talk, but they just don't have time. Maybe if we would send them an e-mail, they would get back to us.

We are beginning to learn that the price we pay for the gift of technology is alienation. Empathy and compassion, so necessary to a stable and fulfilling family life, are the products of calm and thoughtful minds. But as your manopause man pushes buttons for immediate reward, he can numb himself to the actual world around him; and reason, perception, memory, and emotion can begin to elude him. In fact, studies have shown that overuse of electronic media can actually rewire the brain.

How much is too much? How can you know when it is time to step in and have a discussion about electronic media with your mano-pause man? Since you can't peer into his brain, you will have to judge by his actions.

Elizabeth Bernstein, writing in *The Wall Street Journal*, suggested some guidelines.[16] If your manopause man can't get through a meal without e-mailing, texting, or talking on the phone, or if he regu-larly e-mails or texts, other than for something urgent, while you or another family member is with him, you have a problem. If he is looking at more than one screen at a time, checking e-mail while watching television, for example, or if he never turns off the phone, you have a problem. If he sleeps with his phone near him, checks his e-mail or texts while in bed, or logs on to his computer while in bed, you have a problem. If you have argued about his use of tech-nology, you have a problem. If he no longer goes outside for fun, you have a problem. And most telling of all, if, when the family is hanging out together, each of you is looking at a different screen, you have a problem that is encroaching on your entire household. You may be fortunate to be with a manopause man who has already considered this and has made an active decision to stay in real life and limit his use of technology. Good for you. If, on the other hand, you find yourself with a manopause man who is enmeshed in his media, you must bring his overuse to his attention, and explain how it is negatively affecting your family and you. Just as anything done in excess, from exercise to model building, can detract from spend-ing precious family time together, so can an addiction to electronic media. Remind him that he is modeling behavior for his children that they will carry with them throughout their lives. Agree on some ground rules that will let him communicate effectively when neces-sary, without being constantly plugged in. And once those ground rules are set, involve the entire family in abiding by them.

**TIP:** Consider suggesting to your manopause man that you and your family turn a trip into a "technology vacation." Go somewhere with no televisions, and then agree to turn off your personal technology. Doing this can be an eye-opening and uplifting experiment. In a new place, with many distractions, your "withdrawal" won't be as difficult as it might be at home. You will probably discover that this uninterrupted time will give you the ability to have an honest, un-invaded, quality experience together.

## New Family Values for Your Manopause Man

Cynics may point out that with life expectancy nearly double what it once was, the idea of lifelong marriage is hopelessly passé. We change and grow as we age, and life, of necessity, moves on. But looking at your manopause man from that point of view and assuming his metamorphosis will lead him toward discontent with you and his children, through no fault of your own, would be a mistake. For many of us, midlife and beyond can be the best and most loving years of our family relationships.

Our men's cultural code is one reason. As Neil Chethik explained in his book *VoiceMale*, "Most American men—the flesh-and-blood variety—embrace their roles as fathers and husbands. I found in my research that the values of duty, honor, and taking responsibility are far from forgotten by men in our culture. Certainly, most men struggle to fulfill the ideals they set for themselves in this area. But they recognize that being a 'real man' requires that they are honest and respectful and willing to sacrifice."[17]

For the younger generation of family men, the traditional image of the benevolent patriarch positioned on a pedestal, calling the shots from on high, is being replaced by a deepening need for family intimacy and connection. Among these men, the number who are sharing domestic work at home, and the number of college-educated men who are willing to sacrifice pay and lose promotions in exchange for a work schedule that allows them to spend more time with their families, are both rising. If you have any doubt of how pervasive this new image of masculinity is becoming, you have only to look to Procter & Gamble. One of the world's biggest and most effective marketers of household goods has now started a website, Manofthe house.com, aimed directly at men, advising them on everything from disciplining children to having good sex with their wives.

While your manopause man may not have come from an environment that embraced and fathered with these newly developing family values, the fact that they are blossoming all around him gives you wonderful tools to help him transition into his new roles. By pointing out the new male zeitgeist, you can help him feel comfortable reconnecting with his children in a way that has less to do with possessing and controlling them, and more to do with understanding and guiding them. Instead of seeing his sons and daughters slipping away and separating themselves from him, your manopause man can learn to understand that while they may move on to form their own lives and families, he will be with them forever, having helped to shape their character and values. Because of the bonds that grew out of the triumphs and failures they have shared, he will always have emotional ties to them. And even when his children are not under his roof, he can still be a profound influence in their lives.

As to the relationship between the two of you, with proper nurturing and a few modifications, it can be the happiest in your lives together, filled with spontaneity and growing intimacy. If you can help your manopause man look at the source of his fears and the causes of his irritation and anger, he can learn not to use it against you. Instead, in this time of stress and change, he can draw upon his sense of manly service and begin to see you and his family as his greatest source of fulfillment.

CHAPTER ELEVEN

# MANOPAUSE
## MEN AT WORK

Have you ever wondered why your manopause man carries his work with him, wherever he goes? Maybe it's in his briefcase, maybe it's on his cell phone, maybe it's in his truck, or maybe it's just in his constantly churning mind. While *you* may not realize it, to him a paycheck is just one part of a much bigger package. To be fair, he may not realize it either, but in the deepest recesses of his psyche, *what* he does and the degree to which he is recognized for doing it is *who* he is. If you have any doubt about that, think back to the last party you attended. Or the last time your man was thrust into a group of new people—in particular, when he found himself in the midst of a cluster of men he had never met before. What was the first question they asked each other? It's a pretty good bet that question was, "What do you do?"

To men, "What do you do?" is a loaded question. It's the grown-up version of a little boy's, "Mine is bigger than yours." What he does is central to a manopause man's existence. It is his calling card with other men, and one of the main characteristics that gives him his identity in society. It is the lure that brings him the attention of

229

women, and a means by which he proves his continuing worth to his family. For many men, work is their very reason for being. In your manopause man's mind, it may be the measure of the man he has become. And that is why, at midlife, negative changes in his work life can tap into a deep well of manhood anxiety.

## The Prehistoric Imperative

Any sense of falling short in your manopause man's work can produce a sense of failure. It harkens all the way back to a prehistoric time, when men's success at hunting and providing was mankind's most important key to survival. This primal necessity to "bring home the bacon" was slowly honed and refined through the ages, until society made earning and providing an integral requirement for any man's entry into adult society. He may no longer have had to hunt to survive, but a man had to produce something worthwhile in order to gain recognition in the eyes of others.

Today, your manopause man knows in his gut that his work and his accumulated success are major factors in determining his social status and the amount of approval he gets from the people around him—most of all, you. It is the way society judges whether he is stable and worthy of respect. If he is a good provider, he is judged to be a good man. This is the way he has been taught to show his love for his wife and his family.

By midlife, any intelligent man has gotten the message, loud and clear, that he is not only working to pay the bills but also to be someone. And he is no doubt convinced that his greatest sense of accomplishment will come from toughing it out, practicing self-sacrifice, and succeeding in this traditional male role of triumphant worker. This makes it frightening for a manopause man if he begins to feel the hot breath of younger men at his heels, trying to scramble right past him on their climb to the top. Or if he begins to get the feeling that he no longer has what it takes to get ahead. Or, finally, if he hates what he does and dreads having to do it for the rest of his life.

### Failure Not Allowed!

"He worked himself to death." It's an interesting expression and one that can be truer than we might like to acknowledge. How many manopause men have pushed themselves so hard trying to prove themselves that their bodies gave out? Dr. Levant explains why this is possible: "not only because men have been trained to put work before all else, but because they've also been trained to blind themselves to the price they pay for doing it. Men are so thoroughly trained to numb themselves to their emotions and ignore signs of physical distress that they don't even know when the demands of work are pushing them up to or past the limits of their endurance."[1]

This isn't surprising. From the time they are born, parents coach their male children to toughen up by soothing them less often than their female counterparts if they fret. And those baby boys respond by learning to carry on without complaint.

Since performing is the main thing they have to fall back on, traditional men count far more on work for their self-esteem than women do. That's why many manopause men need all the "bells and whistles" they can get: the largest office, the highest salary, the most deferential staff. Sometimes, those perks are even more important to them than the job itself. Let's face it: when someone's life is devoted to work, any job can get boring. Those high-profile rewards are important; they keep a man's interest engaged. They also establish who is winning the game. As Alain de Botton, the Swiss essayist and philosopher says of his fellow men, "We may seek a fortune for no greater reason than to secure the respect and attention of people who would otherwise look straight through us."[2]

As women, our identities are often defined by our relationships. But men's are defined by the "success score" they rack up. It's no wonder manopause men are so shaken if the rules of the game begin to shift as they age. They know that they risk losing the approval of their parents, peers, and most devastatingly, women.

### Men Work for Sex

You can see it in any animal group; the alpha male seeks power because it's the aphrodisiac that makes him the group's greatest stud—the one with the best chance of passing on his genes. It's not so different for humans. For us, it's not just raw muscle that equals power; more often than not it is money and other assets that are earned through a combination of brainpower and hard work.

Men in every culture and class share the ambition of winning the most beautiful and fertile women. And women have their own fantasy. While we may tell men what we want is warmth and sensitivity, it is not the entire truth. What is often most important to us is our man's success, and the fact that he has the financial resources to raise our children and take care of us. "Sexy" men don't have to be great-looking, as long as their bank accounts have an attractive balance. Standing on a bulging wallet can make a man tall, handsome, and very appealing. From a reproductive point of view, women desire men who are heroes—heroes who have triumphed in the fight for success.

Starting from the time they are boys, men begin to discover that sex isn't free. As Warren Farrell, Ph.D. explains in *Why Men Are the Way They Are*, very early on boys see the "genetic celebrities"—the good-looking sports stars and class presidents—with the best-looking girls on their arms. They realize that being with one of those young women will get them accepted, too. And if they're not part of the lucky gene pool, they learn that they have to take risks and perform in order to get attention. Being a "success celebrity" is their way in.[3] And as men mature, work is the most obvious way to gain success.

By the time they are grown, most men realize that prosperity and achievement are their keys to a more lasting form of acceptance. With them, men gain respect from their peers and attention from the women they want—women who might otherwise look right through them. Success in work is their hero's shield against the vulnerability they might otherwise feel.

So if you are with a manopause man who is beginning to feel a little less secure about his place in the world of work, understand that the root of his problem lies much deeper than a difference of opinion with a younger colleague, or a bonus that may not seem quite up to his usual standards. One of the things he may be most worried about is your continuing acceptance of him as a man.

## What's Testosterone Got to Do with It?

Men feel more like men when their testosterone is high, and one way to get it there is by being a winner at work. Animal research has demonstrated a "winner effect": a hormonal jump that happens whenever success at a task produces a reward. These boosted hormones lead to brain changes that encourage faster decision making, increased risk taking, and a pumped-up determination to win. The "loser effect" is just as pronounced; the animal with a record of falling short stops trying as hard, and takes fewer risks.

One reason our manopause men like to win at work is because it makes them feel more male. In April 2008, a *Newsweek* article reported on a study that showed that stock traders who start the workday with high testosterone levels make more money on that day than low-testosterone colleagues.[4] A hot day on the market sends up the winners' levels of testosterone even more. But the high hormone level generated by extreme success also leads to clouded judgment, and the occasional spectacular failure. Winning can't go on forever, and by midlife, the chancy hormone-driven decisions that help get high-testosterone men to the top can come home to roost. Winning can make their decisions faster, but it doesn't make them better. This should be a comfort to a manopause man whose testosterone is declining.

## In the Workplace, Men's Importance Is Shrinking

If your manopause man is consistently searching for that success-driven testosterone boost, don't be surprised. He is increasingly caught between a rock and a hard place, and he may be feeling justifiably threatened. In today's global, knowledge-based economy, almost every growth area for employment is more suited to women's brain wiring and innate skills than to those of a traditional man. According to *Newsweek* in September 2010, "of the 15.3 million new jobs projected to sprout up over the next decade, the vast majority will come in fields that currently attract far more women than men. Men dominate only 2 of the top 12 job titles expected to grow the most between 2008 and 2018: construction worker and accountant. The rest, including teachers, registered nurses, home health aides, and customer service reps, remain heavily female. . . . Men, unlike women, still feel limited to a narrow range of acceptable masculine roles—a range that hasn't kept pace with the changing employment landscape."[5]

That landscape may be changing even more for your manopause man than for the average man, since the top ten in-demand jobs in 2010 didn't even exist in 2004. And because mobility is the order of the day, the U.S. Labor Department estimates today's students will have had 10 to 14 jobs by the time they are 38. In any given workplace, half of the employees will have been there for less than five years.[6] This is quite an adjustment for our manopause men. And there is one that is even bigger.

According to a Pew Research Center study released in October of 2010, 22 percent of men are now married to women whose education and income exceed their own.[7] In 2010, for every two men who earned a college degree, three women graduated. Women also became the majority of both the workforce and its management ranks.[8] As the Age of Testosterone ends, your manopause man, who grew up convinced he was a member of the dominant sex, may now be asking himself whether he still holds the keys to economic success in a time when it's not "who you know," it's "what you know," and where size and strength matter less than communication skills and social intelligence.

> *"The best way to appreciate your job*
> *is to imagine yourself without one."*
>
> **— Oscar Wilde**

Who said that it's a man's world? The icing on the cake for your manopause man is the fact that for a male executive who is looking for a new position when he is in his 50s, the odds are stacked against him. Baby boomers, who were convinced that they were the exception to the rules that restricted prior generations, are finding they are just as vulnerable to being without a job as their fathers and grandfathers were before them. Maybe more so, since today's tech-heavy job market is tilted toward students fresh out of college and graduate schools.

It's no wonder manopause men are feeling fearful and insecure. In a global economy, where corporations are competing against countries with younger, cheaper workers, and where joblessness in workers 55 and over is growing, manopause men can be made to feel superfluous, replaceable, and, in the process, possibly emasculated.

### He Takes Manopause to the Workplace

Knowing the intrinsic value of work to your man, you can't help but wonder how he is feeling as he works his way through manopause. For most men, work gives them a sense of mastery, which helps them to forge ahead in the face of life's many challenges. During manopause, they may find increased competition, a questioning of their superiority, and a feeling of fatigue from all of their years of hard work. Or, worse yet, they may find themselves transitioning into lesser responsibility, or even losing their job. How can you help your man to weather these challenges? Start by remembering the many things he derives from his work.

When Sigmund Freud was asked what a normal person should be able to do well, he replied that they should be able to love and to work. But by the time they are reaching manopause, most men have been working for many years. Some of them may still be filled with energy and a thirst for achievement. Some of them may be expanding their focus from a singular need to conquer, to one which includes giving back. In other, less fortunate cases, men may be drained by the years of constant punishment and pressure, and they can lose their drive and their will to win. Or, they may have realized that as hard as they try, they will never make it to the top. Accepting this may be a struggle. In the latter cases, coming to terms with work during the manopause years can be challenging.

## Fearing the Change in Status

Status can mean everything. How many offices of manopause men have you visited where the walls proudly display degrees, newspaper articles, and pictures of them posing with celebrities and politicians? Look again. Some of those politicians and celebrities are no longer in the spotlight, which confirms a man's worst fears: that everyone, including himself, is vulnerable, and that all men are replaceable. This is proof positive that a man's status is ephemeral. Seeing that one minute you're "in" and the next you're "out" can make a man feel very insecure.

*"The harder you work, the harder it is to surrender."*

**— Vince Lombardi**

In an economy rife with corporate restructuring, business failures, and a general sense of job insecurity, even manopause men at the top of the food chain know that the titles they have and the power that comes with them can disappear. They may try to ignore this lack of control because it threatens their self-image as good providers. They may push on, hoping they can win if they can just stay in the game. But somewhere, deep inside, they recognize the possibility of loss. The men who cling most desperately to the dictates of the *man*dates are often the ones in command, who fear that without the power their positions confer, they will be nothing.

Unfortunately, because traditional men have been trained to be the strong and silent caretakers of others, most feel they can't confide the stress they are under to anyone, even you. If you are living with a manopause man, you should keep in mind that one of the things he most dreads is disappointing you and your family. Remember how large a part of his self-esteem is tied up with his work and with his pride in providing for you. If office problems begin to pressure him, reassure him that his worth is far greater than any job he may hold, especially to you.

For a man who is no longer finding satisfaction in his work, manopause can be a difficult and discouraging transition. If his years of labor are not paying off the way he expected, he can feel cheated. He might also feel that he's losing his identity, as the *man*dates encourage men to draw their self-esteem directly from their work. Following these rules, men are afraid that if they can no longer produce at the same high level, they will be seen as failures, and the psychic toll of facing that possibility is a terrible weight on them. With your help he can discover that the income he earns is just *part* of his identity.

Your man might also be concerned about a loss of power. Heeding the *man*dates, most men thrive on the feeling that they are in control of events around them, and that they have the ability to make things happen. Naturally, they are threatened by anything calling that belief into question. One way to assist your manopause man in moving past this is to help him see that external power is something he never fully owned; the only power that is truly his is the one to run his own life in the way that will make him most happy and fulfilled. Reinforce the idea that your man is much more than his job whenever you get the chance. Point out his other good qualities—those he has control over—and help him figure out how to use those in an activity or business enterprise that will give him satisfaction.

One of the other concerns men have is about a loss of income. While this concern is completely legitimate, it is often blown way out of proportion. Men have been consistently taught to measure their worth by the material possessions they have amassed and the financial accomplishments they have achieved. Facing the possibility of those rewards and the recognition that comes with them being lowered can be so daunting to a manopause man that it can affect every part of his life. As Dudley Danoff, M.D., explains, "Next to sexual issues, the areas that affect a man's self-image the most are those having to do with work and money. When a man suffers a financial setback or comes up short in his career goals, his masculinity takes a beating."[9]

To the extent that a man has shame or fear, it can multiply with the size of his fortune. Psychologist Dennis Pearne, Ed.D., tells us that the more money a man has, the greater his worry may be about losing it. His possible loss may prey on his deepest feelings about money: that he didn't deserve it in the first place, or, alternatively, that since he is entitled to his wealth, anger at its loss is perfectly justified.[10] Be aware that for your manopause man, a threat to his earnings may tap into all his former deprivations, both physical and emotional. And do what you can to remind him that physical possessions do not equal happiness. It is the strong man who can remain standing through all hardship, and this is the type of strength and accomplishment you are looking for.

## Reacting to Change in Status

If he is confronting a possible loss of identity, power, or money, your manopause man may find himself fighting fear of mortality, depression, health-related conditions, and other negative behaviors. Men shape so much of their mature lives around their work, if they feel they are no longer appreciated in the workplace, they can begin to wonder what meaning their existence has had.

-------------------------------------------------------------

**TIP:** If your manopause man's energy seems to be ebbing, you might consider whether it has something to do with dissatisfaction at work. If you think it does, encourage him to look inward and honestly assess whether he is happy with his position.

-------------------------------------------------------------

When a man fears a loss of status, he can be very good at hiding his anxiety. The fact that it isn't obvious doesn't mean it isn't there. Once worry sets in, it can distort reality and jumble thinking. It can become more difficult to make decisions, and to avoid mistakes. Performance suffers, which makes his brain alert him that he should worry even more, ramping up a never-ending cycle.

Did you know that fear can be more harmful than reality? Research has unearthed the fact that bad news is actually easier to deal with than irresolution. In studies, people who felt chronically insecure about their jobs reported significantly worse overall health and were more depressed than those who had lost them.[11] If your manopause man is being stressed by work uncertainties, it is time to have an objective talk, and possibly to take action to find out if changes in his work situation are a potential reality, or simply in his imagination.

The other side of this coin is the manopause man who does feel secure about his work but, having done it for decades, is bored by its predictability. Or, he may be burned out if he has driven himself hard to arrive at his spot in the pecking order, without taking proper care of himself emotionally and physically. As the old proverb tells us, "the devil finds work for idle hands." Not knowing what to do with himself, he might respond by slowly drifting off into depression. Or, he might look for new challenges outside the framework of business. If this is your man, he could be open to the excitement of risky behavior, whether it comes in the guise of extreme sports, new women, or excesses in drinking or drugs.

How will you know if a potential change in his work status is hitting your manopause man hard? You may find yourself repeating things, because he doesn't seem to be able to listen as well. He may have less patience and blow up at you and your children over unimportant things. He may even have some physical symptoms like headaches, sleeplessness, rapid heartbeat, and indigestion.

------------------------------------------------

**TIP:** Anxiety is every bit as contagious as the flu, and once you catch it, your tension may build to a point where you can no longer be helpful and supportive to your manopause man. So if you notice any of these symptoms, you should calmly bring them up, talk them over, and perhaps even help your man find professional help, before they infect you, too.

------------------------------------------------

### He Brings the Workplace Home

You've seen it the entire time you've been together: your man's mood at home can change as radically as spring weather changes from sunshine to showers; it all depends on how his day went at work. So it shouldn't surprise you that as he is asked to make adjustments in his professional identity, they can ricochet into his time with you and your family. A manopause man who is preoccupied with career-related problems may be too distracted to pay full attention to the things that are happening at home.

Add to this the fact that slights at work often dredge up emotional pain from his past—pain that was inflicted by members of his family as he grew up. True, his boss might not be his parent, but he or she *is* occupying a similar position of authority. Maybe your manopause man, in his heart of hearts, never really felt that his parents believed in him. And now, in these surprisingly vulnerable years, if his skills are questioned by his superior in any way, his self-doubts can blossom out of proportion, multiplied by his feelings about the past.

You are not his mother, either. But when he is feeling sensitive, something as simple as your tone of voice can push him back into his feelings about being dependent on her or maybe even dominated by her. If this happens, your manopause man can resist anything you have to say, just to prove that he is now self-sufficient. Instead of resenting him for his stubbornness, understand that he has now stepped into a common *man*date: never show weakness, be strong and silent, instead of accepting help. This is the *man*date that makes him afraid to tell you how much stress he is really under at work. He may try to relieve that pressure, while still appearing to be strong, by letting it boil over into anger.

Manopause is a time of life when men can have a very short fuse. The more your partner feels he has sacrificed, the faster he can bristle, at the most surprising times. Men, who have given up much of their lives to fulfill their assigned roles as protectors and providers, can feel as if they are owed for their unwavering unselfishness. That is why they can erupt unexpectedly when they feel they are not getting the full attention they are entitled to.

When Charlie, a CPA, came home late one night after battling with an important client about a tax problem, he found his teenage children fighting over who was getting the car for the night and his wife on the phone, volunteering for a charity event. Charlie blew up, screaming that his dinner wasn't on the table. Everyone was shocked. They couldn't understand his overreaction. They didn't realize that Charlie was expressing a sense of hurt that his hard work and his commitment to providing for them was not being given appropriate recognition.

Worries about competition at work, amassing enough savings for a future retirement, changes in health and family—these, and other things, can shake a man's emotional equilibrium. For most men, work is their most obvious source of power. If they begin to imagine they are being threatened at work by younger people moving up, or by technology that reminds them they are facing the possibility of losing their edge, they can feel weakened and ineffectual.

Granted, you can't always shield your relationship from things that happen in the workplace. But you can prepare yourself to shore up your manopause man, and yourself, to withstand them. You can learn to recognize when he needs help, find ways to encourage him to communicate about his feelings, and steer him toward solutions.

## Where Do Women Fit In?

Manopause can be a time of great challenges in any relationship. Part of that is due to men instinctively fearing that in the eyes of their women, they are replaceable. If she senses he is insecure, or flagging in his role as provider, she may move on to a man who is more capable. In theory, men are right. Many women do have a dream of being married to a husband who brings them both status and a large paycheck. That's what a hero would do. So *you* may have to get real and acknowledge the financial realities of his midlife workplace. Not doing so could put too much strain on him and break both him, and your relationship.

Trust your instincts. They can tell you when your man has doubts about his work. And if he does, you can shore up his belief in himself by assuring him that your love for him is still growing. Try to get him to open up with honesty and intimacy. If he does trust you, help him vocalize his fears. Explain to him that while you are not with him at the office, you suspect things might be going on there that are upsetting him. Confide to him the ways that he is displacing his frustrations with work onto you and his immediate family. In the process, be sure to communicate how his behaviors are making you and your children feel.

### How to Work with a Manopause Man

Maybe you are confronting a manopause man at work, instead of at home. He could be the man you report to in the corner office, or the co-worker in the one next to you. Or, he might be reporting to you. Whichever he is, in order to maneuver around him, you will need to understand something about your different needs and work styles.

## His and Hers at Work

In a study of chimpanzee societies, Frans de Waal, ethnologist and primatologist, observed that females formed "circles of friends," while males built power-based hierarchies.[12] When human females go to work, they are much the same way. Instead of viewing ourselves as isolated entities, we tend to look at our role in the office in terms of our relationships with fellow workers and our place in the organization as a whole. Women at work want to connect with the people around them, have people understand each other, and be appreciated for what they do. Many of us are "good girls," who crave teamwork and harmony in our workplaces.

Men are very different. Dr. Levant explains that they naturally compete, not connect. "At work that's how a man achieves and excels—by competing and going for the win."[13]

One reason our work styles don't match up is because we are socialized very differently. As Gail Evans explains in *Play Like a Man, Win Like a Woman,* girls and boys both play games, but boys play to win, while girls look to games as opportunities to build connections.[14] Boys are pretty clear about it. If they want to improve their friendships, they do that after the game is over. Any boy who has played in a ballgame knows that setbacks can be overcome and momentum can shift. To them, being down on the scorecard is an opportunity to claw their way back up. Girls, on the other hand, who have been encouraged to think that they prove their value by behaving well and bringing home good report cards, can be knocked off balance if they are told they have made mistakes.

Each sex's style can contribute wonderful things to the workplace, but there is one thing you should keep in mind. Since men are still making most of the rules in business, it behooves you to understand how their minds work.

## The Office as a Substitute Family

When you go to the office, you carry your family dynamics with you. A *New York Times* article from December 2008 cut to the heart of it when it said that "workplace roles and the dynamics among colleagues can go much deeper than those somewhat superficial stereotypes, especially in a nation where many people spend as much time with colleagues as they do with their families, where the office so often mirrors the family . . . A boss is not just a boss, in the view of some psychologists; he can be a stand-in for a disapproving and distant father. An unpredictable, easily angered manager can be a thinly veiled rejecting mother. Colleagues competing for the boss's attention are siblings in rivalry."[15] Have you ever noticed that the reaction you feel to some small happening during your workday is vastly out of proportion to what has just transpired? There is a very good chance that it has triggered some underlying feeling you have about your place in your family and the way they treated you in the past.

Working with a manopause man adds yet another layer of complication to the mix. If you are already walking into your office toting fears of a domineering or unpredictable father in your visceral briefcase, interfacing with a manopause man who is irritable, defensive, and feeling his own self-esteem is at risk can be exactly the sort of situation you instinctively want to retreat from. Without thinking, you may fall back on mechanisms that helped you cope, as a child, with threats in similar situations. By doing this, you run the risk of inadvertently re-creating the same sorts of predicaments you lived through as you were growing up. This is why, if you find yourself uncomfortable with your manopause co-worker, you must first look to yourself.

If you are working with a manopause man, you may be starting with some cultural limitations simply due to your nature as a woman. We tend to take things personally. If a man snaps at us, we often assume we did something wrong. In the workplace, if we get a curt answer, we can leap to the conclusion that there is something off base about our ideas, and that notion can fill us with self-doubt. It rarely occurs to us as a first thought that there is something out of kilter with *him*; that he is acting out of his own male life-passage.

As women, who are innately empathetic, we are less comfortable with infighting than the men around us. Not only do our brains lead us to be this way, girls are often taught to be passive, while boys are encouraged to stir the pot and make things happen. We like to avoid arguments, because we want to be perceived as "nice." And on those occasions when we do express anger, we often double back quickly with an apology, attempting to keep our relationships intact, particularly in a work environment. Men, on the other hand, are compartmentalizers, who are much better equipped to draw the line between business and personal relationships, and to understand that disagreements don't necessarily indicate a lack of support and loyalty. They can hear the word *no* as an opportunity, while we perceive it as an indication of our lack of preparation, or a judgment that we aren't perfect.

Some of these female traits are inborn and some of them are socially imprinted on us, but all of them can skew our thinking when we deal with manopause men in the workplace. So as you navigate through your world of work, remember that your distinctly female compass may be sending you in some false directions. Don't allow it to steer you away from dealing with your manopause co-workers in the mode they most clearly understand and respect.

---

**TIP:** Keep in mind that women are generally more sensitive to emotional nuance. So in the work environment, be careful not to read things into a man's comments and physical presentation that he never intended. Be careful not to overthink!

---

Add your personal family dynamic to your universal female traits, and you are truly stirring a jumbled stew. Not too many of us meditate on it, but each of us grew up playing a certain role. As Brian Des Roches, Ph.D., explains, even in the workplace, "people may act out more emotionally based roles that they learned in their families."[16] Your specific part in the play largely depended on the mechanics of the family in which you matured. Maybe you were the super-achiever. You could have been the rescuer or the people-pleaser. Or were you the victim, or the rebel? Don't be surprised if you search for your comfort zone by falling back into your assigned role when faced with an irritable, judgmental manopause co-worker. Your assignment becomes one of recognizing your childhood patterns and learning not to fall back into them, or to overcorrect or overreact because of them. It's easy to see where trouble can arise when we look at Gerri.

Gerri, newly turned 40, was excited about joining the architectural firm that had recently offered her an entry-level position. Her last decades had been spent raising her children, and she was eager to get out into the workplace and put her degree to use. Soon she was on the job, in a cubicle next to a young man who had been hired the year before, both of them working under the guidance of the renowned head of the firm. Within weeks she found herself losing confidence and becoming depressed. Every exchange she had with her boss seemed to point to the fact that in his view, she was coming up short. And while his comments seemed benign on the surface, she imagined that her co-worker saw her as woefully unprepared for her position. It wasn't until she went to her parents' home for her mother's birthday dinner that Gerri realized what was happening. As her father, a university professor, questioned her about her job, his comments consistently pointed out the things she *hadn't* done, instead of the things she was accomplishing. He then switched the conversation, telling her about her older brother's latest promotion. Thinking back, Gerri could see that her feelings were triggered by a lifelong pattern of her father favoring her brother and undercutting her sense of worth and accomplishment. She returned to her job with a new attitude. Instead of filtering her boss's comments through the lens of her father's eyes, she took what he said at face value and used his input to improve her work. And instead of seeing her co-worker as a better-qualified competitor, she saw him as a valuable source of advice on how to work successfully within the firm.

## Blame It on Your Manopause Co-worker

Your male co-workers who are engaged in a manopause struggle are easy to recognize. They are the men who are demanding, yet insecure; judgmental at the same time they are caught up in their own denial; strangely uncommunicative, yet sometimes inappropriately flirtatious. Before you judge them too harshly, remember that just as you are playing a part, so are they. And they play this part all the more fiercely during manopause because they are looking for something familiar in this time of change, confusion, and uncertainty. Men are as locked into family roles as you are. Looking at you, their subconscious minds may refer back to their mothers, their sisters, or even their wives, and their response to you will be shifted according to their feelings about your designated alter ego. So if, at times, you wonder how your manopause co-worker drew certain conclusions about you and your work, ask yourself who you really represent to him.

In their confusion about who they are and where they are going, manopause men may push for more power and grip tightly to the control they already have. Maybe your co-worker is nudging you out of the loop, and intentionally withholding information from you. Look to the source of that behavior, and you will see a traditionally thinking manopause man who is trying to appear strong at your expense. An insecure manopause boss may tell you he is open to all of your ideas, and then push you out his office door if you actually arrive to present them, because he wants to feel too important to deal with your suggestions. He's the man who will keep everyone at a meeting waiting for his arrival, because it is only the "little guys" who are on time.

Another way for a manopause man to reassure himself of his continuing importance at work is by always occupying center stage, being the focus of attention. Who, after all, can see younger talent coming up behind him if he keeps all eyes focused on himself? Is he using ridicule against you? Perhaps that is because he is beginning to worry about losing ground and becoming inferior. And the patronizing manopause man is trying to convince himself that his physical and mental changes aren't real, by implying that he is more experienced and knowledgeable than you are.

Another key indicator of manopause co-workers is depression. If a man is giving you the silent treatment, a passive withdrawal, it may actually be midlife anxiety and stress. And just as at home, depression can evidence itself as anger—anger aimed at you. A third iteration of this syndrome is the paranoid manopause man, who interprets any remark that is not 100 percent behind him as a sign of your potential disloyalty.

Ironically, if the manopause man in question is also the man in charge, he is rarely aware of his behavior and the effects it is having on you and the other people around him. Management consultant and behavior therapist Larry Harmon, Ph.D., of Physicians Development Program, is hired by hospitals to analyze the causes of staff attrition. He explained to us that highly skilled surgeons, normally in the manopause age range, are sure they are beloved by people who work under them. In reality, when interviewed, the staff members reveal these uber-manopause doctors are driving them from their jobs. Often demanding, short-tempered, and disrespectful, these renowned physicians alienate co-workers by dishing out blame and expecting unceasing praise. When the doctors are confronted with this news, they are shocked, having bought into the praise their underlings are giving them. These are unempathetic, insecure manopause men who are trying to maintain their herohood. And the last thing they are willing to hear is that they are the ones causing the staff exodus by being wrong, weak, and mortal. This eye-opening experience doesn't just happen in the medical profession.

Jessica was the longtime assistant to the head of an international business consulting firm. Their working relationship was both cordial and respectful for its first years. But as her superior passed through his 50s, things began to change. To her embarrassment, instead of discussing her suggestions, he would publicly override her and point out only the ideas he disagreed with. Instead of giving her credit for suggestions he liked, he would take it for himself. And when things went wrong for him, he would vent his frustration on her. Jessica, who was raising a family and needed her job, held her tongue. Until the day her boss asked her to give some comments to the editor of a business journal that was writing an article on him. Although she knew she was taking a risk, she also knew that she couldn't continue working in the environment he had created. She replied that she probably shouldn't talk to the editor; her boss might not like what she would say. This was an eye-opening revelation for her boss. It gave him the incentive to take Jessica to lunch, where she was able to explain how she was experiencing their working relationship. Luckily, he took what she said to heart. While their interaction isn't perfect, Jessica, by being honest, managed to open the door enough so that when her boss steps over the line, she can point it out to him and be heard.

## Knowing When You Have a Manopause Work Problem

At what point should you decide that trying to work with a manopause man may be futile? Step back and take an objective look at yourself. Are you stuck in old role-play patterns? Are you losing your creativity? Is your productivity falling? Are you continuing to fight similar battles with the man in question, and predictably losing them? Do you spend your hours at the office feeling nervous and disrespected? Do you go home feeling discouraged and angry, without any specific cause?

If this describes you, you are not only frustrating yourself, you are wasting your time and talent. Tackling your office manopause problem, learning how to avoid the potential traps, and then deciding whether it makes more sense for you to go or stay can reenergize your work life and restore your sense of adventure and fun on the job.

## How to Handle Your Manopause Work Problem

If you are working with a manopause man, the first thing you might want to do is reframe your mind-set. Don't take it personally if you are feeling singled out and picked on. The *man*dates encourage men to hide their self-doubts behind a shield of machismo, and if that fails, to blame the people around them for much of what is going wrong. Are you feeling isolated and out of his loop? Everyone likes to edit the people around them in a way that makes them feel comfortable. And for men, they are often most at ease surrounded by their own sex.

Understand that one sure way to place yourself directly in the crosshairs of a psychologically vulnerable manopause co-worker is by challenging his ego. To you, self-esteem may be more about building relationships than having your name on the letterhead. But to him, it is all about tangible rewards and keeping score. Men like to be perceived as masters of their environments, at midlife even more than before. Every time *you* look like a winner at work, your manopause co-worker may wonder whether *he* is the loser, and has slipped a rung down the ladder.

So if you *are* "winning" at work, remember that manopause men worry a great deal about how people are seeing them, and they tend to keep careful track of the amount of respect they are receiving. Be happy you are achieving good things, but be careful about celebrating your triumphs in ways that seem to be at his expense. Men who are worried about how they are being evaluated can react defensively. There is no reason to deliberately put yourself in his line of fire.

Let's say that despite your best efforts in the workplace, you *do* end up in the line of fire. You can either retreat, whimpering, or you can dig down for new levels of strength. If he plays games trying to embarrass you in front of others, or hoping to diminish your status, the best way to react is not to. If you go on about your business, refusing to be manipulated, he is the one who will be reduced in the eyes of the people around you.

Hopefully, instead of spending your days in the office steering clear of your manopause co-worker, you can sit down and negotiate a new working relationship. This will not only be good for your work life, it will help clear your head, since confronting and dealing with your anxiety is a much better way to lessen your discomfort than bottling it up inside.

As Gail Evans points out in *Play Like a Man, Win Like a Woman,* the best way for you to handle your manopause work problems is with self-confidence. Approach the meeting with a plan. Men have learned from the games they play that the way to win is by developing a strategy, and you should do that, too. Know ahead of time exactly what it is you want to walk away with. Instead of worrying about proving that you're right, be prepared to accept partial blame for the situation. You are both acting out childhood roles in ways that have been counterproductive, so don't focus on past problems; instead, propose solutions. Understand ahead of time the thoughts you want your manopause co-worker to walk away with, and be prepared to communicate them succinctly. Remember, men aren't wired to have long, self-examining discussions; they are aimed straight at the goal. And don't regurgitate his manopause behavior back to him; that will only make him more defensive.

If you are feeling wary of this conversation, ask yourself why you are letting your manopause co-worker have such influence over your feelings. Most probably it has less to do with him than it has to do with your own outdated family patterns. So leave them behind, take charge of your destiny, and feel empowered to make the kinds of choices you were too afraid to risk as a child.

Even if you are well prepared, you may find that trying to change the workplace behavior of your manopause co-worker is an impossible dream. This can be a lot like an unsatisfying midlife marriage—you now have the choice of staying, stewing and grumbling; or gracefully moving on. Consider this. If you are feeling abused, chances are that other people you work with are as well. And though you might try to detach yourself emotionally from the situation, their disappointment and anger can infect you.

------------------------------------------------------------

**TIP:** If you want to have a balanced and happy life, this might be a good time to head for the door. This is especially true if 1) you find yourself settling for a lower quality of work, 2) you lack the energy to keep moving at a productive pace, or 3) you want to call in sick for questionable reasons.

------------------------------------------------------------

A manopause man may think that he wins by holding on to his territory and refusing to give ground. But as a woman, you know that he won't necessarily be the player who has the most marbles at the end of the game. The real object of playing is to feel good about yourself and proud of what you do.

## Reshaping the Way Your Manopause Man Looks at Work

*"There's a time when you have to separate yourself from what other people expect of you, and do what you love, because if you find yourself 50 years old, and you aren't doing what you love, then what's the point?"*

**— Jim Carrey**

When the rules he has labored under begin to subtly shift as your man enters midlife, it can shake his foundations and send shock waves through your family, as well as through his "family" of co-workers. Some manopause men find themselves feeling "unmoored" as they transition into the second halves of their work lives. This is a very

251

unsettling sensation for them, but it's one that doesn't necessarily have to happen—not if we help our men to reshape their understanding of the place and significance of work in their lives.

Your partner is starting with some strikes against him as he tries to shift his thinking about work. While it is no longer as directly linked to survival as it was in eons past, remember the culture still values men more for what they do than for who they are. You can add to this an unfortunate stereotype that as a man ages, the "worker side" of him becomes less productive. Reassure your man that studies show these assumptions are far from the truth. *The New York Times Magazine* reported in December 2009 on a study that pitted men over age 50 against men under 30.[17] They were tested on risk taking, competitiveness, and cooperation. The "over 50s" more than held their own. As the article explained, "Older workers don't suffer from the deficiencies that a lot of people think they do." In fact, Malcolm Knowles, an authority on adult learning, tells us that from adulthood to middle age, men's ability to learn does not decrease. Any declines that tests do show may simply be due to the fact that manopause men's motivation and goals are shifting. Gary Small, M.D., concurs, and explains, "When we reach middle age, there's a sweet spot where our brain cells are actually firing more rapidly than they do when they're younger."[18]

Point this out to your manopause man and remind him of the wonderful plasticity of the brain, which continues to remodel itself on a continuing basis. Let your partner know that men who make a habit of thinking affirmatively can reinforce and permanently change their brain's tendency to automatically do just that. A continuing interest and excitement about life, developing new passions, and learning new things, can help him harness greater cognitive powers and foster stronger brain pathways. These pathways can aid him in reaching solutions faster and being more effective in the workplace. Psychiatrist Oliver Sacks, M.D., wrote in a *New York Times* editorial in January 2011 that "by simply thinking about an old problem in a new way, all of us can find ways to stimulate our brains to grow."

Our growing understanding of the brain's plasticity is just one factor in what seems to be a trend; manopause men are working longer and better than ever before. You can chalk it up to longer life spans and continuing consumption, or the energy the baby boomers have provided. But a recent report from the *Rand Review* tells us that "Americans have reversed a century-long trend toward early retirement and have raised their workforce participation rates."[19] New websites, like Jobs4.0, aimed at mature workers over the age of 40, are multiplying and flourishing. And one out of every three people who formerly worked for someone else is now his or her own boss. The even more exciting news for your manopause man is that this is all to the good. In 2010, cross-national data from 13 developed countries showed a correlation between postponed retirement and the delay of cognitive declines. In other words, "working" will keep his brain "working."[20] As we move toward a new economy, with service- and technology-based jobs replacing work that requires physical strength, there's a better chance than ever that if your manopause man truly wants to continue to work, he will be able to find avenues that lead him there.

### Working on the Future

Manopause is the time of life when a man should catch his breath, look inside, and reassess his notions of the kind of work that will let him live more richly through his next phase. Perhaps that reassessment will tell him that he is still challenged and invigorated by his career. He may find that it really suits him. His accomplishments may be giving him great pleasure and internally empowering him. In the best case, he can imagine himself continuing to enjoy and reap rich rewards from his work for many years to come.

If your manopause man is not so lucky, it may be time for him to break free of the preconceived *man*date notions about work and to take a hard look at what would give him true inner satisfaction. After absorbing the concept that his job is what he does, not who he is, he can have the opportunity to transition into a whole new level of growth and awareness. He may even discover passions he didn't know he possessed.

*"We make a living by what we get, but
we make a life by what we give."*

**— Winston Churchill**

At midlife, many men discover a very gratifying experience by taking the expertise they have amassed, and sharing it with someone who wants to learn. This new "work" encompasses giving back, helping others, and passing on knowledge. Instead of abandoning everything he has done up to this point, your manopause man can add to it in self-fulfilling ways. If this possibility interests him, help him to transition into it by figuring out what about his present work is still vitally important to him, and what can be dropped or changed. This can be a difficult analysis. But done successfully, it can move him toward his next successful phase in life. Compromise is key to the process. Keep in mind that when your manopause man abandons one goal, it is easier to move on if there is another goal already in mind. Help him understand that quitting an old and outworn goal may display more courage than staying and trying to fight a losing battle. Leaving it behind, he will feel a sense of accomplishment; a sense of success.

Beyond mentoring, the world of volunteering is on the rise, and midlife men are fully participating in giving of themselves. In 2009, President Obama signed into law the expansion of the AmeriCorps Nation program for community service, providing for a more than tripling of the number of federally sponsored community service volunteers in areas of health care, education, clean energy, and conservation.[21] Whether it is giving back to the community through volunteering or choosing a second career to share expertise, helping others makes midlife men feel good. So does finally fulfilling long-held dreams.

*"No man has ever risen to the real stature of spiritual
manhood until he has found that it is finer to serve
somebody else than it is to serve himself."*

**— T. Woodrow Wilson**

## New Roads Can Be Good Roads

Various services are popping up to give people an on-the-job taste of what it would be like if they were to change their careers and pursue something that has only been a dream. And many companies are now offering programs that pay for employees to receive an education while working. In 2010 it was reported that approximately 50 companies nationwide offered employee-controlled education accounts. This gives new meaning to "learning on the job." Partially as a result of this, college enrollment for midlife students is up. The administrators from Johns Hopkins University, Dartmouth College, and the University of Oklahoma estimate that more than 10 percent of liberal arts graduate students are now over 55. All of this is contributing to a growth spurt in businesses started by Americans over 55.[22] A study performed by Babson College and Baruch College says that they were responsible for starting 18.9 percent of all new businesses in 2008, compared to just 10 percent in 2001.[23] And the highly respected career of teaching, also known as the "Power Hobby," is also a choice people make to pass forward their experience and expertise.[24]

---

**TIP:** There are many options for online learning too. Some of the world's top universities, including Stanford, Harvard, and MIT, are offering free online classes. Encourage your man to check out what's available.

---

## *"Working" on Your Manopause Man's Happiness*

Moving into a new phase of his work life can be a wonderful thing for your manopause man if he approaches it with an open, honest mind and heart. Maybe he will find that his decades of nose-to-the-grindstone working have kept him from enjoying artistic aspects of his personality that he never knew were in him. He could unearth community-based passions. And surely he will learn, with your help, that he can feel indispensible to your family in ways other than just financially providing for them. Perhaps he will do this by expending more of himself in relating to his children and nurturing them. In the best of all possible worlds, newfound emotional intelligence will help him teach those children a better set of "work rules" than the ones he was raised on.

There is a misperception that material success provides happiness. Hundreds of studies have shown that once basic needs have been met, additional monetary success does not add to people's sense of well-being. Someone who gains stature simply through the material objects he accumulates is always on shaky ground. Even the most hard-gained possessions can be easily lost. They don't bring about the good feelings in the heart that come from giving to someone or receiving from them.

So what should his new definition of success be? Your man should be striving to win respect for the things that last: his experience, his integrity, and his generosity of spirit. Your female wisdom needs to teach him that the greatest respect he can gain is generated by his personal feelings about himself, not by acceptance from others. Then he will understand that the fastest way he can lose respect is if he values his peers' opinions of his worth more than his own.

Happiness comes from within. Your manopause man should be trying to find that very happiness and peace inside himself as he goes through his period of change. To do so, he may have to look deeper and more spiritually at the meaning of his life and at his purpose for being on this earth. You know your manopause man well. You have learned how full his reservoirs of innate characteristics and behaviors, both negative and positive, are. Using that information, and listening from your heart, you can help him look honestly at his work life and understand that it isn't *what he does* that makes him who he is; it is fully understanding *who he is* that will help him find his happiness.

# YOUR NEW
# AND IMPROVED
# **MANOPAUSE MAN**

The *man*dates are rules, but unlike the Ten Commandments, they are not divine, unchangeable, or graven in stone. The *man*dates are cultural—the product of human thought and action. And reconfiguring them, even disobeying them, might be more of a gift than a transgression. The rules that the *man*dates enforce on your manopause man are confining, damaging, and limiting. They put his "feeling self" in a collision with the culture every day, as he strives to prove his manhood. That is why they need to be changed.

Now that you have a better understanding of what your manopause man is going through, you can bring your female brain, the brain that is so much more attuned to feeling and experiencing emotions, to bear, and show him that the *man*dates are made of malleable clay. They can be stretched and reworked without shattering. And like clay, the more they are manipulated in your warm women's hands, the stronger and truer they will become. The way for you to start the process is by helping him redefine his "manhood."

## Redefining Your Manopause Man's Manhood

*"We don't receive wisdom; we must discover it for ourselves after a journey that no one can take for us or spare us."*

**— Marcel Proust**

Help your manopause man take the "wise" road on the journey ahead. Hopefully it will be long and extremely satisfying. He should not pit his wishful superior strength against the reality of his physical maturity; his yearning for immortality against the actuality of his mortality; his *man*date heroism against his true vulnerability. These conflicts intrinsically involve loss of control and set him up for failure. But heroes can't fail. Help him reinvent his manhood in different and more positive terms, ones that allow him to be back in control. That way he can feel triumphant.

This is a heroic task, one that takes endurance, innovation, creativity, fortitude, inner strength, and conviction. At midlife, when his manhood is being challenged to its utmost, you have been given an opportunity to encourage your manopause man's true strength to flourish. Help him spread his wings, rise like a phoenix, and soar. As Dr. Gary Small told us, the mature brain is stronger, thanks to more life experience and more emotional maturity. And because of that, your manopause man is primed to redefine his manhood. He just may need a push from you.

Inspire him to try. There is absolutely no downside to your man reexamining who he is, what is important to him at this stage of his life, and what can be discarded. These are things that if he were to look at them honestly would have very little meaning to him. Refocusing his mind-set can be achieved. Dr. Louann Brizendine says, "We can use our intelligence and determination both to celebrate and when necessary to change the effects of sex hormones on brain structure, behavior, reality, creativity, and destiny."[1] If your manopause man is aware that the biology of his brain is responsible for driving his impulses, and he doesn't like what he is doing, then he can choose to act differently. It is in his power; he has the ability and the freedom to change for the better.

Your manopause man should begin by truly accepting that change is inevitable. He can find control in the way that change is handled. He should examine how the culture influences every move he makes, and how the manopause years act as a magnifier of society's dictates. With this insight, he can then work on changing the way he interprets the things that are happening in his life.

Encourage your man to envision life not as a mountain, which at midlife turns into a slippery, uncontrolled slope toward death, but as a basketball game. Halftime simply represents the end of his first adulthood and the beginning of his second. Like any game, the second half can be both more thrilling, and more rewarding.

Unfortunately, our society has not fully adjusted to the reality of today's men living longer and more productively. Your manopause man needs to rise above this outdated and damaging thinking in order to maintain his confidence and inner strength. He must always keep in mind that how he plays in the second half of the game of life can make all the difference to the outcome.

## The New and Improved Mandates for Your Manopause Man

Strive for goals? Maintain control? Be strong? Remain a hero? Your manopause man can achieve all of these *man*date requirements by reexamining those terms. By doing so, he can pass through midlife constructively, rediscovering who he is and what is most important to him. So in the hope of helping him redefine his manhood, we are proposing a new and improved set of *man*dates:

1. Find your authentic self

2. Accept change

3. Become emotionally intelligent

4. Reconsider the definition of strength

5. Be your healthiest self

6. Rethink sex to include emotional intimacy

7. Redefine your definition of success

8. Discover deeper meaning and intimacy in relationships

You've learned about each and every one of these as you've worked your way through *Manopause,* but we thought it would be helpful to spell them out—to put them in the spotlight for you to refer back to as reminders. Please keep in mind that these *man*dates are continually evolving, as our world is constantly changing. It is imperative to recognize they are not carved in stone; they are merely suggestions to get you and your manopause man discussing ways to rethink his "manhood."

## Some Simple Suggestions for You

Take advantage of this time of change by seizing the opportunity to model a new and deeper form of intimacy between the two of you. Keep in mind both of your deep human needs, the types of intimacy you can include in your lives together, and the levels of communication that will get you there.

As you maneuver through midlife with your manopause man, you need to monitor your own actions and be aware of how they are contributing, both negatively and positively, to his voyage. With the deck rocking under him, this can be a challenging journey. Do your best not to complicate it.

Women have inquisitive minds. Our curiosity throws us in myriad directions, while our men's minds work in a more linear, systematized way. You are in a wonderful position to bring information back to your man that provides him with a clear picture of what is happening to him, both physically and mentally. Thanks in part to his hormonal decline, his desire to connect to you is more alive than ever. Take advantage of that.

But before you can jump into action, you have to be aware of where you stand. How can you expect your man to change his thinking if you don't change yours? It's time to shed your own traditional *man*dates, the limiting ones that stifle forward growth and thinking. Throw away those impediments that have been imbedded in your mind since you were a girl. Like the one that says he alone must be the "superhero" for your family. It is time for you to gain the confidence in yourself to free him from that pressure.

At first he may not want to talk about manopause. Be sensitive to the possibility that he is feeling humiliated or flawed when you suggest ideas that you believe will help him. Try to identify with the frustration he is experiencing, consciously or not, as he hides what he is really feeling in the hope that he will continue to appear strong and Herculean to his family, to his peers, and most important, to you. Show him you accept his shortcomings and welcome his honesty. Be patient with him. Lifting the pressure of your expectations and his own will help him stand taller. Instead of letting him fall back on defense mechanisms, encourage him to accept the caring feelings, from you and from others that will, very often, fill him with positive energy and produce worthwhile results.

When your manopause man seems down or distant, tread carefully while trying to cheer him up. In his mind, he may feel you are minimizing the seriousness of his concerns. Help him open up. Be his sounding board. Allow him to tell you how he feels. Enable him to express his feelings by encouraging him to use his emotional vocabulary, particularly words that help to evoke positive emotions.

Never forget the differences between your brain and your man's brain. Approach your communication in a way that takes advantage of your man's gender traits. Be prepared with real-life facts and scientific information to back up what you are telling him. Don't let your eagerness to talk override his attempts to communicate. Observing these guidelines lets you present things in a way that resonates with him, without threatening him. Reframe your goal; it isn't to change him. He is different than you, and always will be. Isn't that what you want? Be content to know where those differences lie, so that you can work around them when a gender-based conflict arises.

Frame your suggestions as compliments. Consistently show your appreciation for your manopause man's positive actions, before you point out the things he might want to change. He should always feel your love and support. Compliment even the smallest things. When the urge to criticize comes over you, consider why you are about to say something negative. Is it to benefit him, or simply to make your own life more convenient and pleasant? Analyzing your authentic motivation can help you moderate your words to achieve the positive effect you are hoping for.

As your manopause man digs deep down into introspection and expresses his vulnerabilities, send him the message that you are with him no matter what he confides, and that nothing he is telling you makes you fear that he is falling apart. To the contrary: you are impressed and proud of the strength he is showing by attempting to face his demons and reveal them to you.

Use your love, understanding, and empathy to build a platform from which he can grow, and your love relationship can flourish. The most satisfying relationships require complete honesty and vulnerability. As he opens up in the most intimate of shared moments, he will learn to form real trust with you that will lead to deep bonds; a true connection.

Pace yourself as your manopause man readjusts his outlook. Be careful not to push him too far or too fast in any direction; it could backfire by causing him to resist. Understand that the process of moving into a new set of *man*dates will take time. It will be an imperfect journey, but one that is going to surprise you in ways that make it well worth taking.

Always remember that while your manopause man may be working to find his way, so are you. Use these unprecedented ideas to help free your manopause man from the stale traditions of the past, to help him maintain the undeniably irresistible, eternal manhood qualities you love, and help him move forward into a deeply felt and richly fulfilling future.

And, finally, spread the new *man*dates. Our men live almost twice as long as they used to. With every passing day, we are increasing our scientific awareness of what men experience both physically and mentally, in ways that let us understand them more deeply, and relish them fully for each of those added years.

It is our hope that *Manopause* has given you knowledge and a new way of thinking that you can use to "survive his changing life." Take what you have discovered in this book, and pass it forward. Talk to friends, raise your children with it in mind, communicate your newly formed perspective to all those you care about, and encourage a culture-wide change in outlook. Share this new way of living alongside your manopause man with the women you care for and respect. You will be giving a gift to the men you love, and to everyone around you. Helping people accept the new *man*dates will encourage a shift in the cultural canvas so that we all can have richer and more gratifying lives with our manopause men.

# ENDNOTES

## Chapter Two: What It Means to "Be a Man"

1. Gilmore, *Manhood in the Making,* 12.

2. Ibid., 11.

3. Ibid., 17.

4. Kindlon, Thompson, *Raising Cain,* 79.

5. Ibid.

6. Gurian, *What Could He Be Thinking?,* 63.

7. Ibid.

8. Interview with Heidi Kraft, Ph.D., *CNN Newsroom,* aired May 12, 2009, http://edition.cnn.com/transcripts/0905/12/cnr.02.html.

9. Diamond, *The Irritable Male Syndrome,* 112.

10. Dabbs, *Heroes, Rogues, and Lovers,* 84.

11. Ibid., 142.

12. Ibid., 141.

13. Ibid., 129.

14. Andrew Sullivan, "The He Hormone," *The New York Times Magazine,* April 2, 2000. http://www.nytimes.com/2000/04/02/magazine/the-he-hormone.html?pagewanted=all&src=pm.

15. Brizendine, *The Female Brain,* 5.

16. Carol Mithers, "The Male Brain: What's Really Going On in There," Oprah.com, (August 2009): Oprah.com/relationships/Understanding-the-Male-Brain.

17. Dozier, Jr., *Fear Itself,* 28.

18. Ibid., 30.

19. Baron-Cohen, *The Essential Difference,* 1.

20. Ibid., 2.

21. Ibid., 5.

22. Gurian, *What Could He Be Thinking?,* 11.

23. Brizendine, *The Female Brain,* 128.

24. Ibid., 120–121.

25. Ibid., 125.

26. Maura Dolan, "UC Berkeley police say girls' demeanor, appearance raised suspicions about Phillip Garrido," *The Los Angeles Times,* August 28, 2009: http://latimesblogs.latimes.com/lanow/2009/08/uc-berkeley-police-say-girls-demeanor-appearance-raised-suspicions.html.

27. Amen, *The Brain in Love,* 86–87.

28. Levant, Ed.D, ABPP, *Masculinity Reconstructed,* 8–13; and Michael Kimmel, Ph.D., "Interview: Michael Kimmel, Ph.D.," PBS, http://www.pbs.org/kued/nosafeplace/interv/kimmel.html.

29. Steven Leder, "God's Loneliest Creatures," *Reform Judaism* magazine.

## Chapter Three: The Manopause Problem

1. *Harvard Health Letter,* Harvard Medical School, July 2006.

2. Daniel D. Federman, M.D., and Geoffrey A. Walford, M.D., "Is Male Menopause Real?" *Newsweek,* January 15, 2007: 46–48.

3. Sheehy, *New Passages,* 313.

4. Tan, *The Andropause Mystery,* 9.

5. Ibid.

6. Bernard Fallon, M.D., *Erectile Dysfunction: Frequently Asked Questions,* http://www.uihealthcare.com/topics/medicaldepartments/urology/erectiledysfunction/index.html.

7. Dozier, Jr., *Fear Itself,* 3.

8. Ibid., 11.

9. Ibid., 129.

10. Ibid., 207.

11. Sheehy, *Understanding Men's Passages,* 69.

12. Ibid., 152.

13. Dozier, Jr., *Fear Itself,* 209.

## Chapter Four: Good Men, Bad Behavior

1. Levant, *Masculinity Reconstructed,* 84.

2. Dozier, Jr., *Fear Itself,* 132.

3. "Denial," Encyclopedia of Mental Disorders, 2007–2012, http://www .minddisorders.com/Del-Fi/Denial.html.

4. Michael Winerip, "They Warned Us About You," *The New York Times*, January 23, 2009, http://www.nytimes.com/2009/01/25/fashion /25winerip.html?_r=1&page20wanted=all.

5. Michael Winerip, "Doc, Make Me New Again, *The New York Times*, February 13, 2009, http://www.nytimes.com/2009/02/15/fashion /15generationb.html?pagewanted=All.

6. D'Vera Cohn and Paul Taylor, "Baby Boomers Approach Age 65—Glumly," Pew Research Center Publications, December 20, 2010, http://pew research.org/pubs/1834/baby-boomers-old-age-downbeat-pessimism.

## Chapter Five: Your Manopause Man's Emotional Awakening

1. Levant, *Masculinity Reconstructed,* 152.

2. Ibid., 78–79.

3. Pink, *A Whole New Mind,* 165.

4. Ibid., 159.

5. Brizendine, *The Female Brain,* 4.

6. Gurian, *What Could He Be Thinking?,* 94.

7. "Emotional Flooding: How Do We Stop the Conflict?" Wellsphere, April 23, 2009, http://www.wellsphere.com/relationships-sex-article /emotional-flooding-how-do-we-stop-the-conflict/654347.

8. Robert A. Emmons and Michael E. McCullough, "Counting Blessings Versus Burdens: An Experimental Investigation of Gratitude and Subjective Well-Being in Daily Life," *Journal of Personality and Social Psychology* 84, no. 2 (2003): 377–389.

9. Timothy Smith, Michael McCullough, and Justin Poll, "Religiousness and Depression: Evidence for a Main Effect and the Moderating Influence of Stressful Life Events," *Psychological Bulletin* 129, no. 4 (2003): 614–636.

10. John Tierney, "For Good Self-Control, Try Getting Religious About It," *The New York Times,* December 29, 2008, http://www.nytimes.com /2008/12/30/science/30tier.html.

11. Jeremy K. Kark, M.D., Ph.D., et al, "Does Religious Observance Promote Health? Mortality in Secular vs. Religious Kibbutzim in Israel," *American Journal of Public Health* 86, no. 3 (March 1996): 341–346.

12. Jon Kabat-Zinn, "Opening to Our Lives: Jon Kabat-Zinn's Science of Mindfulness," American Public Media, On Being, April 16, 2009, http://being.publicradio.org/programs/2009/opening-to-our-lives.

13. "Is Meditation Push-Ups for the Brain?" *UCLA Medicine* (Fall/Winter 2001): 2.

14. Jane Brody, "Biological Role of Emotional Tears Emerges Through Recent Studies," *The New York Times,* August 31, 1982, http://www.nytimes.com/1982/08/31/science/biological-role-of-emotional-tears-emerges-through-recent-studies.html?pagewanted=all.

15. Jane Brody, "Personal Health," *The New York Times,* February 22, 1984, http://www.nytimes.com/1984/02/22/garden/personal-health-002144.html?pagewanted=all.

16. Leder, "God's Loneliest Creatures."

17. Sue Shellengbarger, "Beyond Facebook: the Benefits of Deeper Friendships," *The Wall Street Journal,* November 9, 2010, http://online.wsj.com/article/SB10001424052748704635704575604353719548676.html.

18. Danoff, *Penis Power,* 62.

## Chapter Six: Emotions and Behaviors Go from Bad to Worse

1. Mayo Clinic staff, "Male Depression: Understanding the Issues," MayoClinic.com, November 15, 2008, http://www.mayoclinic.com/health/male-depression/MC00041.

2. Bob Murray, Ph.D., "Facts About Male Depression," Uplift Program, August 5, 2005, http://www.upliftprogram.com/facts_depression_men.html.

3. Mayo Clinic Staff, "Anger Management: Your Questions Answered," Mayo Clinic.com, http://www.mayoclinic.com/health/anger-management/MH00075.

4. "Anger and Hostility Harmful to the Heart, Especially Among Men," *ScienceDaily,* March 9, 2009, http://www.sciencedaily.com/releases/2009/03/090309191505.htm.

5. Mayo Clinic Staff, "Anger Management: Your Questions Answered."

6. Robert T. Zackery, "Anger Management: Recognize and Understand Unhealthy Behaviors," CNN.com, July 18, 2005, http://cgi.cnn.com/HEALTH/library/MH/00075.html.

7. Mary Ann Moon, "Antidepressant use doubles in less than 10 years," *Skin and Allergy News,* September 2009, http://www.skinandallergynews.com/index.php?id=372&cHash=071010&tx_ttnews[tt_news]=4337.

8. Speaking of Faith with Krista Tippet, "Opening to Our Lives: Jon Kabat-Zinn's Science of Mindfulness," National Public Radio, April 16, 2009, http://being.publicradio.org/programs/2009/opening-to-our-lives/transcript.shtml.

9. Dozier, Jr., *Fear Itself,* 210.

10. Karen Kaplan, "Your Whole World Smiles with You," *Los Angeles Times,* December 5, 2008: A1.

11. Martin Seligman, "Learned Helplessness Guru Martin Seligman quotes," Self Development Centre, http://www.kigem.com/en/content .asp?bodyID=21.

## Chapter Seven: Testosterone and Your Manopause Man

1. Joe Spataro interview with Robert Tan, M.D., http://pinksunrise.com /mta/tan.htm

2. Sharon H. Fitzgerald, "Male Menopause: Fact or Myth?," *Medical News, Inc.,* May 23, 2011, http://www.medicalnewsinc.com/male-menopause-fact-or-myth-cms-356.

3. Janice Willingham, "Why Men Can Have Hot Flashes, Too," http: //ezinearticles.com/?Why-Men-Can-Have-Hot-Flashes-Too&id=763745.

4. M. M. Shores et al., "Low Testosterone Is Associated with Decreased Function and Increased Mortality Risk: A Preliminary Study of Men in a Geriatric Rehabilitation Unit," *Journal of the American Geriatrics Society* 52, no. 12 (December 2004): 2077–2081.

5. The Impact of Low Testosterone in Chronic Diseases, presentation at the American Association of Clinical Endocrinologists, 2003 Annual Meeting and Clinical Congress.

6. M. M. Shores et al., "Increased Incidence of Diagnosed Depressive Illness in Hypogonadal Older Men," *Archives of General Psychiatry* 61, no. 2 (February 2004):162–167.

7. Elizabeth Barrett-Connor et al., "Bioavailable Testosterone and Depressed Mood in Older Men: The Ranch Bernardo Study," *Journal of Clinical Endocrinology and Metabolism* 84, no. 2 (February 1999): 573–577.

8. "Testosterone and Aging: Clinical Research Directions," Institute of Medicine of the National Academies (November 11, 2003): http:// www.iom.edu/Reports/2003/Testosterone-and-Aging-Clinical-Research-Directions.aspx.

9. J. G. Rabkin et al., "A Double-Blind, Placebo-Controlled Trial of Testosterone Therapy for HIV-Positive Men with Hypogonadal Symptoms," *Archives of General Psychiatry* 57, no. 2 (February 2000): 141–147.

10. Sheehy, *New Passages,* 203.

11. Ibid.

12. Shannon Brownlee and Jeanne Lenzer, "Do I Have Cancer?" The New York Times Magazine, October 9, 2011: 43.

13. E-mail correspondence, April 6, 2011.

14. Mayo Clinic, DHEA, http://www.mayoclinic.com/health/dhea/NS _patient-dhea

## Chapter Eight: Manopause Sex, His Penis, and Your Relationship

1. Berkowitz, *He's Just Not Up for It Anymore,* 130.

2. National Survey of Sexual Health and Behavior, Center for Sexual Health Promotion, School of Health, Physical Education, and Recreation, Indiana University, Bloomington.

3. Amen, *Sex on the Brain,* 12.

4. Brizendine, *The Female Brain,* 5.

5. Danoff, *Penis Power,* 113.

6. Lisa Belkin, "Your Old Man," *The New York Times Magazine,* April 5, 2009, http://www.nytimes.com/2009/04/05/magazine/05wwln-lede-t.html.

7. Myron I. Murdock, M.D., F.A.C.S, "What is Male Erectile Dysfunction or Impotence?," http://advancetherapynetwork.com/health/erectile_dysfunction/index.html.

8. Katherine Esposito et al., "Effects of Intensive Lifestyle Change on Erectile Dsyfunction in Men," *The Journal of Sexual Medicine* 6, no. 1 (January 2009): 243–250.

9 John Hanc, "In America's Gyms, More Than a Touch of Gray," *The New York Times,* March 4, 2010: F7.

10. Charlotte E. Grayson Mathis, M.D., reviewed "Want Better Sex? Stop Smoking," WebMD feature, http://men.webmd.com/features/want-better-sex.

11. Danoff, *Penis Power,* 144.

12. Kindlon, *Raising Cain,* 209.

13. A. B. O'Donnell et al., "The Health of Normally Aging Men: The Massachusetts Male Aging Study (1987–2004)," *Experimental Gerontology* 39, no. 7 (July 2004): 975–984.

14. Sheehy, *Understanding Men's Passages,* 186.

15. Ibid., 184.

16 Ibid., 186.

17. Ibid., 184.

18. John E. Morley, M.D., "Impotence," Cyberounds, http://www.cyberounds.com/cmecontent/art94.html?pf=yes.

19. Sheehy, New Passages, 201.

20. A. B. O'Donnell et al., "The Health of Normally Aging Men: The Massachusetts Male Aging Study (1987–2004)," *Experimental Gerontology* 39, no. 7 (July 2004): 975–984.

21. E. O. Laumann et al., "Sexual Dysfunction in the United States: Prevalence and Predictors," *Journal of the American Medical Association* 281, no. 13 (April 7, 1999): 1174.

22. Gillick, *The Denial of Aging,* 3.

23. Spark, *Sexual Health for Men,* 108.

24. Boteach, *The Kosher Sutra,* 5.

## Chapter Nine: Intimacy with Your Manopause Man

1.  Smalley, *Secrets to Lasting Love,* 210.

2.  Fisher, Helen, Ph.D., "How to Build Intimacy in Your Relationship," *O, The Oprah Magazine,* October 2009.

3.  "Types of Intimacy," University of Florida Counseling and Wellness Center, http://www.counseling.ufl.edu/cwc/types-of-intimacy.aspx.

4.  Smalley, *Secrets to Lasting Love,* 28.

5.  Sheehy, *New Passages,* 313.

6.  Catharine Paddock, Ph.D., "Scientists Find Gene That Affects Pair-Bonding Behaviour in Men," September 4, 2008, http://www.medicalnews today.com/articles/120395.php (accessed March 12, 2012).

## Chapter Ten: Family Matters at Manopause

1.  Sean Macaulay, "Dad-olescence: The New Midlife Crisis," *The Daily Beast,* October 27, 2009, http://www.thedailybeast.com /articles/2009/10/27/dadolescence-the-new-midlife-crisis.html.

2.  Kindlon, *Raising Cain,* 107.

3.  Evans, *The Divide,* 88.

4.  Kindlon, *Raising Cain,* 94.

5.  Levant, *Masculinity Reconstructed,* 260.

6.  Elizabeth Bernstein, "I'm Very, Very, Very Sorry… Really?" *The Wall Street Journal,* October 18, 2010, http://online.wsj.com/article/SB1000142405 2702304410504575560093884004442.html.

7.  Evans, *The Divide,* 134.

8.  "Marital Status: 2005–2009 American Community Survey 5-Year Estimates," U.S. Census Bureau: http://factfinder2.census.gov/faces /tableservices/jsf/pages/productview.xhtml?pid=ACS_09_5YR _S1201&prodType=table.

9.  Bruce Feiler, "The Joys of Vicarious Divorce," *The New York Times,* August 29, 2010: ST2.

10. Michael McCullough, Ph.D., "The Forgiveness Instinct," *Greater Good,* http://greatergood.berkeley.edu/article/item/forgiveness_instinct.

11. Michael Cieply, "All That Logging in Makes Dropping Out Much More Difficult," *The New York Times,* March 17, 2011: C3.

12. Aaron Smith, "Mobile Access 2010," Pew Internet (July 7, 2010): http://www.pewinternet.org/Reports/2010/Mobile-Access-2010.aspx.

13. Pamela Paul, "Cracking Teenagers' Online Codes," *The New York Times,* January 22, 2012: ST1.

14. Michael Cieply, "All That Logging in Makes Dropping Out Much More Difficult."

15. Matt Richtel, "Attached to Technology and Paying a Price," *The New York Times,* June 7, 2010: A1.

16. Elizabeth Bernstein, "Your BlackBerry or Your Wife," *The Wall Street Journal,* January 11, 2011, http://online.wsj.com/article/SB1000142405274 8703779704576073801833991620.html.

17. Lakshmi Chaudry, "Men Growing Up to Be Boys," *In These Times,* March 17, 2006, http://www.inthesetimes.com/article/2526.

## Chapter Eleven: Manopause Men at Work

1. Levant, *Masculinity Reconstructed,* 189.

2. de Botton, *The Consolations of Philosophy,* 57.

3. Farrell, *Why Men Are the Way They Are,* 114.

4. Mary Carmichael, "Bubble and Bust," *Newsweek,* April 13, 2008, http://www.thedailybeast.com/newsweek/2008/04/13/bubble-and-bust.html.

5. Andrew Romano and Tony Dokoupil, "Men's Lib," *Newsweek,* September 20, 2010, http://www.thedailybeast.com/newsweek/2010/09/20/why-we-need-to-reimagine-masculinity.

6. "Did You Know 4.0" Video, www.youtube.com/user/xplanevisualthinking.

7. Nicole Santa Cruz, "Women Out-Earning, Out-Learning Men in More Couples," *Los Angeles Times,* January 20, 2010, http://articles.latimes.com/2010/jan/20/nation/la-na-marriage20-2010jan20.

8. Hannah Rosin, "The End of Men," *The Atlantic,* July/August 2010, http://www.theatlantic.com/magazine/archive/2010/07/the-end-of-men/8135/.

9. Danoff, *Penis Power,* 241.

10. Christine Haughney, "In Tough Times, Even the Billionaires Worry," *The New York Times,* September 10, 2008: SPG2.

11. Alina Tugend, "Coping Skills and Horrible Imaginings," *The New York Times,* January 3, 2009: B6.

12. Blum, *Sex on the Brain,* 265.

13. Levant, *Masculinity Reconstructed,* 200.

14. Evans, *Play Like a Man, Win Like a Woman,* 28.

15. Sarah Kershaw, "Family and Office Roles Mix," *The New York Times,* December 4, 2008: E1.

16. DesRoches, *Your Boss Is Not Your Mother,* 25.

17. Lia Miller, "The Myth of the Deficient Older Employee," *The New York Times Magazine,* December 13, 2009.

18. Lisa Stark, "Baby Boomer Brain Power," ABC News, January 30, 2012.

19. Nicole Maestas et al., "When I'm 64: How Aging U.S. Baby Boomers Have Begun to Carry That Weight," *Rand Review* (Summer 2010): 23.

20. Gina Kolata, "Taking Early Retirement May Retire Memory, Too," *The New York Times,* October 12, 2010: D1.

21. Rebecca Cole, "National Service Programs to Get a Boost from Obama," Los Angeles Times, April 22, 2009, http://articles.latimes.com/2009/apr/22/nation/na-service22.

22. Christine Larson, "Older, and Wiser, Students," *The New York Times,* October 23, 2008: SPG12.

23. Elizabeth Olson, "Education on the Company's Dime," *The New York Times,* March 4, 2010: F9.

24. Steven Greenhouse, "Starting Over at 55," *The New York Times,* March 4, 2010: F1.

## Conclusion

1. Brizendine, *The Female Brain,* 7.

# BIBLIOGRAPHY

Amen, M.D., Daniel G. *The Brain in Love*. New York: Three Rivers Press, 2009.

———. *Sex on the Brain*. New York: Three Rivers Press, 2007.

Astrachan, Anthony. *How Men Feel: Their Response to Women's Demands for Equality and Power*. New York: Anchor Press/Doubleday, 1986.

Barash, David P. and Judith Eve Lipton, M.D. *The Myth of Monogamy: Fidelity and Infidelity in Animals and People*. New York: Henry Holt and Company, 2001.

Baron-Cohen, Simon. *The Essential Difference: The Truth About the Male and Female Brain*. New York: Basic Books/Perseus Books Group, 2003.

Beckwith, Michael Bernard. *Spiritual Liberation*. New York: Atria Books, 2008.

Berkowitz, Ph.D., Bob and Susan Yager-Berkowitz. *He's Just Not Up for it Anymore*. New York: William Morrow, 2008.

Blum, Deborah. *Sex on the Brain: The Biological Differences Between Men and Women*. New York: Viking, 1997.

Boteach, Shmuley. *The Kosher Sutra*. New York: Harper Collins/Harper One, 2009.

Brassfield, Marissa. "19 Common Defense Mechanisms," *Lifescript*, http://www.lifescript.com/soul/self/growth/19_common_defense_mechanisms.aspx (accessed February 3, 2010).

Brizendine, M.D., Louann. *The Female Brain*. New York: Morgan Road Books, 2006.

———. *The Male Brain*. New York: Three Rivers Press/Crown Publishing Group, 2010.

Broder, Ph.D., Michael S. *The Art of Staying Together: A Couple's Guide to Intimacy and Respect*. New York: Hyperion, 1993.

Burnham, Terry and Jay Phelan. *Mean Genes: From Sex to Money to Food*. New York: Perseus Publishing, 2000.

Buss, David M. *The Evolution of Desire: Strategies of Human Mating*. New York: Basic Books/HarperCollins Publishers, 1994.

Carr, Nicholas. *The Shallows*. New York: W. W. Norton & Company, 2010.

Crenshaw, M.D., Theresa. *The Alchemy of Love and Lust*. New York: G. P. Putnam's Sons, 1996.

Critser, Greg. *Eternity Soup*. New York: Harmony Books/Crown Publishing Group/Random House, Inc., 2010.

Dabbs, Ph.D., James McBride. *Heroes, Rogues, and Lovers*. New York: McGraw-Hill, 2000.

Danoff, M.D., Dudley. *Penis Power*. Bloomington, Indiana: AuthorHouse, 2009.

de Botton, Alain. *The Consolations of Philosophy*. New York: Pantheon Books, 2000.

DesRoches, Ph.D., Brian. *Your Boss is Not Your Mother*. New York: William Morrow and Company, Inc., 1995.

Diamond, Jed. *The Irritable Male Syndrome*. New York: Rodale, 2004.

———. *Surviving Male Menopause*. Naperville, Illinois: Sourcebooks, Inc., 2000.

Dorsen, M.D., Peter. *Dr. D's Handbook for Men Over 40*. New York: John Wiley & Sons, Inc., 1999.

Dozier, Jr., Rush W. *Fear Itself: The Origin and Nature of the Powerful Emotion That Shapes Our Lives and Our World*. New York: Thomas Dunne Books, 1998.

Evans, Gail. *Play Like a Man, Win Like a Woman*. New York: Broadway Books/Random House, 2000.

Evans, Nicholas. *The Divide*. New York: G.P. Putnam's Sons, 2005.

Farrell, Ph.D., Warren. *Why Men Are the Way They Are: The Male-Female Dynamic*. New York: McGraw-Hill Book Company, 1986.

Gillick, M.D., Muriel R. *The Denial of Aging: Perpetual Youth, Eternal Life, and Other Dangerous Fantasies*. Cambridge, Massachusetts: Harvard University Press, 2006.

Gilmore, David D. *Manhood in the Making: Cultural Concepts of Masculinity*. New Haven, Connecticut: Yale University, 1990.

Gray, Ph.D., John. *Men Are from Mars, Women Are from Venus*. New York: HarperCollins Publishers, 1992.

Grothe, Dr. Mardy and Dr. Peter Wylie. *Problem Bosses: Who They Are and How to Deal with Them*. New York: Facts On File Publications, 1987. Gurian, Michael. *What Could He Be Thinking?: How a Man's Mind Really Works*. New York: St. Martin's Press, 2003.

Hart, Archibald D. *Unmasking Male Depression: Recognizing the Root Cause to Many Problem Behaviors, Such as Anger, Resentment, Abusiveness, Silence, Addictions, and Sexual Compulsions*. Nashville, Tennessee: W. Publishing Group/Thomas Nelson, Inc., 2001.

Hill, M.D., Aubrey. *The Testosterone Solution: Increase Your Energy and Vigor with Male Hormone Therapy.* Rocklin, California.: Prima Publishing, 1997.

Kimmel, Michael. *Guyland: The Perilous World Where Boys Become Men.* New York: HarperCollins, 2008.

Kindlon, Ph.D., Dan and Michael Thompson, Ph.D. *Raising Cain: Protecting the Emotional Life of Boys.* New York: A Living Planet Book, Ballantine Books, 1999.

Levant, Ed.D., ABPP, Ronald F. *Masculinity Reconstructed: Changing the Rules of Manhood—at Work, in Relationships, and in Family Life.* New York: Plume/Penguin Group, 1995.

LeVay, Simon. *The Sexual Brain.* Cambridge, Massachusetts: MIT Press, 1993.

Levinson, Daniel J. *The Seasons of a Man's Life.* New York: Ballantine Books, 1978.

Luskin, Ph.D., Fred. *Forgive for Good: A Proven Prescription for Health and Happiness.* New York: Harper One/HarperCollins Publishers, 2002.

———. *Forgive for Love.* New York: Harper One/HarperCollins Publishers, 2007.

Milsten, M.D., Richard and Julian Slowinsky, Psy.D. *The Sexual Male: Problems and Solutions.* New York: W.W. Norton & Company, 1999.

Morgantaler M.D., Abraham. *The Viagra Myth: The Surprising Impact on Love and Relationships.* San Francisco: Jossey-Bass/Wiley, 2003.

O'Connor, Peter A. *Facing the Fifties: From Denial to Reflection.* Crows Nest NSW (Australia): Allen & Unwin, 2000.

Pink, Daniel H. *A Whole New Mind: Why Right-Brainers Will Rule the Future.* New York: Riverhead Books/Penguin Group, 2005, 2006.

Pinker, Steven. *The Blank Slate: The Modern Denial of Human Nature.* New York; Viking, 2002.

Radwan, M. Farouk, "Ego Defense Mechanisms," SelfGrowth.com, January 9, 2010, http://www.selfgrowth.com/print/572695 (accessed March 22, 2010).

"Real Men. Real Depression." nih.gov, March 2003, http://wwwapps.nimh.nih.gov/health/publications/real-men-real-depression.pdf (accessed July 2010).

Rinpoche, Yongey Mingyur. *The Joy of Living: Unlocking the Secret and Science of Happiness.* New York: Crown Publishing/Harmony Books, 2007.

Selhub, M.D., Eva. *The Love Response.* New York: Random House, 2009.

Sheehy, Gail. *The Silent Passage: Menopause.* New York: PocketBooks/Simon & Schuster Inc., 1991, 1992, 1993.

———. *New Passages: Mapping Your Life Across Time.* New York: Random House, 1995.

————. *Sex and the Seasoned Woman: Pursuing the Passionate Life.* New York: Random House, 2006

————. *Understanding Men's Passages: Discovering the New Map of Men's Lives.* New York: Random House, 1999.

Shippen, M.D., Eugene and William Fryer. *The Testosterone Syndrome.* New York: M. Evans and Company, Inc., 1998.

Smalley, Gary. *Secrets to Lasting Love: Uncovering the Keys to Lifelong Intimacy.* New York: Simon & Schuster, 2000.

Spark, M,D., Richard F. *Sexual Health for Men: The Complete Guide.* Cambridge, Massachusetts: Perseus Publishing, 2000.

Tan, M.D., Robert S. *The Andropause Mystery: Unraveling Truths About the Male Menopause.* Houston: Amred Publishing, 2001.

University of Southern California, "Shifting Blame Is Socially Contagious," *ScienceDaily,* November 19, 2009, http://www.sciencedaily.com/releases/2009/11/091119194124.htm (accessed March 22, 2010).

Van Hoose, William H. *Midlife Myths and Realities: An Upbeat Approach to Enjoying the Transitions of the Middle Years.* Atlanta, Georgia: Humanics, Ltd, 1985.

Zal, H. Michael. *The Sandwich Generation: Caught Between Growing Children and Aging Parents.* Cambridge, Massachusetts: Perseus Publishing, 1992.

Zilbergeld, Ph.D, Bernie. *Better Than Ever.* Norwalk, Connecticut: Crown House Publishing, Ltd., 2004.

# ACKNOWLEDGMENTS

*Manopause* came to fruition beyond our most optimistic imaginings because of the contributions of our "uber-agent," Jillian Manus. Her insatiable hunger to improve the world and to empower women was our inspiration to help women understand the world of men at midlife, and to help both men and women enhance their relationships. Her magnetic enthusiasm, creativity, and unrelenting drive motivated us to immerse ourselves in the subject matter and deliver an all-encompassing book. She taught us to look at things in ways that encouraged disparate ideas to cross-fertilize and blossom. We would not be in a position to write these acknowledgments, let alone celebrate the publication of this book, if it weren't for her. We thank Jillian from the top and bottom of our hearts.

We are extremely grateful to our editor, Laura Koch, who has contributed in so many ways to this work. She continually demanded excellence, in the very nicest way, as we crafted revisions and worked to fashion a narrative in which medical science, anthropology, culture, and the personal experiences of so many could fuse together and come alive. Her consistent sense of humor, her sensitivity and calm in the midst of chaos, and her incisive intelligence were invaluable to us during this process.

We are indebted to Louann Brizendine, M.D., who early on validated the need for this book, and who, in long and stimulating conversations, gave us new directions to explore, and offered incalculable insight. Her voracious curiosity about hormones and the way the brain functions is inspiring and addicting. For all of her wisdom, expertise, enthusiasm, and friendship, we can't thank her enough.

It is no surprise that a lifelong friend, Eva Ritvo, M.D., went above and beyond to help us with *Manopause*. We thank her for sharing her intellect and giving us invaluable guidance, especially in the area of depression. Even at "crunch time" her positive spirit was an inspiration. We appreciate her encouragement and loving support beyond measure.

We offer sincere thanks to Rabbi Steven Leder for lending his wisdom and his spiritual leadership to this work. *Manopause* has been greatly enriched as a result.

In light of the breadth of the material we have tried to cover in this book, we have been especially reliant on and grateful for the help of friends, business colleagues, and those who are experts in areas where we are less well-versed. In addition, we offer thanks to doctors Gary Small, M.D., Jane Beresford, Psy.D., Larry Harmon, Ph.D., Neil Martin, M.D., Dudley Danoff, M.D., Howard Liebowitz, M.D., Estelle Shane, Ph.D., and the many other professionals in the world of science who gave invaluable guidance by providing scientific information and clarification. We have truly appreciated these contributions.

We are grateful to Reid Tracy and Patty Gift of Hay House, Inc., who believed in and supported this book from the outset. And to the creative and marketing teams at Hay House who helped to make it come to life.

A big thank you to all of those we love, both close family members and dear friends, who have eagerly and wholeheartedly supported this project, and who have offered their understanding when we were short on time and long on stress while researching and writing. In particular, we thank Marlene Friedman for her constant encouragement, Stacy Mandelberg for her skillful reading talents and on-target comments, and Giselle Fernandez and Colleen Martin for graciously sharing their time and connections. And to all of our girlfriends and acquaintances, who have listened to us, and who have shared their private thoughts and intimate experiences, we are forever grateful.

*Manopause* sits on the shoulders of work done by many others over the last decades, both professionally and nonprofessionally. We thank the scientists, researchers, and writers whose work help to clarify the many aspects of manopause for us. As writers and commentators, we are only as worthwhile as our readers and listeners, thus we thank all of you, in advance, for helping this work to have a positive impact.

Our never-ending thanks go to the many men who, spurred on by the women who love them, will open their minds to the teachings of this book, and by following its advice will lead happier lives, making the world a better place for generations to come.

And finally to each other, for sharing a screen and filling the two chairs in front of it for the last 22 years . . . it's a continuous thrill.

# ABOUT THE AUTHORS

**Lisa Friedman Bloch** and **Kathy Kirtland Silverman** have shared a long and successful writing career. They bring to *Manopause* an extensive background as social commentators and a deep knowledge of the male sex honed through decades of observation, research, and personal experience. Their previous nonfiction book, *Dr. Richard Marrs' Fertility Book,* has been dubbed, "The bible of infertility for consumers." It presented the latest in medical technology, as well as giving practical advice to surviving the fertility process. Its comprehensive section on the emotional consequences of fertility treatment utilized advice from Dr. Marrs and other nationally recognized experts, which was blended with deeply felt personal experiences as reported by numerous couples at varying stages in the process.

In addition to their nonfiction writing, Bloch and Silverman have spent years writing and producing network television, cable, and feature motion pictures. Their expertise lies in dramatizing true-life stories and adapting best-selling biographies for the screen.

## HAY HOUSE TITLES OF RELATED INTEREST

*YOU CAN HEAL YOUR LIFE, the movie,* starring Louise L. Hay & Friends
(available as a 1-DVD program and an expanded 2-DVD set)
Watch the trailer at: **www.LouiseHayMovie.com**

*THE SHIFT, the movie,*
starring Dr. Wayne W. Dyer
(available as a 1-DVD program and an expanded 2-DVD set)
Watch the trailer at: **www.DyerMovie.com**

*ECSTASY IS NECESSARY: A Practical Guide,* by Barbara Carrellas

*THE FATIGUE SOLUTION: Increase Your Energy in Eight Easy Steps,*
by Eva Cwynar, M.D.

*REWIRE YOUR BRAIN FOR LOVE: Creating Vibrant Relationships
Using the Science of Mindfulness,* by Marsha Lucas, Ph.D.

*THE SECRET PLEASURES OF MENOPAUSE,* by Christiane Northrup, M.D.

All of the above are available at your local bookstore,
or may be ordered by contacting Hay House (see next page).

We hope you enjoyed this Hay House book. If you'd like
to receive our online catalog featuring additional information
on Hay House books and products, or if you'd like to find out
more about the Hay Foundation, please contact:

Hay House, Inc., P.O. Box 5100, Carlsbad, CA 92018-5100
(760) 431-7695 or (800) 654-5126
(760) 431-6948 (fax) or (800) 650-5115 (fax)
**www.hayhouse.com**® • **www.hayfoundation.org**

*Published and distributed in Australia by:* Hay House Australia Pty. Ltd., 18/36 Ralph
St., Alexandria NSW 2015 • *Phone:* 612-9669-4299 • *Fax:* 612-9669-4144
www.hayhouse.com.au

*Published and distributed in the United Kingdom by:* Hay House UK, Ltd.,
292B Kensal Rd., London W10 5BE • *Phone:* 44-20-8962-1230
*Fax:* 44-20-8962-1239 • www.hayhouse.co.uk

*Published and distributed in the Republic of South Africa by:* Hay House SA (Pty),
Ltd., P.O. Box 990, Witkoppen 2068 • *Phone/Fax:* 27-11-467-8904
www.hayhouse.co.za

*Published in India by:* Hay House Publishers India, Muskaan Complex,
Plot No. 3, B-2, Vasant Kunj, New Delhi 110 070 • *Phone:* 91-11-4176-1620
*Fax:* 91-11-4176-1630 • www.hayhouse.co.in

*Distributed in Canada by:* Raincoast, 9050 Shaughnessy St.,
Vancouver, B.C. V6P 6E5 • *Phone:* (604) 323-7100
*Fax:* (604) 323-2600 • www.raincoast.com

## Take Your Soul on a Vacation

Visit **www.HealYourLife.com**® to regroup, recharge, and reconnect
with your own magnificence. Featuring blogs, mind-body-spirit news,
and life-changing wisdom from Louise Hay and friends.

Visit **www.HealYourLife.com** today!